BACK FROM THE BRINK

BACK FROM THE BRINK

An Apocalyptic Experience

MICHAEL EDWARDES

COLLINS
8 Grafton Street, London W1
1983

William Collins Sons & Co Ltd
London · Glasgow · Sydney · Auckland
Toronto · Johannesburg

British Library Cataloguing in Publication Data
Edwardes, *Sir* Michael
    Back from the brink.
    1. BL Limited   2. Automobile industry and
    trade—Great Britain—Management
    I. Title
    338.7′6292′0924   HD9710.G74B65

Copyright © William Collins Sons & Co Ltd 1983
ISBN 0 00 217074 4

Photoset in Linotron Sabon by
Rowland Phototypesetting Ltd
Bury St Edmunds, Suffolk
Made and printed in Great Britain by
William Collins Sons and Co Ltd.

For Mary –
and Susan, Judy and Penni

Contents

Preface

Early in October 1977, I was asked, at short notice, to take on the awesome task of running British Leyland; of bringing about its recovery. I reported for duty 28 days later, and now, five years later, my assignment at BL is over. Others will continue with the task.

This book describes those five years; the fine people I worked with, and what they achieved; the remarkable sense of commitment that there is inside the company, and the sheer determination that BL should survive, which it has, and that it should succeed, which it richly deserves to do.

Deciding to write this account was no straightforward matter, despite the persuasiveness of those who thought it needed to be done. Quite apart from the time and effort involved – every spare moment for 16 weeks – I had a number of misgivings. Was I too close to the action to be capable of an objective analytical account? Would it end up as a lengthy apologia for everything we had done? Yet if ever there was a book looking for an author, this was it. BL has too often captured the public interest for the wrong reasons. Its struggle for survival, and more recently for full recovery, deserves a record which explains the complexity of the problems and pressures, for BL presents a microcosm of the issues affecting British industry as a whole.

The story needed to be told from the inside, if it was to add anything to the tons of press cuttings already in existence. It could not easily be published by a current employee, if the flavour of the more sensitive political and employee relations dimensions was to be conveyed in more than a passing fashion. And if these sensitive issues were to be fairly treated, it was essential that they be covered by someone who had been closely involved in the events as they occurred. There being few other candidates for the author's job, I took a deep breath and plunged in.

Where discussion or correspondence, which were private at the time, cover on-going issues which could embarrass BL or the Government, I have refrained from using the material: collaborative discussions which are still continuing would be a case in point. On the other hand, where issues are no longer 'live', or where they have been the subject of a fair amount of public coverage, I have taken the view that publication at this point is not against the public interest.

If despite the careful consideration I have given to each instance, I nevertheless offend anyone, I apologise. My objective is to explain how the present system works, and I have drawn on all the appropriate material except where I felt that it was improper to do so.

MICHAEL EDWARDES
St Francis Bay, December 1982

Base Camp

On arrival at BL at 9.30 am on Tuesday, 1st November, 1977, I had to fight my way through the doors. Not that my new colleagues tried to keep me out, although some might willingly have done so! It was simply that the journalists and television crews waiting on the pavement on that cold autumn morning wouldn't let me in. In late 1977 British Leyland was big news and bad news.

That first morning I had been delayed by reporters at my home in Richmond, which had been under siege for some days. My neighbours understandably were disenchanted with the 'knock-on' effect my new job was having on their lives. An enterprising photographer persuaded a neighbour to give him a vantage point to catch me leaving the house at 7.30 am.

Following the announcement of my appointment I immediately laid my hands on the first BL model I could find. My Chloride company car, a Ford, would have caused an uproar. Unfortunately its replacement, a Triumph Estate, had just been phased out of production, and this tit-bit did not go unnoticed by the press, as I pulled away from the house. I learned the hard way that anything to do with British Leyland caused intense interest.

As I drew alongside the pavement in Piccadilly I was astounded to see more than 100 pressmen – photographers, newspaper reporters, television crews – all scrambling for a story.

Was I going to close British Leyland down? What was I going to do about the factory at Speke, Liverpool, where 2,000 employees building the Triumph TR7 sports car had chosen my first day with the company can go on strike? Can the company survive? And the bizarre but predictable, what had I eaten for breakfast? I was able to be positive on that question, for I never eat breakfast. But I was silent on the big issues, and it was three months before I was prepared to make any public comments on things that mattered. It was a deliberate decision not to make off-the-cuff judgments on issues which needed to be carefully thought through, and that required at least a couple of months of intensive study.

I avoided going to the dark green monolithic headquarters, Leyland House, in Marylebone Road, and went instead to an unpretentious building not far from Piccadilly Circus, which was to be my base. What had to be done – my plan was to devolve authority, drastically cut headquarters staff and put much greater responsibility back where it belonged, at the operational level – was far better conducted away from the corporate headquarters. So I accepted Lord Stokes's offer of his office 'over the shop' astride the British Leyland sales showrooms at 41 Piccadilly. Since his retirement in 1975 there had been no less than three Chairmen – I was the fourth, including Donald Stokes, in less than two years. At the beginning of my secondment, he was the Honorary President. Number 41 Piccadilly was a labyrinth of corridors and small offices and was shared with other tenants. It was also on the corner of Sackville Street – another piece of colour and background which several journalists couldn't resist, since the word 'sack' seemed to loom large in their minds.

The questions, filming and photography went on for about 15 minutes, with reporters spilling across the pavement and into the morning traffic. Not for the last time the side street was filled with ITV and BBC Outside Broadcast vans. 'Would I be able to bring about the recovery of British Leyland?' asked a pretty young reporter. 'Yes, if I have to stand on my head to do it.' The press let me off lightly at the time for that injudicious remark.

At first I felt able to trust only three people in a company of about 198,000, and I would bet that the feeling was mutual – at that stage 197,997 didn't know what to make of me, and it took a few months for mutual trust to develop. The three people had come with me from Chloride: John McKay, Communications Director; Sheila Witts, my personal assistant, with her particular flair for judging people and situations; and Margaret Evans, my always cheerful secretary.

Inside Number 41 the atmosphere was almost as frenetic. My colleagues, the nucleus of my office, were getting to grips with the practical problems: there were pressing organisational problems to be looked at, and a framework of meetings to be arranged. Bill Barlow, the new Chairman of the Post Office, quickly solved the telephone problem and he remembers this well, for it was also his first day as Chairman of that vast institution. The new phones were installed within 24 hours and we were in business – communication being everything.

The early pressures were to continue not for weeks or months, but for three years, as we faced an avalanche of issues and crises. The first priority was to come to grips with reality – as opposed to the images, politics, postures, and all the stage-managing that goes on within a company that is in deep trouble.

Just how grave the problems were was illustrated by the fact – then kept a closely guarded secret – that British Leyland was once again on the point of running out of money. Industrial disruption and strikes throughout the previous ten months of 1977, characterised by the toolmakers' strike in the early part of the year, resulted in the production loss of 250,000 vehicles. This was a quarter of the company's total planned production for the year and it caused a cash haemorrhage. There was simply not enough money to pay the wages from November 1977 onwards, and there was no possibility of going to the Government for immediate funds as the Labour Administration had problems of its own, with a 'hung' Parliament. Besides which we were not yet in a position to put forward a sensible Corporate Plan. Without a viable Plan there could be no justification for further government funding. The best the Government could do was to provide comfort letters, to assure the banks that they were aware of the transactions.

The banks did not put much weight on the comfort letters, and this emerged during the negotiations when the late Lord Armstrong, Chairman of the Midland Bank, invited my wife and me to a dinner at rather short notice. The Midland Bank's involvement in the loan was crucial, for we already knew that at least one major London bank was not prepared to subscribe to the loan. It was, frankly, a question of convincing him and a Board colleague – over drinks after dinner – that we knew what we were about, and that the company had a real chance of survival. And so it was the clearing banks and not the Government that came to our rescue, after intense but speedy discussions. They chipped in loan facilities of £80 million to keep us going through the crisis period with the existing government assurances as their only security. We owed the three clearing banks a debt of gratitude that went beyond the material debt, for this was an act of faith if ever there was one. I well remember the relief we felt when the message came through, 'We've got the money.' There was no need to ask 'What money?' When this good news arrived the irony did not escape me that British Leyland's immediate cash crisis was being eased by the private sector, but what about the irony of my own situation?

It is odd how one has moments of reflection when all around is chaos – how one's mind flashes back to some memory that links to the present. Here was I, an exponent of free enterprise, solemnly presiding over one of the largest public sector lame ducks of all time. What was I, of all people, doing in this job? It was in sharp contrast to all my experience, and the business philosophy I had started to develop and put into practice well before I had finished university in South Africa. It all began with 'Lucy'. It was back in 1949, a year before I took my final examinations, that I first saw her. I loved 'Lucy' from the first moment; she was all I'd ever hoped for. She had a tremendous personality and I still think of her with tenderness. Freshly painted, she looked a picture: bright green in front and deep red behind. She was indeed a gorgeous specimen of a 1938 Chevrolet, with her narrow cab up front, and her vast platform behind.

Her payload was a little over three tons according to her makers, but her actual capacity for carrying oil drums knew no bounds, and on the flat stretch along Algoa Bay between the Mobil Oil depot and down-town Port Elizabeth, she had no difficulty in topping four tons – £150 of sheer joy. She was named after *Put your shoes on Lucy* then the popular song at Rhodes, where my business partner Brian Mills and I were both at university in Grahamstown. 'Lucy' was our regular vacation project, and she never let us down throughout 1949 and 1950. My partner and I were very much the free-wheeling entrepreneurs and the haulage venture funded our holiday fun. We were very proud of 'Lucy' and the business she allowed us to develop. Nobody owed us a living. The risk was ours, the profit was ours. There I was, a student, with a tiny holiday business – the classic capitalist. Here at Nuffield House, dealing in millions, even in billions, I was in no sense a capitalist, for I was a hired manager with no material stake in the enterprise.

I was brought sharply back to British Leyland's problems when Pat Lowry, Director of Personnel, and now Chairman of the Government's Advisory, Conciliation and Arbitration Service, walked in: 'Look at this, four typed pages of disputes.' In those days there were disputes in half of our 50 British factories day in and day out, and the list often ran to five sheets. Those pages made unhappy reading, and they brought a sharp end to my philosophical ruminations. It was to be three years before the daily dispute sheets dwindled to the point where I was able to discontinue them.

I know that Pat Lowry, who had been in industrial relations before his BL days, when he worked for the Engineering Employers' Federation, was as depressed about the dispute record as I was. He had lived with confrontation for most of his working life, and three years later, when he was offered the chairmanship of the Government's arbitration service, he saw this as a fitting culmination to his long career in dealing with industrial problems. He had all the experience needed and all the contacts – and, most important, the stature.

The pattern of that early period was of relentless 70- and 80-hour working weeks, often with breakfast and evening meetings at each end of the day; of interminable meetings at the office during the week and at home over weekends. The participants on the other side of the table often changed at intervals of 20 minutes as people queued up to have their say. Some wanted assurances which they seldom received, others argued the case for organisational changes, staff changes, changes in their own duties, but rather more often advocating no change at all. This, the inertia school, was the one I needed to resist firmly, for a company in our sort of difficulty could not survive by maintaining the status quo. Others, from outside the company, came to plead or even cajole and threaten, for British Leyland had an impact on a great many people. In the early months internal politics manifested itself in a running battle to persuade me to stop 'living rough' in Piccadilly; to enter the corporate warmth of Leyland House, which had accommodation for 1,000, and in its heyday accommodated some 600 headquarters' and International Division personnel. On my rare visits there I found no enthusiasm and a stifling atmosphere, rather like being in a luxury liner, without portholes; corridors between closed doors, behind which people seemed to work in a vacuum, at least two steps removed from the 'nuts and bolts' of the business, which was in the Midlands, in Oxfordshire, in the North West of England and in Scotland.

Of course, many people there worked positively and conscientiously, but the centralised concept disturbed me, for it wasn't only cost we were determined to save, but the knock-on effect of bureaucracy: the 'second-guessing' of Cars headquarters in Coventry and of Commercial Vehicles, centred at Leyland, Lancashire.

These divisional headquarters, in turn, 'second-guessed' and had a suffocating effect on the operational management in factories around the country.

I was sure that if I allowed myself to get drawn into Leyland House it would slow down the decentralisation process. I would be seen (or thought) to have gone native, and this would inhibit the fundamental shift I planned to drive through. The process whereby you don't so much dish out authority, as have it 'pulled' from you naturally by people in charge of their own operations where products are developed and made and sold. This doesn't happen easily if there are layers of intermediary staffs, at divisional and headquarters level.

I was not wedded to Nuffield House, but if we moved it would be to a smaller building which would accommodate the key people we really needed centrally, rather than the several hundred corporate staff which then existed. The company, in particular the Cars operation, was too centralised. Too many decisions which should have been taken at factory or divisional level, where the facts were known, were being taken at Marylebone Road in London. It was like wading through treacle. The organisation was unsatisfactory in other ways: the International Division was quite separate from United Kingdom design, product development and manufacturing, and this exacerbated their understandable scepticism about products, costs of products, and delivery promises. The Cars operation in Britain was vertically organised – the 'buck' would pass from one man to the next, until it reached overburdened top executives, without people down the line sharing the load or being deeply involved (and therefore deeply committed) to the decisions made. People simply did not have manageable jobs and they couldn't get their arms around the trees. What was needed therefore was decentralisation, with existing people not required centrally being redeployed to the operating companies outside London; those not needed would have to leave the company. We certainly did not need a headquarters building to house so many people. I made this philosophy clear on many occasions, but the subtle and not so subtle pressures to move to Marylebone Road continued until they became a standing joke between Pat Lowry and me, for he was usually the ambassador for the Leyland House contingent. He regularly used to raise the subject along the lines, 'Morale isn't good there. They can't understand why you won't join the team directly, be with them; what is your real motive?' I reminded him that even the Ryder Report, which had been the company's blueprint for recovery since 1975, advocated decentralisation, but it had never happened. I was determined to put an end to the dead-hand of central control.

And so the modest offices in Piccadilly became the nerve centre for the company and remained so until October 1979, when we moved into four floors of an office block in Portman Square, giving us just sufficient space to accommodate the key corporate staff needed. We had sold Leyland House before finding the new accommodation, and this forced the pace.

The Leyland House saga was symptomatic of an ingrained attitude which was widespread throughout the company. Yet in those first weeks as we separated the real from the unreal, some first-rate people emerged from within the company – some still in their 30s – and the top team started to reform. New relationships were quickly established, but trust and confidence came later. It could hardly have been otherwise; managers generally were demoralised and demotivated as some braced themselves for yet another reorganisation, while others were determined to stop changes of one and every sort!

It was therefore not surprising that internal rumour and gossip should be rife and that much of it would be gratefully received in Fleet Street, where interest in British Leyland continued to be intense. Inevitably 'leaks' occurred and these grew into a stream of conjecture, speculation, and, on a few occasions, highly damaging misinformation which seemed to be maliciously created.

One particularly bad incident concerned speculation about the future of the Speke factory, while a decision was still being taken as to whether to close it. The report stated categorically that the decision had, in fact, been made. I decided to bring home to people just how seriously we viewed the disloyalty epitomised by this flow of mischievous rumour. We needed a man of acknowledged stature to become involved and be seen to be involved in stamping out this irresponsible practice.

I had just flown back from Detroit when I read the Speke story in the *Sunday Telegraph*. I can't recall how I got hold of Lord Goodman's home telephone number on that Sunday afternoon (for my wife and I only came to know him well and enjoy his company much later on), but a couple of hours later I was ensconced in his

London apartment, seeking advice as to how we could discourage the leakage of confidential information from the company. What came out of this and a later discussion with that remarkable man, was the proposition that we should provide some disciplinary therapy. Lord Goodman, together with Brian Neill, QC, were formally empowered by the Board to investigate the 'security' of top managers and to recommend how best to tighten our security system. We felt certain that the leaks were emanating from senior people, for matters as sensitive as the possible closure of Speke, should have been known to no more than 20 people. But Arnold Goodman figured that if his 'Inquiry' team sat at Leyland House and was seen to interview streams of people, this would have a restraining influence on the culprits – even if the perpetrators were not included directly in the trawl.

Ostentatiously in the glass mezzanine above the foyer at Leyland House, Lord Goodman and the Queen's Counsel interviewed each member of the main Board, and exhaustively went through the top management. At the same time we issued a letter to employees reminding them that disclosure of commercial information could result in dismissal without compensation.

The Goodman Inquiry made its presence felt, and to everyone's relief thenceforth the flow of 'leaky' information was reduced to a trickle. The Report was a masterpiece, and served as a model for tightening security in the company. The primary cause of the security problem was low morale, but this had to wait its turn as there were many urgent priorities in those first days and no shortage of advice from all quarters. It is always difficult to 'fix' morale until there is stability; and we were not ready to stabilise, for we were in the process of managing change on a vast scale.

Meanwhile, mail poured into my office at the rate of many hundreds of letters a week – all demanding my attention. After all what is the Chairman paid to do, if not to correspond with Members of Parliament, company executives, union leaders, and others who expect instant and personal attention? During the first few weeks there were 1,300 letters purely on the subject of my appointment. Half of them made it clear that I needed my head examined but almost all of them were nevertheless warm in their encouragement. The routine 'personal' mail poured in at the rate of 1,700 letters a month, as it continued to do for a further three years.

In the early days, in this mountain of mail I particularly remember a long letter from the then Secretary of State for Trade, Edmund Dell, complaining at poor Land Rover deliveries and now that a new Chairman was at the helm, could he be assured that all this nonsense would come to an end forthwith. I replied that all that stood between us and proper deliveries of Land Rover was £250 million of capital expenditure to modernise the Land Rover factory at Solihull and double its production capacity. It might just take a few months to set in motion. Perhaps a year or two would solve the problem. Edmund Dell's letter was written, I'm sure, with the best intentions, but it illustrated the gap between the public expectation and what was practical given the range and depth of the problems to be resolved, and the vast investment needed to make an impact on the Dickensian facilities at most of our factories.

We really were at the wrong end of a sheer cliff face and the climb would require energy and resilience. I wondered frankly whether the job could be done at all, and if it could, whether I was the person to do it. My family and close colleagues never had any doubts and the Government and the NEB Board (management and unions) had supported the appointment. They must have thought I had a chance, and this in itself was a good start.

My business life had been spent neither in the motor industry proper, nor in the public sector with all its machinations; nevertheless I felt that my unconventional upbringing and my subsequent experiences were more appropriate to the challenge than might have appeared at first sight.

2

Early Experiences

What was different about my early life? Perhaps that I wasn't spoonfed and that I was encouraged to get on with things.

I had a wonderful father, who had his own inimitable way of bringing up children. He saw life as an obstacle course and, as a part of their education, his children were required to practise on real live obstacles. He was the sort of father who many close friends accused of having had little to do with my sister's and my upbringing, for it was my mother who was the more involved and who was the more accessible – and the more understanding. He was an avid reader and must have been familiar with the prayer attributed to the Chinese philosopher who on being asked what he wanted most for his son replied, 'I pray only that he will live in interesting times.' This, my father helped me to achieve! Had he forseen what I was destined to take on, six thousand miles away northwards across the Atlantic, he would have been even more convinced that his spartan approach was right, for my early life had a major impact on my attitudes as a manager, and I doubt if I could have coped with those five exciting but demanding years had it not been for my upbringing.

When I was seven years old we would head into the South African wilds to go fishing for the weekend. In those days the mountain passes on the road to Kromme River were indescribably dangerous, and the roads being made of gravel and clay, were a nightmare in either wet or very dry weather. Furthermore, there were 52 gates – each way – in 1938. It was my job to open and close each one. We would leave home on a Friday evening, usually with a couple of friends, and return exhausted late on Sunday night. This took place in winter as well as summer, which was fine for the adults who kept warm by drinking brandy and milk with a dash of coffee while I remained cold, shivering in a light mackintosh and giving my muffled replies through a scarf. The winter nights were long and cold, and it was better to be in the boat on the river than on land – at least in the boat we had the warmth of paraffin lamps.

My father's insistence that I should become self-sufficient and resourceful is well illustrated by an incident with an outboard motor. My old friend Mike McKiever, all of 15 years old like me, was at the tiller when it happened. We were catching springers by flashlight at the mouth of the river, where it flows between banks of sand as white as ivory into the Indian Ocean. We kept an eye on the beam from Cape St Francis lighthouse, to establish our bearings. We had to be careful for on an outgoing tide we could have soon found ourselves right out at sea, especially on the sort of moonless night that was best for catching the elusive springer or mullet – spotlight on one's forehead and scoop net in hand. A dark night with only the Southern Cross to light up the sky, takes some beating for its vast blackness; everything is so much bigger than in Europe, and the young fisherman feels he is in a very little boat with a very little motor surrounded by a dark immensity. Suddenly there was a gurgle, and then dead silence. The Bendix outboard motor had gone over the stern, in deep water. My father's reaction, when we rowed back to the shack, was quite predictable – 'We'll leave some eggs, milk and bread for you; when you have found it phone me and I'll drive out to fetch the pair of you.' We found it after eight days of grappling and diving. The lesson was clear and simple: you make your own mistakes and you correct them yourself. No one looks after anyone from the cradle to the grave. If my father taught me anything, it was that. I spent many school holidays on the river, messing about with outboards, jalopies, and 'lighting plants' – learning the mysteries of Exide batteries some 30 years before I became Chairman of Chloride.

My education was geographically narrow in the sense that St Andrew's College, where I was a schoolboy, was just across the road from Rhodes University but both institutions had, and still have, a reputation for producing embryonic entrepreneurs.

At Rhodes, where I studied law, I had put a toe in the water with 'Lucy', but it was not until I came to leave that I began seriously to think of earning a living. Knowing a little about the haulage business I was led quite naturally into a further enterprise – a contract for planting grass sports fields at a local school. My assets were a few pounds in cash. The first entry in the ledger reflected this wealth; 'one axe and "bush chopper" – £3.' Fortunately the manager of the Main Street branch of the Standard Bank knew me well, for he had been an amused onlooker when we took on our original vacation projects. He was willing to advance limited funds – but only against a firm contract. Fortunately, a contract materialised almost immediately. A friend, Bob Lovemore, was in the process of turning down a request to grass some new playing fields because he was too committed to his farm and his property affairs to tackle it on his own.

Bob and I went into partnership – Lovemore and Edwardes (Pty) Limited was formed for this one contract. At 20 years of age I was an owner proprietor, and very proud of it. But I no longer had 'Lucy'. A by-product of the contract was pine trees; as the main contractor knocked them down, so I was able to buy the timber, saw it into logs, and sell it. I formed another company, V. E. Lawns (Pty) Limited which sold the timber to the local saw mills for cash every Thursday evening. Pay day was Friday – my cash flow was positive, and I never fully utilised the overdraft. But I did want a lorry, for the contract haulage cost was eating into my timber profits. When I found a lorry, back I went to my friend at the Standard Bank. 'She's in good running order and only £90 fully licensed.' 'Why so cheap?' 'Well, Searles, the coal merchants, are pensioning her off because she can't make the Port Elizabeth hills fully loaded. As my timber is located above town, she'll run down to the saw mills fully loaded and return uphill empty.' And so one 1934 GMC truck had a new lease of life, and I had a bargain. Less skittish than 'Lucy', my foreman, George Jonas, and I drove her away, sitting way above the road behind her enormous square bonnet. She went slowly, but with dignity, as a 17-year-old truck should.

While my enterprises ticked over, my father and a close friend decided to merge their rather disparate businesses into the Cape Battery Company. My father's partner, Len Maytham, was the Exide battery distributor for South Africa's Eastern Province, stretching from Mossel Bay in the West, across to a point beyond Grahamstown in the East. The merger was not a wise one, for though the franchise was good and profitable, these friends of long standing turned out to be less en rapport in a business relationship. Nevertheless, out of this liaison came a great opportunity for me. To Port Elizabeth's shores, in early 1951, came a remarkable York-shireman, H. V. Schofield, a main Board director of Chloride, whose headquarters were in Grosvenor Gardens, London. HVS was one of three men who ran Chloride in the late 1940s and into the 1950s, and he was no typical Englishman. He was larger than life. When I say that his way of showing appreciation to his host was to stand on his very bald pate after a good dinner, it will be apparent why he appealed to a young 20-year-old colonial like me.

On the day of HVS's arrival in Port Elizabeth the 'other' half of my father's merger invited him to dinner at which I was privileged to be present. Although I had no intention whatever of being involved with the family business, I got on well with HVS and he invited me to join him the following day for a cup of tea at Port Elizabeth's Marine Hotel at 4.00 pm, straight from work.

I believe he was amused to see me arrive in khaki shorts and shirt, with long khaki stockings – the regular apparel of someone in 'contracting'. He showed no surprise, however and came straight to the point. 'Now Michael, I know you aren't keen to go into your father's business, but why not broaden your horizons by having two years in England with Chloride? You can return to your own business afterwards.' My immediate reaction was, 'What would I do with my businesses in the meanwhile? I've just started them.' 'Put in a manager while you are with us.' Looking back, I suspect there was a conspiracy at work between HVS and my father. I was tempted. Yet I went on, 'How would I afford to live in England?' 'We'll pay you £5 a week and you can top it up with the income from your businesses here.' Now that was not a lot of money, even in 1951; but the offer to learn the business from beginning to end as a management trainee, with no obligation to join Chloride at the end of it, was difficult to resist. So in July 1951 I sailed from Port Elizabeth in the *Edinburgh Castle* to start a whole new career. Three months later I had my 21st birthday in London at a flat in Great Cumberland Place, literally two blocks from BL's present head-quarters in Portman Square. Each morning during the past three years I have driven past that first London flat with some nostalgia.

After two years in London – and some time spent in other parts of Britain, clocking in at Chloride's Duckinfield submarine battery factory for the early shift, and later managing a battery and electrical wholesale subsidiary in Tunbridge Wells – I fell for the inevitable offer to join Cape Battery Company, and sailed for South Africa in January 1953. When it split from my father's business, I remained and subsequently was asked to join Chloride proper, as assistant sales manager in South Africa. We put Exide on the map, literally, for while Chloride was well established as an industrial type battery, its automotive product, Exide, only went into local manufacture there in 1953. It has never looked back.

Mary Finlay and I met in October 1958, when she was the bridesmaid at the wedding of mutual friends. Her father had established Safmarine, the South African shipping line, a few years earlier, where he and 'Bomber' Harris (of wartime fame) were the joint managing directors. The shipping line went from strength to strength. Today it is substantial with a large fleet of ships, and it is highly profitable, having weathered recessions which many larger competitors around the world were rather less able to handle. The idea of their daughter marrying an unknown fellow from the Eastern Province – 'some sort of salesman in a battery company' did not immediately appeal to Jock and Doris Finlay. As Mary said to me: 'It's nothing personal, it's just that they always had in mind a Lord or at least a Knight!'

The Safmarine business typified the entrepreneurial resource which still abounds in South Africa – a country with untold potential, with people of all races who have a great capacity for work and innovation. I only wish more of this drive could be diverted towards solving the political and social problems. The leadership resource in mining, industry and business is capable of managing change, but change needs to be effected on a grand scale with a political dimension – then southern Africa would indeed be transformed. As it is, there are reactionary, myopic political forces which attract odium and international criticism from South Africa's friends, as well as her enemies. A more progressive attitude would replace opprobrium with massive investment, and enthusiastic support. Although the present Government recognises this, it is also aware that politics are the art of the possible. While time is not on its side, speeding up the action could well leave the Government vulnerable to an electoral challenge from the extreme right wing. The Government would certainly argue that it is planning deep and far-reaching racial reforms, but is implementing them more slowly than it would wish; that is, at a pace which will avoid too high a price in electoral terms. If the Government can't muster support for its policies it won't be there to implement the reforms.

It is interesting how countries which have major internal problems invariably have exchange controls. South Africa's exchange control regulations are a case in point, for if ever a country should not need to curb the flow of funds, that country is the gold-blessed, platinum-blessed Republic. She abounds in minerals and natural resources and, above all, in people who have initiative. Those countries which are bold and progressive in political and social outlook do not require exchange controls to keep money within their borders – the United States and Germany are prime examples. Now Britain has once again achieved the distinction – a bold Chancellor supported by a bold Prime Minister has done what many other countries can and should emulate. What Russia and the Eastern block dare not do, for the outflow of roubles would build into a torrent.

No one who has been brought up in South Africa can fail to love the country: no one who has lived there can fail to admire what so many larger-than-life individuals have achieved. But most far-sighted South Africans accept that change must be managed right from the top, at the political and social level, and that no amount of progress by individuals and companies acting alone will bring about the sea change in the racial scene that is long overdue. This means that businessmen will have to become more deeply involved in political and economic policy formulation and implementation. The present structure of society is seen by the world at large to be inequitable – the hope among leading industrialists is that recent initiatives will accelerate change, and that change will be so clearcut and effective that investment will flow naturally to the sunny southern tip of Africa. Investment is vital if the people of South Africa are to be gainfully employed and the greatest service that the world at large can do to ease social strain in South Africa is to continue to invest while pressing for appropriate liberalisation. But the greatest challenge of all is to lead people to do the right things, and there is much that the industrialist can do in the employee relations field, given recent legislation that has sought to remove many of the barriers.

In April 1980 I was given an honorary doctorate in law, by my old university, Rhodes, in the lovely miniature city of Grahams-town, nestling like a great amphitheatre between the hills. The graduation ceremony was on top of one of those hills, and my address to the graduands was on the subject of change for I believe that change is the big issue in South Africa. Even the Great Hall from my days at Rhodes had given way to a new Hall – the original, in which I had been a teddy bear in the Teddy bears' Picnic, I had watched burn to the ground in 1950. Eight hundred of us in our pyjamas poured out of the 'Men's' and 'Women's' residences at 2.00 am to watch the spectacle. But at the graduation ceremony I spoke of more serious and fundamental change.

> If I have reached any conclusion from my experiences so far, it is this: if there is a touchstone to human attitudes, that touchstone is change. How nations, how businesses, how men and women come to terms with change is a measurement of themselves.

In the late 1950s a second great figure emerged in Chloride – the late Edward Powell. I never dreamed then that ten years later I would succeed him first as Chief Executive and then as Chairman. Edward Powell was appointed Group Managing Director and later Chairman and, as a result of the confidence he then, and afterwards, showed in me, I found myself at the age of 33 with my own command. 'Sort out Central Africa. The Federation is bound to be broken up, and we need to safeguard our markets in Northern Rhodesia and Nyasaland. We can't supply from Southern Rhodesia indefinitely.' How right he was.

And so in 1963, four years after my first meeting with Edward Powell, my wife, two daughters – Susan and Judy – and I moved with our few worldly possessions to Salisbury (now Harare in Zimbabwe) where we spent three fascinating years. Our third daughter, Penni, was born during those eventful times. Then, as now, she showed calm and self-possession in a crisis.

With help and encouragement from the young Dr Kenneth Kaunda, who was in the wings waiting to take over from the British Administration, we set up a factory in Northern Rhodesia. Soon after 'KK' became President of what is now Zambia, he and Chloride Zambia went on to do great things. Despite dire warnings from one or two of my London-based colleagues about the political risks, it was a very good investment. Neither Zambia nor President Kaunda ever let us down.

The reorganisation of Chloride's affairs in Central Africa was a rewarding experience. As the political pressures on the Federal structure became impossible to withstand, the spectre of tariff barriers loomed up. Mary and I were at the Victoria Falls for a long weekend in the mid-sixties when the news broke; the Zambian President had had a particularly unpleasant contretemps with the

Rhodesians, and was about to put up tariff barriers across the Zambesi. A quick phone call was made to Salisbury, and oxide mills and other equipment from our 'second' factory in Bulawayo were loaded on to three Leyland-Albion Clydesdales. Two days later, when the Customs posts went up, our load was well on its way past Lusaka heading for Kitwe. The new factory in Kitwe, which had depended on Salisbury for lead oxide, was potentially self-sufficient within 48 hours of the political decision being announced, and within a few weeks it was producing oxide. Chloride Zambia became profitable from the very beginning and in due course we built up exports to Katanga and elsewhere. We merged with a local battery business that had been set up by an enterprising expatriate Englishman, Bill Edwards, and our combined business made Zambia totally self-sufficient for all types of car, truck and tractor batteries. A success story that has stood the test of time.

We also set up a small plant in Malawi, purchased the major competitor in Salisbury, the Atom Battery Company, and each part of what had been the Central African Federation became a profitable and free-standing part of Chloride's African venture. Just as well, for on the 11th November, 1965, came Southern Rhodesia's Unilateral Declaration of Independence, and with it the final break-up of commercial and other links between Zambia and Rhodesia. Soon after UDI Edward Powell asked me to see him in London. He persuaded me to return to Britain where I had lived and worked as a trainee manager 14 years earlier. My family stoically accepted the change and the five of us flew out of Salisbury with fond memories of what is now Zimbabwe.

We settled in Redditch in Worcestershire. Before I became Chief Executive, and later Chairman of Chloride, I took on two successive restructuring tasks. Each was bigger than the Central African reorganisation, but neither involved top level political contact. In Central Africa, I had dealt with, at the age of 33, ministers and Presidents-designate but it was to be some years before my political experiences in Africa could be utilised in Britain.

After a comprehensive restructuring of the Group's nickel cadmium (or Nife Alcad) battery business at Redditch, I was invited to join the Main Board just as I turned 39. Eighteen months later Edward Powell plunged me into the heart of the business, following a palace revolution at the Group's major Exide battery subsidiary in Britain, and I had the fascinating task of breaking it down into three distinct businesses. The effect on profitability was instantaneous. Within 18 months profits increased from £600,000 a year to £5 million a year. This was quickly followed by my appointment as Chief Executive of Chloride and then Executive Chairman. For most of this period, until he retired, I worked closely with Edward Powell who remained Chairman while I was Chief Executive, and he agreed to remain on the Board as deputy Chairman when I succeeded him as Chairman. We worked very well together.

Profits literally took off. In six years between 1971 and 1977, when I went to British Leyland, pre-tax profits for the Group increased from £3.5 million to £26 million. It was one of the most satisfying periods of my commercial life, involving the application of virtually all my experience gained over the years.

In all I spent 26 years in an executive role at Chloride adding professional management to my original owner-proprietor experience. Both careers were intensive in management development terms, and led naturally to the biggest challenge – the five years at BL. Chloride with its 20,000 employees towered over my own little business which employed 200 at its peak. British Leyland, as it was when I went in, employed just under 200,000. But during all those 30-odd years I was a capitalist only at the outset – as half owner of Lovemore and Edwardes and when I owned V. E. Lawns. Thereafter I was a professional manager.

There is much nonsensical talk about ownership. The social distinction between state and large private sector company ownership escapes me. The real difference is to do with accountability. In the case of BL the primary shareholder is the reluctant taxpayer, the man in the street, with the Cabinet acting as his investment agent – using his hard-earned money willy-nilly in what they perceive to be the 'national interest' sometimes against their own better judgment. In the case of the Chloride Group, the primary shareholder is that same man in the street, and his investment agent is a great institution, be it pension fund or insurance company. He can be more selective – have more say in how his cash is dispersed – particularly in respect of his choice of savings institution or insurance company. In both cases the 'primary' owner of the shares is the man in the street. The major difference is that in the case of the state-owned companies he can only have a major say in investment policy once every five years, at the polls. Even Members of Parliament have little influence on a determined Cabinet, particularly if the Government is in an unassailable parliamentary position.

But not everyone agrees that the best climate in which to work is where private enterprise, initiative, and the demands of the open market determine success or failure. Nor does everyone agree that rewards should be commensurate with the size of the challenge and the energy and skill applied by the individual – with his ability to solve problems and face challenges. After some years in Britain I have observed that there are many who would rather live with mediocre leadership than overcome their reluctance to pay relatively high salaries. This is the way to industrial ruin, for employment in British industry depends upon companies becoming competitive before whole sectors disappear. Those who eschew firm leadership, or will not pay for it; who are not prepared to stand up to militancy; who view state ownership as the Utopian solution, will watch unemployment soar still further, as our share of world markets continues to decline. For every 1% of world markets lost, 250,000 British people are added to the dole queue. And in the past 20 years Britain's share of world trade has dropped from 16% to 8.5% – a sorry tale.

I am in no doubt that the private sector is better able to cope with competition, to handle industrial and commercial issues; it works better for the man in the street, both in his role as customer and in his capacity as an investor of hard-earned savings. For the private sector system gives the individual more say in how his money is invested. In neither case is there much sign of old-fashioned monopolistic capitalism for few of the myriads of investors who provide the institutions with cash are wealthy people – any more than is the average taxpayer, who funds the state-owned industries. And investment via state ownership is far less democratic, for let us not fool ourselves: the nucleus of the Cabinet, a mere handful of people, make the big decisions on behalf of millions. The left wing may huff and puff, but that is how it works in practice.

But of course, there is a practical distinction between private and public sector companies, and it has to do with attitudes and accountability. In the private sector employees know the company is vulnerable to takeover, to failure, to market forces. So do its managers. There is a great incentive to survive. In the public sector these motivations are severely diluted, and the enterprise has less edge. In my own little business I made the decisions, and I thrived or slumped – I took the profit but I took the risks, success or failure were both for my own account. In the private sector 'quoted-on-the-Stock-Exchange' company, the Board and management make the decisions, but seldom own more than a fraction of the company. The banks and other shareholders constrain excesses, and can and do bring about changes at the top. In most state-owned companies there is not the same feeling of vulnerability and employees and even managers feel protected by government muscle. The Secretary of State's criteria are not always commercially orientated. Reality is blunted, the pain is reduced, the consequences of actions do not come screaming through; the strike that would kill off a private sector company hardly makes a dent on Her Majesty's Treasury. When the new BL Board took over at the end of 1977 this feeling of invulnerability, of sheer complacency about the present and the future, permeated the company. There was a conviction at middle manager, staff, and shop floor level, that the Government would see the company through its vicissitudes, whether they were externally imposed or, more usually, simply self-inflicted. It was therefore difficult to inculcate a sense of realism, for realism could well be suspended at any time for social or political reasons. How then can one create the right degree of accountability when other than commercial considerations can be brought to bear? I would argue that the theory of state ownership is one thing – the problem lies in its practical application. This is why one seldom comes across a well run state-owned business.

How then did I come to believe that the recovery of British Leyland could be effected; that a strong Board could overcome the deficiencies of the system – and that I could play a meaningful role in achieving this? My first tentative involvement with the company occurred in March 1975 and the next two years were to give me an inkling of how it might be done. How a strong Board might neutralise the inherent weaknesses of enforced state ownership – enforced in British Leyland's case because the company was in no condition to be returned to the private sector.

3

Into The Hot Seat

Early in 1975 Sir Don Ryder, who had recently been appointed Industrial Adviser to the Prime Minister, Harold Wilson, asked me – out of the blue – to become a member of the proposed National Enterprise Board. He said that the appointment had been cleared with the Prime Minister and the Chancellor of the Exchequer, Denis Healey, but there remained a formality to be gone through: I might need to meet the Secretary of State for Industry, for he would make the appointment. In the event the Secretary of State, Tony Benn, did want to meet me. I was aware of the reason for the meeting because Sir Don Ryder had given me a broad hint that my appointment to the NEB had been delayed for some weeks while Tony Benn instigated an investigation into my activities in Rhodesia.

One morning I was summoned to see Tony Benn at his office; I had no sooner joined him at his coffee table than he exposed his political philosophy in one sentence: 'Our job in Government is to look after all our people from the cradle to the grave.' I know that those were his exact words because I scribbled them in my notebook while I waited for the lift after our meeting. Each year I have transcribed them into my engagement book just in case I should ever forget how centralist Tony Benn's philosophy really is.

The meeting was genial: Tony Benn has a seductive charm and I am in no doubt it is this, rather than logic, which wins people over to his point of view. But no amount of charm could hide the fact that he saw the NEB as his machine for carrying through extreme socialist policies; and bringing further chunks of industry under government control. This he seemed determined to do. As I sat opposite him I wondered just how much weight he and his 'cradle to the grave' philosophy carried in the Labour Government. As the Prime Minister had already made the decision about my appointment it seemed that Tony Benn had no real say in the matter. So perhaps his influence was less than some people were led to believe?

Indeed, it is significant that all decisions on NEB membership had to have Harold Wilson's approval while Tony Benn was Secretary of State for Industry.

Why had Tony Benn looked into my three-year stint in Rhodesia? Quite properly, I believe, as I had been a non-executive director of TEPCOR, the Tobacco Export Promotion Corporation, before UDI. To serve on TEPCOR was considered to be a public duty, as it helped employment, helped the balance of payments and contributed to the Rhodesian economy in a positive way. The tobacco crop of £40 million was important to Rhodesia in 1965 and TEPCOR's main role was to boost tobacco exports. When UDI was declared on the 11th November, 1965, the TEPCOR operation had to go underground internationally, and like every facet of Rhodesian life it felt the confrontation with Britain, but quickly adjusted to the new situation. My resignation from TEPCOR took immediate effect upon my transfer to London, but the Board were kind enough to invite me to a farewell luncheon, attended by Lord Graham. Lord Graham, before he became Minister for Defence, had held the Agriculture portfolio, and had appointed me to TEPCOR. I remember that day at the Meikles Hotel very clearly for Lord Graham leaned across and asked, 'Michael, do you think "they" will bomb Salisbury, or perhaps Lake McIlwaine; and are they capable of landing paratroopers?' I didn't have an answer to that and thought at the time that the Minister of Defence (designate) was rather better placed than me to hazard a guess.

I could understand why Tony Benn wanted me investigated; nevertheless, he came to the conclusion that my activities in Rhodesia were beyond reproach and that I was a fit person to join the NEB.

But I, too, had doubts about my suitability for a different reason. Business and industry (quite rightly in my view) had grave reservations about the NEB's interventionist role, even if the wilder utterances from Tony Benn about state control and direction were set aside. Yet there was a consensus among my colleagues, both at Chloride and in the Confederation of British Industry, that it was essential to have some free enterprise voices among the industry and union representatives, particularly if the NEB was to wield power and influence. Edward Powell strongly advised me to take it on, which I did with some diffidence. Bill Duncan, a deputy Chairman of ICI, was probably under similar pressure and for the same reasons, and he made a major non-executive contribution on the NEB.

At the NEB's inaugural dinner Tony Benn made it clear that the funds being made available to the NEB, by his Government, were quite inadequate for his purposes: he saw it as a vehicle for doing a far more ambitious job; a figure of £10,000 million was mentioned as a target. Some of us at the dinner were unlikely bed-fellows, to put it mildly, and this attitude caused some concern. The notion that the NEB might buy up private companies on a large scale was horrific, but in relation to the actual funds available from the Treasury, it was also absurd, and in the event it never happened. There was a feeling that the Prime Minister and the Chancellor of the Exchequer were keeping a tight rein on Tony Benn; my own view is that he was being humoured. I doubt if Tony Benn shared my sentiments.

Whatever the internal politics in Whitehall, the NEB was charged with overseeing the state shareholding in Rolls-Royce, the aero engine company, and British Leyland, among others. And so from the unique vantage point of the NEB, I watched with both fascination and horror the 'Leyland' saga unfold.

The company – previously called the British Leyland Motor Corporation – had been formed in 1968 as the last in a long line of mergers going back to the early 1950s. The main amalgamation to form BLMC was triggered off on the initiative of Prime Minister Harold Wilson, Tony Benn, and Sir Donald Stokes – later to become Lord Stokes. The company was a single business in name only for each of its constituent parts consisted of the proudest individual names in the British motor industry: Austin, Morris, Jaguar, Rover, Triumph, Leyland. Even after they were ostensibly brought together under the BLMC banner each was determined to go its own way, until the respective company barons retired or resigned. At this point, quite late in the day, an attempt was made to centralise the whole business. The only thing this attempt had in common with the *laissez faire* policy of the earlier years, was that it, too, was doomed to fail.

Jaguar and Rover were not in fact self-sufficient in cash generation before they were absorbed, and the merger did nothing to ameliorate this. The model range was complex and in some areas (like the Rover and Triumph 2000 models) they competed directly with one another and there was no real attempt at rationalisation.

The managers and shop-floor employees of these once proud and independent vehicle makers showed their resentment at being thrown together willy-nilly by respectively fostering internal politics, and shop-floor unrest.

BLMC consistently failed to earn enough profit to reinvest in new products and facilities, leading to inadequate development and engineering of new vehicles, which in turn, led to falling sales and revenue. In December 1974, the company ran out of money and the banks would not extend borrowing facilities any further. BLMC sought government assistance.

The Labour Government's solution for coping with the BLMC collapse was to appoint Sir Don Ryder to two quite separate roles: Industrial Adviser to the Prime Minister, and Chairman designate of the NEB. In the former capacity he was to provide a public 'prospectus' for government funding of the company. This became known as the Ryder Report. In his NEB role he was to appoint directors, officers, channel government funds and monitor the progress of BLMC and other NEB companies. In both roles he exercised a dominating influence on those who were appointed to work with him.

As part of a major reconstruction of BLMC the Labour Administration offered to buy out the publicly quoted shares, and become the main shareholder combining with some 90,000 individual shareholders who preferred to keep their shares, presumably for sentimental reasons (I kept my few shares for that reason).

And so for the second time in the company's history centralism was at work. The Labour Government, having sanctioned the merger in 1968, picked up the pieces and took direct responsibility for its future. That the renamed British Leyland could not be saved without the injection of vast sums of money was painfully clear.

The Ryder Report was published in April 1975: four months later its assumptions on key issues like levels of sales, model rationalisation, the size of the workforce and industrial relations were severely questioned by the powerful All Party Parliamentary Expenditure Committee, which rightly subjected the highly optimistic Ryder blueprint to searching analysis.

The Committee highlighted the Ryder assumptions that BLMC would retain its share of the British car market at 33% while increasing European sales by no less than 25%. 'We are not satisfied that the Report's market forecasting was carried out sufficiently objectively, or, indeed sufficiently thoroughly.' The Committee added:

> If there were overcapacity in the European industry, or if the strong possibility of a price war in the European industry, or if the strong possibility of a price war in the European market were realised or if an increase in the price of cars relative to incomes were to damage the UK market then BLMC's increased sales would be placed in jeopardy.

The Committee also cast doubt on the value of the Ryder Report as an independent study stating: 'It is clear that the Ryder team relied to a considerable extent on BLMC's own view of the future.' This future was tied closely to a concept study the company had done covering a ten-year period on the basis that there would be 'a fairly free availability of cash.' In other words, the Ryder team assumed very substantial public funds would be available and planned on that basis. In this they were right – in most other assumptions they were not.

The Expenditure Committee got to the core of many of the Ryder Report's deficiencies but it did not have enough influence to block the Government rescue, and many of the Report's basic flaws were only revealed in the light of the impossible task faced by the British Leyland management between 1975 to 1977 in 'running the business according to Ryder.'

A third report was also published in 1975 which took a broader view of the motor industry. It was the work of the Government's 'Think Tank' (the Central Policy Review Staff), and its main conclusions were both accurate and depressing. It envisaged an unprecedented level of competition within the European motor industry for at least a decade; it pointed to serious weaknesses in the British car industry, with 'too many manufacturers, with too many models, too many plants, and too much capacity. These are the responsibility of management.' Just so! The report continued:

> Other severe weaknesses are poor quality, bad labour relations, unsatisfactory delivery record, low productivity, and too much manpower. With the same power at his elbow as his Continental counterpart the British car assembly worker produces only half as much output per

shift. It is not too late to correct these weaknesses. They basically arise on the shop floor, and it is on the shop floor that they must be corrected.

This was in line with my view, except that I would have given more emphasis to the lack of acceptability of many models being made by British Leyland and its British competitors; not only on grounds of quality and reliability but also because many models were simply not up to European standards. This weakness could not be put at the door of the average employee. The report went on to say:

> To improve productivity investment alone is not enough. The basic problem is attitudes – attitudes of both management and labour. The future of the industry lies in its own hands.

While all these issues were well understood in some quarters, the over-optimistic Ryder Plan remained the bible for the company's recovery between 1975 and 1977.

The NEB role was restricted to overseeing the implementation of the Ryder Plan – the Board having no say whatever in its findings. To the best of my knowledge Sir Don Ryder (later Lord Ryder) consulted none of the NEB members on the plan, and any suggestions or comments were dismissed on the grounds that his Industrial Adviser role was insulated from his NEB role – a quite bizarre situation.

During the period 1975–77 there were a number of changes at the top of British Leyland. Sadly, Sir Ronald Edwards died within months of becoming non-executive Chairman, and Sir Richard Dobson was appointed in his place, but Lord Ryder continued to exercise considerable day-to-day control of the business over the heads of the British Leyland management. Yet as the months progressed it became increasingly clear that the Ryder Plan was being overtaken by events. He had postulated expansion, when in reality the company lacked the models, the efficient manufacturing facilities and a management determined to get to grips with gross over-manning and over-capacity. Money alone couldn't do the job. In the short term expansion was not practicable with ageing models. Nevertheless, the NEB assumption that the Ryder Plan was still tenable persisted until shortly after Lord Ryder resigned, in the summer of 1977. During this time the British Leyland Board was obliged to go along with the charade. And while the British Leyland Board was constantly looking over its shoulder at the NEB, the NEB's role was ambiguous, mixing strategic policy with operational direction. The problem was that Lord Ryder felt the need to exercise executive responsibility from his Grosvenor Gardens eyrie at the NEB, presumably because he was the author of the Ryder Report. I come to this conclusion because he did not try to exercise executive authority in the case of Rolls-Royce, another NEB subsidiary. Lord Ryder literally visited British Leyland's factories and exhorted employees and unions to lift themselves out of the malaise. This undermined the company's management, and it made no impact on the disillusioned workforce. Meanwhile, militant representatives of the workforce exploited the situation to the full. The three-tier employee participation structure – a cornerstone of the Ryder remedy to solve the entrenched industrial relations problems – only produced a bureaucratic paperchase dissipating management resource and effort. Some management decisions were delayed by months while the joint consultative machinery tried unsuccessfully to grind out a consensus. Procedure and consultation to avert industrial relations problems appeared to overwhelm decision-making and action-taking, yet during this time the number of disputes rose sharply. This industrial unrest came to a head in February 1977, in the most disastrous dispute ever faced by the company, when toolmakers in the car factories went on strike. Ironically, it wasn't over pay.

The unofficial Toolroom Committee, comprised of skilled workers, had for a long time fought to have separate bargaining rights and to receive official recognition. The company had rightly refused, fearing that this would cause a knock-on effect with other specialist groups within the company; and that the already over-complicated framework of bargaining would collapse. Furthermore, the toolmakers' union, the Amalgamated Union of Engineering Workers, was adamantly opposed to recognition of this splinter group. Nevertheless, a large majority of toolroom and mechanical maintenance employees in the Cars Group felt so strongly about their case that they went on strike from the 21st February, 1977, and it wasn't until a month later on the 21st March, that they agreed to return to work. At its peak there were 40,000 Cars employees either on strike or laid-off. The men were frustrated because they felt that the Transport and General Workers' Union had been all too successful in narrowing differentials in their bid to establish an egalitarian society, and that neither management nor their own union had fought for them to any effect. Their strike was the result of sheer frustration. (I fully understood their point of view, as I told the toolroom leader, Roy Fraser, when I visited Cowley in 1978, but I also stressed that bringing the company down was no way to prosecute their case.)

The dispute marked a direct intervention in the company's affairs by the then Secretary of State for Industry, Eric Varley, when he froze government funds for the company. Whether he was right to intervene is debatable, but he did not lack courage. There was a management vacuum to be filled; and he filled it. But the British Leyland Board played their part: they said publicly that they would ask the Government through the NEB not to continue funding the business until there was a satisfactory outcome to the strike. More significantly they were also prepared to dismiss the men for being on an unofficial, unconstitutional strike, and it was this that brought the strikers to their senses. That 1977 was truly a nadir in the employee relations history of the company can be seen from the fact that by the end of the year over 250,000 vehicles had been lost through strike action. This at a time when there was still a strong demand for British Leyland's medium-sized cars, which were later to decline in popularity, as competitors introduced updated models.

As a result of the 1977 toolroom strike Eric Varley asked the NEB to carry out yet another review of the future of British Leyland; its overall conclusions were that the company had made just enough progress to offer the hope of recovery and future viability, and that further funds from the Government of up to £100 million should be released. These recommendations were based almost entirely on the company's relatively good performance in the three-month period following the resumption of work after the toolmakers' dispute, and did not take into consideration the prevailing downward trend in production, productivity and market share. But from that point onwards the combination of a growing crisis of confidence amongst dealers, tighter trading conditions, projected exchange rate movements, internal and external disputes, and a further fall in market share, showed that it was impossible for the company to achieve its targets. The situation was exacerbated by the unfortunate worldwide publicity that arose from a well-publicised court case, when an employee of the company made allegations of bribery and corruption based on documents which turned out to be falsified, thus increasing the frenetic interest in British Leyland's affairs.

With the resignation of Lord Ryder as Chairman of the NEB – I believe he found the intense press and public interest in him and in the NEB distasteful – the Deputy Chairman, Leslie Murphy, took over. With a background in the oil business and then in merchant banking, he was well placed to judge just how parlous a condition British Leyland was in. Leslie Murphy – knighted in 1978 – saw that changes at the top were urgently needed, for the complexity and depth of its problems made British Leyland a classic management case study: ageing models, declining market share, highly publicised disputes and strikes, chaotic individual bargaining arrangements involving 17 different unions across 50 factories, no consensus on the Board, a strategy based on the unachievableRyder Plan and a world image so damaging that the company craved only for silence, which it didn't get.

By the beginning of October 1977, finally, it became clear that there could be no confidence in the official projections and that the company's Ryder Plan objectives were not achievable. A week or two earlier, I had spent two hours over lunch with Sir Robert Clark, a member of the British Leyland Board, discussing the situation, and I agreed with his view that it was virtually beyond recall; that if something was to be done about it it would have to be done fast.

As an NEB member I watched these problems looming up with some apprehension. During the Ryder period it had been impossible to contribute, unless he paid one the rare compliment of seeking personal advice before or between Board meetings. Debate at the Board itself was discouraged, and even when he sought advice privately one felt that he had already made up his mind; that he was endeavouring to win one over to his point of view rather than seek one's opinion.

Post Ryder, the NEB became more genuinely involved, and it didn't take long for its members' views on Leyland to emerge – changes at the top were a pre-requisite to the company's survival. Most of us saw that even with Board and management changes the Ryder Plan could not be executed successfully; the first thing to do was to establish a team at British Leyland who would face up to and define the more limited objectives which were clearly needed.

Then came the bombshell. I was at my Chloride office when Leslie Murphy telephoned – could he see me urgently. Ten minutes

later I was in his office the other side of Grosvenor Gardens. Bluntly
he asked me: 'Are you willing to take on British Leyland?' I was
momentarily taken aback, but within half a minute I realised that
there was a certain logic to the proposition. Despite Lord Ryder's
protective attitude towards British Leyland at NEB Board Meetings
I had made my misgivings and criticisms known. Also I had observed the chaos, albeit at 'second hand'. I knew more about its
problems than most managers not directly involved. But despite the
logic my first reaction was 'No', particularly as Leslie Murphy saw
the job as a dual effort: Ian MacGregor, the Scots-born New York
businessman who had stepped down as Chairman of the AMAX
Corporation would be the new British Leyland Chairman, and I
would be Chief Executive. Ian MacGregor was already a non-
executive director of British Leyland.

The way Leslie Murphy put his proposal reminded me of a
similar tête-à-tête 18 months earlier in Sir Richard Dobson's office
at British American Tobacco on the Thames Embankment; a
recollection that caused me to ponder on how these things were
sometimes done in Britain. At that time I had called on Sir Richard
Dobson to invite him to join the Chloride Board as a non-executive
director, when to my amazement he pre-empted the discussion by
saying, 'I know why you've come, I've just had MacGregor on the
telephone from New York.'

I was dumbfounded. 'But he has no idea why I'm here.'

'Oh, yes he has, he's already invited me to take over as Chairman of British Leyland following Ronnie Edwards's death.'

Here I was, a member of the NEB; I had been with Lord Ryder
the previous day and British Leyland was our major problem child;
yet I knew nothing whatever about the proposal that had been put
to Sir Richard Dobson. Sir Ronald Edwards's death had, of course,
left a big gap, which Sir Robert Clark was filling admirably as acting
Chairman. It was said that he chaired the Board very crisply during
the interregnum, until a new Chairman was appointed. Clearly Sir
Richard Dobson found the offer very tempting; he asked me what I
thought he should do. First, I had to disabuse him of his assumption
that the NEB directors had been consulted about the proposal, and
then I spelled out why I thought he should think twice about
accepting the offer. I believed that it was impossible to do the job in
tandem. A company in that state needed, at least for two years, an
Executive Chairman with great authority, and dual responsibility at

the top – he was being offered the job of part-time Chairman which was unlikely to work. In the event Sir Richard Dobson succumbed to the temptation, and no one gained from the exercise. Indeed it was the continuing disarray at British Leyland that caused me to be sitting opposite Leslie Murphy, 18 months later.

'Who knows of this proposal? Does Richard Dobson know?'

'Only MacGregor; Bill Duncan, you and me.'

'I couldn't take it on without Richard being a party to it.'

'I can't involve him, or the rest of the British Leyland Board, until I'm sure you will accept, because Ian can't take on the Chairmanship – due to his recent commitments at Lehmans in New York – unless you take on the operational responsibility.'

'I can't let Chloride down – you say you want this to be settled and put into effect within a month; the Chloride Board would have to release me at uncomfortably short notice – it wouldn't be fair on them.'

'Nevertheless, will you talk to your Board? And if necessary allow me to argue the "national duty" aspect. British Leyland is insolvent again; we can't get funds through Parliament before it rises, and we must re-establish some semblance of confidence. The clearing banks will have to be persuaded to help us out and that will mean convincing them that we have credible leadership. The situation is extremely difficult.'

I muttered something about not being prepared to split the top role anyway, but that I would think about it while in the United States, where I was heading the next day on Chloride business. I spent an anxious couple of days there weighing up whether it was a workable job. British Leyland seemed to be in utter chaos; I was very doubtful about the centralised management structure and the capacity of its top management to pull it out of its nose-dive.

That weekend I attended Chloride meetings in Washington, where my executive colleagues, who knew nothing of the recent events, must have found me somewhat preoccupied. Furthermore, our meeting at the Madison Hotel was interrupted five or six times by calls from London and some of my colleagues began to wonder whether there was a takeover bid for Chloride! Meanwhile my mind was inevitably focusing on the British Leyland issue. Was my own background experience right for what had to be done? Could the job be done at all?

On the other hand, it might just be done, given substantial funds to restructure, de-man, modernise, and drive through the product plan. But that would require a free hand, and the minimum of NEB and government intervention. Furthermore, it would be no bad thing if I were not directly employed by British Leyland and therefore the Government, for this would give me greater freedom. Perhaps a secondment? I telephoned Leslie Murphy from Washington. 'I wouldn't accept less than the combined role of Chairman and Chief Executive. I want a free hand, including the right to change the Board on "day one". The Chloride Board might go along with a secondment, provided we agree a management charge sufficient for Chloride to make appropriate pension arrangements with me. I can hardly return to my old job at the end of a three-year absence.' I also knew from preliminary talks with Sir Geoffrey Hawkings, Chloride's Deputy Chairman, that they would be reluctant to do other than second me. He wanted it publicly understood that I was not summarily breaking my links with Chloride. This suited me from every point of view, for I felt uneasy about leaving Chloride at short notice. These and other issues were tossed across the Atlantic between Leslie Murphy and me until finally we established a basis of potential understanding.

The upshot of these lengthy transatlantic telephone calls was that I was to meet the peripatetic Ian MacGregor at Kennedy Airport – he was returning home to New York on the following day – when I could explain my aversion to a split function at the top. He readily saw my point of view and offered to be deputy Chairman.

This solved one problem, but two things still held me back. Firstly, Chloride was not ready for a change at the top – there was a lot at stake, for the company was set to make record profits for the seventh year in succession. Secondly, those few friends I had consulted were concerned that I would find the British Leyland job utterly frustrating due to likely government intervention, if not intransigence. Others said that I was crazy to put my business reputation at risk. Both points of view were shared by Ian Fraser, now Chairman of Lazards and then on the Chloride Board. The first point required full discussion with my Chloride colleagues, who – apart from Ian Fraser – felt I should do the job as a public duty, despite the obvious inconvenience to them. The latter required a firm assurance from the NEB so that I would be better able to repel boarders, if and when the NEB, the Civil Service or the politicians attempted to intervene unreasonably.

I was still undecided as I flew out of Washington to New York, when the news broke that Sir Richard Dobson was alleged to have made offensive racial remarks at a private dinner where he was the guest speaker; the speech had been taped secretly by one of the guests, and then released to the press. All hell broke loose and there were strident calls for his resignation, for only a few people were aware that a change of Chairman was in the offing. *The Times* newspaper was certainly not aware of this. In its leading article of the 22nd October, 1977, it assumed that his resignation the previous day was entirely due to the damaging publicity.

> Sir Richard Dobson does not measure up to the common caricature, so beloved of the left, of the crude and bigoted industrialist out only to exploit the working classes for his own benefit. He is, in fact, a man of considerable intellect, ability and sensitivity, with an entirely honourable career which has greatly benefited the organisation with which he has been associated. It is particularly unfortunate that he should have become the victim of a few silly remarks he made at a private meeting, recorded secretly and without authorisation, and deliberately leaked to a hostile left-wing journal.

It concluded:

> Whatever his real views are Sir Richard has left the impression that he considers many of the company's customers, and many of its employees, to be inferior people. For that reason, even if it was not the reason he gave, his resignation is right though the occasion was an unhappy one.

Here was I, thousands of miles away from base, mulling over the pros and cons, when the Dobson debacle sharply increased the pressure for my decision; I would have to decide quickly. I remember strolling the length of Central Park weighing it all up for the umpteenth time. It was always the positive factors that came to the fore: it *must* be possible to change the attitudes of management, the staff and the shop floor, therefore, why not have a crack at it? There were good men in the company; I had come across some down-to-earth people who were utterly frustrated about the state of the company. They were ashamed of the depths to which it had sunk.

Could I build on this nucleus of determination, and get it right? I flew out of Kennedy airport thinking more about how I would do the job, than about whether I would do it. I had turned the corner in the decision-making process.

Immediately I got back to London I told Leslie Murphy that I needed to resolve the two questions: Chloride's situation, which was up to me and the Chloride Board, and the need to have a free hand in running the company, which was up to him. I put the second point in writing:

> My main job at 'S' (the code name he and I were using for British Leyland) would be to build a team on a reoriented organisation which would take account of the real needs of that company. It follows that I would expect to have freedom in organisational terms and in the appointment of managers, subject always to the limits of authority which I would agree with the 'S' Board. As I see it, the Government/NEB interest in this is at the level of the appointment of a Chairman and Chief Executive, and the monitoring and termination, where appropriate, of this individual.
>
> My style of management would definitely be to optimise (but not maximise) involvement both of my own Board and of the NEB where the issues are of fundamental importance. I would not want to find myself in a position of reporting daily on detail.
>
> I would hope to reorganise the company with the maximum of disturbance in the sense of redeployment (of managers) but with the minimum termination of appointments given that individuals can be redeployed sensibly. I am not looking for a blood bath, but I cannot promise to have silent evolution – there will have to be some unpopular moves and some demotions and sideways shift of people.

I made it clear that without freedom of action from day one, the job was not for me. Leslie Murphy gave me the necessary assurances without any reservation and one of the major obstacles to acceptance was removed.

This left the other hurdle, and I put the up-to-date position to both Edward Powell and Sir Geoffrey Hawkings. They in turn

consulted the full Board. We quickly agreed on succession arrangements at Chloride; my colleagues there were concerned about the
turn of events but were generally of the view that it was a question of
national duty.

Leslie Murphy had pressed me to give him a decision on Sunday,
23rd October. I again debated the pros and cons with my family,
who never wavered in their belief that I should take on the job, and
on the Saturday, a day before the time was up, I telephoned a very
tense Leslie Murphy to accept. He seemed greatly relieved at my
decision for he had worked at it and on me for 13 days without
letting up. As I remember it he was unusually economical in his part
of the conversation, repeating two words: 'Well done, well done.'

My three-year secondment was to be announced on the 25th
October to take effect on the 1st November, 1977. I had no
reservations when I finally decided to go ahead. There were no
leaks, and the speculation in the press, as to who the new incumbent
would be, was so wide of the mark, that when the appointment was
announced it took everyone by surprise. It was also a surprise to
most of the members of the British Leyland Board, for only Ian
MacGregor and Sir Robert Clark had been taken into the Government's confidence. They were the only two members who subsequently remained on the new Board.

The whole proceedings – offer to announcement – had taken
three weeks, but unlike the five years that were to follow, those days
were long and agonising and went very slowly.

It has always intrigued me that with all the press speculation
that ensued, no one linked me with the job. The speculation came
after I was appointed: had the Prime Minister persuaded me to take
it? Had Eric Varley spent long hours of discussion with me about it?
It was none of these things. There were only two meetings with
Leslie Murphy, followed by a number of telephone calls to clarify
matters. He cleared the appointment with Eric Varley and the Prime
Minister and having obtained the full backing of the NEB, he
obtained my acceptance. It was as simple as that.

On the day of the announcement an opportunity came to take
the first steps, although it was still a week before I was due to take
over. And a fruitful day that turned out to be, for a key non-
executive director was to come on board who one day was to
become non-executive Chairman of BL.

4

First Steps

On the day of the official announcement I happened to be at the annual luncheon for Companions of the British Institute of Management of which I was then a Vice-Chairman. I found it astonishing that so many people had kept the secret, for the only other person in that room who seemed to have an inkling of my new appointment was Roy Close, Director General of the BIM and he was by no means certain about it.

Two weeks earlier he had asked me to take on the chairmanship of the BIM, and I had had to say, 'I can't – for reasons which will become clear to you in a fortnight.' I had by this time drawn up a shortlist of people to replace the predominantly executive British Leyland Board, for I was determined to have a small, largely non-executive, team; a key choice was the Chairman of Glaxo, Sir Austin Bide. By a remarkable coincidence I found myself placed next to him as we listened to strong words about the 'Leyland' problem from our colleagues at the table. This seemed to be the main topic of conversation for the news of Dobson's resignation was reverberating around London. 'Who would be silly enough to take on the job?' I found it extremely amusing, for I rather agreed with them. Sir Austin Bide was quite oblivious of the impending threat to his freedom. Halfway through lunch I whispered to him, 'I'm the mug; it's being announced at 2.30 pm today, and will you join the "new" Board next week, effective 1st November?' And he did. Two and a half years later he became Deputy Chairman, when Ian MacGregor resigned from the Board to become Chairman of British Steel. Sir Austin Bide proved to be a tower of strength in that key role as we hit problem after problem.

That same afternoon I started the process of meeting the existing Board members individually, seeking the resignations necessary to halve the size of the Board. This meant asking some ten people to retire from the Board; some had made an important contribution, but for one reason or another they would not suit the new situation. Besides Ian MacGregor and Sir Robert Clark, only Alex Park, who had been Chief Executive, stayed, and he resigned within weeks – in mid-December, 1977, when David Andrews rejoined the Board, the only executive director to be so invited. All the other executive directors were asked to resign from the Board. The three new directors were Sir Austin Bide, Albert Frost, ex-Finance Director of ICI, and me.

It was only with difficulty and after Leslie Murphy had prepared the ground that Albert Frost was persuaded to become a non-executive director on the BL Board for he was not keen on the public sector. Eventually he stated his terms: 'My role as Chairman of the Funding Committee must be meaningful, and no Friday Board meetings.' I gave him assurances on both counts. We agreed on a fixed period of time, and coincidentally when Ian MacGregor resigned to become Chairman of British Steel, Albert Frost's commitment to BL was about at an end, and he was able to join Ian MacGregor a few months later. They had always got on well together.

Albert Frost's contribution was greatest when balance sheets were involved. This wasn't surprising for the outspoken Albert Frost is one of the most financially orientated businessmen in Britain. Some of BL's most difficult negotiations related to whether government funds would be in loan or equity form; how much equity was needed to provide a properly geared balance sheet. These issues were meat and drink to him, and he was at the centre of some interesting debates in our meetings and negotiations with the NEB and later with Government.

In 1980, when we had wind of the likelihood of Ian MacGregor and Albert Frost joining British Steel we were able to provide continuity by bringing in first Sir Robert Hunt, Chairman of Dowty, with his superb engineering background, and to succeed Albert Frost as Chairman of the Funding Committee we asked Sir John Mayhew-Sanders, Chairman of John Brown, to join the company. Sir John Mayhew-Sanders is a qualified accountant and has a strong engineering background.

We remained a six-man Board until 1981 when Ray Horrocks joined the Board. At the end of 1977, Ray Horrocks and I had debated the pros and cons of his joining the company, to take over what was then Austin Morris. Eventually we hammered out the sort of role which I knew he could handle and which he felt able to accept. His immediate preference had been for Rover Triumph, but as in those early days we were still under the mistaken impression that only Austin Morris was in a real mess, I pressed him to take on that particular challenge. His track record gave me total confidence in his ability to tackle the job; he is a forceful, hard driving, confident man – not everyone's cup of tea for these very reasons. But he is a first-rate leader and has a professional discipline – what he would describe as orderliness – that makes him the perfect team man, in relationships downwards, sideways and upwards. Neither of us ever regretted the investment of time and patience in coming to a deal: he was the right man at the right time, and has made a major contribution to Britain's indigenous car industry.

Ray Horrocks, David Andrews and I ended up as the executive triumvirate at the top of BL. David Andrews was the only one of the three of us who had had extensive experience in BL itself. During my time with the company he had two quite different roles and he made a major contribution in each. First, as an executive director on the main Board he was responsible for finance, planning, and other central functions, including nursing some of the companies that were potentially for sale. He is a first-rate strategist and before my arrival had managed British Leyland International. When David Abell left the company, David Andrews became responsible for the Truck and Bus operations worldwide and also, later, Land Rover. Out of these moves the present organisation evolved. As the only other two executives on the BL Board, David Andrews and Ray Horrocks shared with me the operational decision-making.

I was determined to have a small Board, for a number of reasons. With such formidable problems facing us, there would be occasions when panic or crisis required speedy communication. Anyone who has cleared a four-page statement, or a long letter to employees, or a complex letter to a Secretary of State, with Board colleagues over a weekend, by telephone, will know that dealing with six people is more than twice as efficient as dealing with fourteen, Six or seven people can get on a wavelength, even if the odd one among them has slightly unconventional ideas. In a Board of fourteen, one is bound to get some ganging up and this distorts decision-making. A large Board has the tendency to baulk at communicating on anything but very big issues; with a small Board informal links are built through the company secretary, and soundings taken on less obvious issues, where colleagues' views can nevertheless contribute to the build-up of thinking. It is easier to consult with a small Board at an earlier stage in the proceedings. The difference is also reflected at Board meetings. In a large Board people instinctively posture; there is an actor in most people, and this comes through when the environment becomes depersonalised. In a small Board the same gesture or comment would be out of place, and would not therefore arise.

Knowing what I now know I would not take on a major restructuring of anything if it meant policy being determined by more than nine or ten people. The fact that BL had one of the smallest Boards for a major public company was a great help, especially from the point of view of strategic debate. It was also helpful to have non-executive directors who were deeply involved in private enterprise businesses; time and again, their support and advice proved to be crucial in shaping the business and taking hard, painful decisions. Despite the demands of executive roles in their own companies, they gave time unstintingly to BL's affairs. They were kept well informed on the major developments at BL through Arthur Large, the Company Secretary. At times of crisis, this often meant Arthur Large contacting them to inform and take soundings during the night and day, seven days a week. Throughout the troubled times there was usually agreement between us on the fundamental issues but consensus was harder won on detail and application! This careful communicating helped to align the differing shades of advice, and the resulting decisions and actions were, without exception, better for the debates.

Above all British Leyland needed a Board that had stature and was of an independent mind, and so could help avert undue NEB or government intervention. In the event this 'independence of spirit' was fundamental in keeping the company free from non-commercial pressures and from periodic attempts by government to interfere and 'second-guess' Board decisions.

My reasons for having a largely non-executive Board were not only to do with people. They were also concerned with the likely impact of tussling with government, and with the militant shop stewards who controlled many of our factories. I suspected the company would have to go to the very brink before the employee relations and other problems could be overcome. In these circumstances it would have been unfair to expect BL executives to make decisions about the company at Board level which would put their own jobs on the line again and again, and over a considerable period of time. What was required was a Board consisting of experienced independent businessmen, whose judgments would be dispassionate and therefore would be carefully weighed by both government and workforce; and a bare minimum of executive directors. People, in short, who were free and ready to resign if need be.

The restructuring of the Board was a vital step, and it had to be done – and was done – in a matter of days, before ranks closed against change. It is always in the first days of a crisis that the situation is fluid; after that the bureaucratic treacle sets again. Anyway, change cannot be managed if the Board isn't right – you must start at the top. The media saw the change of directors in November 1977 in the context of a boardroom blood bath and certainly the scale of departures gave superficial credence to such a view. In practice, it was all done very amicably. As is so often the case, the reality was different from the public perception. The executives who retired from the Board did so with dignity and with the genuine interests of the company at heart; some left the company and have gone on to further their careers in other major businesses.

The change to a predominantly non-executive Board meant that a new executive forum had to be created, at least until such time as we could decentralise the business. In setting up the Advisory Board I followed the management philosophy I had developed and used at Chloride. We would not be autocratic; each and every major management decision would be fully debated, and the Advisory Board would arrive at a consensus and then wholeheartedly put the decision into effect. It would operate in the same way when recommending actions which required Main Board decisions.

The nine-strong Advisory Board consisted of executives who would normally have been on a company's main Board. They were key people in providing the impetus to overcome the widespread inertia and resistance to change. It was formed on the 16th November, 1977, and included seven of the executives whom I had asked to resign from the Main Board. Apart from Alex Park, there was Derek Whittaker, who ran 'Leyland Cars' under Park: he expected the reorganisation of the company to make or break his particular role. In the event the decision went against him and to his credit he took it with understanding and dignity. The others were David Andrews,

IS HE TRYING TO TELL US SOMETHING?

Gemini, the *Birmingham Post*

David Abell, who ran the Special Products operations; Pat Lowry, Director of Personnel; Gerry Wright, Finance Director; and Des Pitcher, Managing Director of Truck and Bus Operations.

A number of these people found themselves in the unenviable position of having to associate themselves with the reversal of earlier decisions, or with courses of action that they might not be involved in seeing through. Yet, like many executives in the company at the time, their only concern was that the company should survive and any personal or personality issues or misgivings were subordinated to the task of breathing life into British Leyland. In this way a consensus evolved on every major issue – except the shape of the organisation itself.

I knew from my NEB involvement, that there was no breakdown of cost information model by model. The speed with which my new colleagues set about making good this mammoth defect, was encouraging; imagine trying to manage a business without knowing the cost of the individual products – it seemed unbelievable, and yet, on investigation, quite explicable. Accountants can only work on information provided to them, and the organisation, including that at factory level, was a shambles. Putting in proper accounting yardsticks and controls was dependent on bringing the day-to-day business under control – without discipline nothing could be done, and very soon we realised that the *sine qua non* of survival was to re-establish the right to manage.

Right back to 1973 the auditors had qualified BLMC's subsidiary company accounts because of inadequacies in accounting and inventory control. When I joined British Leyland the staff unions still refused to allow their members to work weekend overtime at the annual stock-take, so that yet again, in 1978, the Cars accounts were qualified by the auditors. It was not until 1979 that the qualifications were lifted. News of our efforts was music to Leslie Murphy's ears – through 1977 he, his NEB colleagues and I had begun to wonder whether the costing systems and accounting systems would ever be sorted out. That they were, and thoroughly, was due in no small measure to David Andrews, backed up a year later by Frank Fitzpatrick as Finance Director. But until the new team took hold of the situation the finance people were bedevilled by a large measure of indecisiveness on the part of management generally, and it was difficult for them to do their jobs effectively. They were crying out for an environment in which managers managed – and this took more than 18 months to bring about.

During these first few weeks we had established small task forces of executives to examine the key areas of the Cars organisation and to report back rapidly with recommendations on how best to structure product planning, engineering, quality, sales, marketing and other functions. Coordinating these groups was the Cars Organisation Group, or 'COG' as it was known, chaired by Pat Lowry. It was to be a wide-ranging review of the organisation structure. The individual teams were known as 'mini COGs'.

To ensure objectivity we also brought in a firm of management consultants and their representatives sat in on each of the 15 study groups. When the mini COGs reported to COG, some weeks later, I also joined in, and listened as group after group opted to keep the organisation unchanged. Their instinct was for retaining centralisation. At the same time the consultants submitted their report: 'A centralised structure would provide more scope for cost reduction.'

After some hours of debate COG voted 12 to 1 to keep the centralised Leyland Cars structure in being. It was clear that these managers genuinely believed that the existing organisation could be made to work, and they were in large measure supported by the consultants. There were, however, two other factors that made me very wary of their conclusion.

First, there was the need for a massive redeployment of managers over the next months, involving hundreds of terminations and many internal moves, and some external recruitment. There were too many staff men in line jobs, which explained why so little action was evident; why, to take but one example, the capital expenditure programme for 1977 had been hundreds of millions of pounds below target despite the availability of government funding.

There is no better way to achieve mobility of executive management than to change the structure sufficiently to create transparency – that is to create a climate in which each and every job must automatically be subjected to a spotlight; the appropriate staffing of each job (or even whether it should exist at all) must then be thought through in depth. The 'staff man', whose strength lies in analysis and exposition, sets out the problem and evaluates the possible means of solving it; the good 'line man', whose qualities are weighted more towards leadership and drive, carries through the chosen option with speed and effect. The right line man achieves a balance in these things; he seeks advice from his staff men, both at the operational level and at the centre. He will not be diverted. He creates the enthusiasm, which oils the wheels; he turns drive into effective effort.

The second factor was to do with identity. The Cars structure was claustrophobic and its philosophy was a disincentive, in that it provided little, if any, scope for people down the line, or in activities remote from Cars headquarters, to exercise initiative. Great names like Rover, Austin, Morris, Jaguar and Land Rover, were being subordinated to a Leyland uniformity that was stifling enthusiasm and local pride. In fact the Cars operations were split by function and geography; nowhere did the product names appear in the organisational 'family trees'. The manufacture of engines for Jaguar was carried out in the 'Radford Engines and Transmission Plant' under a separate management from Jaguar car assembly, which took place in the 'Browns Lane Plant, Large/Specialist Vehicle Operations'. The Austin factory was designated 'Longbridge Body and Assembly Plant, Small/Medium Vehicle Operations'. The Rover factory was simply known as the 'Solihull Plant', and MG works as the 'Abingdon Assembly Plant'. In addition, the engines for these vehicles were the responsibility of a separate management function. So as well as erasing the marque names, the organisation divided management responsibility so that there was no overall responsibility for individual products. In short, the worst type of corporate centralism was at work; I found it stifling.

It could be argued that both these subsidiary issues could have been dealt with by following the COG recommendation, that is, merely by changing the people, rather than the structure. Yet, if the existing organisation really was workable, and the individual managers were presumably not advocating their own demise, why was the company in a state of chaos? Why was the quality of our products very bad indeed? Why were inventories out of balance and excessive in terms of money tied up? Why were deliveries of cars uncertain and unpredictable? Why were no factories achieving targeted rates of production? Why had disputes run at more than two million man hours for every single month in 1977? Why had managers in some plants abdicated major functions – such as recruitment – to shop stewards? Why was all communication with our employees only effected via the union system? Why were we continually losing good men? Why were dealers defecting to competitors? Why were problems and confidential documents being leaked to the press with embarrassing regularity? These were some of the questions that I had debated with senior executives – and with my main Board colleagues, at less frequent intervals, but with equal frustration.

It seemed to me, in answering these questions, that there was a common thread. We had a classic case, on a massive scale, of faulty executive appointments – the wrong people in simply hundreds of key jobs – and only a change of organisation would provide the fluidity in which personnel changes would be the norm. It had to be done speedily and, like a heart transplant, we needed to sew the patient up as quickly as possible after surgery.

For the only time in my business career I imposed a decision on senior colleagues against an overwhelming majority view; I could not accept COG. At a meeting of the rather large Leyland Cars Board, to the dismay of all but one or two, I told them that we would reject the COG recommendation, and start the process of decentralisation. Names like Austin, Rover, Jaguar and Land Rover, would be resuscitated at factory level, and we would cut headquarters numbers both in London at the corporate level, and in Coventry from whence the Cars operations wielded a second tier of 'central' control. We would restore authority to the factories, rebuilding the roles of factory managers, superintendents and foremen. At that time functions like engineering, employee relations and accounting were being imposed on them from Coventry and elsewhere – it wasn't surprising that factory management had become emasculated, and morale had hit rock bottom.

And so the process of re-establishing management authority began. It took three years, and a few crises, to take root firmly and irrevocably.

Another factor which persuaded me to follow instinct was that the psychological assessments of executives were showing a disturbing trend. The use of assessments as one factor in deciding on a person's suitability for a job is commonplace in the United States of America and among major international companies around the world. They were used extensively in Chloride, but the fact that I began to subject British Leyland executives to them, within days of arriving, gained widespread and usually fatuous publicity. Stories abounded of powerful and high-paid executives lying on couches or playing with bricks – the reality was nothing as fanciful, and had it been, we would have lost good men! What was required was just five hours of intense concentration at a desk. The tests are very demanding and they reveal a great deal about people's basic intellectual capacity as well as their style and approach to management tasks. My experience has been that their use in recruitment improves the success rate in making appointments on straight interviews from 50% to approximately 90%. The procedure reduces the failure rate; it doesn't eliminate error, but it is an invaluable aid to decision-making – even for internal deployment. Assessment is, of course, particularly useful in the case of recruitment when one is not familiar with the executives concerned. But the tests also gave a new opportunity to many existing managers in the company to slot into new and often more appropriate jobs.

During the first week of November, we persuaded Eric Jones, the Welsh and Edinburgh trained psychologist, to fly to England from Johannesburg, to give us some months of his time. With Eric Jones assessing four to five managers a day we began to build a picture of the strengths and weaknesses of our top 300 people, starting with the executive directors. His work was later supplemented by other skilled psychologists, including Dr Ken Miller of Independent Assessment and Research Centre, so that by 1981 we had the benefit of in-depth assessments on no fewer than 2,000 managers.

Dr Charles Bahn was another key figure in our task of fitting people to jobs. A professor of Psychology at the John Jay College of Criminal Justice, part of the University of New York, he is also consultant to numerous public and private bodies such as the New York Police Department, the US Navy and the Exxon Corporation. Like Eric Jones, Charles Bahn's basic interest is assessment of individual capacities and capabilities, and he is also an expert in the creation of teams. He has spent long and fruitful hours during the last three years, helping us to decide the most likely effective deployment of whole management groups in BL. He has great faith in the strength of management we now have and which he and Eric Jones played a significant part in helping us to create.

Of the top 300 managers, 60 were recruited externally by selective search plus psychological assessments, and although the remainder were found within the company, they had to be assessed and appraised because there was the need for extensive redeployment, and I could not be sure that internal appraisals were always objective. Of the other 240, no less than 150 managers found themselves in new positions, often because of the need to get 'line' people into 'managing' jobs and 'staff' people into basically advisory jobs. Too often there were staff men – excellent men – getting nowhere in jobs that required tough line types. Over the first months a few managers left the company of their own accord, but many more were asked to leave. In most cases we allowed the manager to 'resign' but in truth most of these people were dismissed, and were paid termination payments. We helped them to keep their reputations intact by inviting them to resign. Many were good men, but changes were needed; some had lost credibility, often through no fault of their own, others had been over-promoted and needed to start again elsewhere. Nevertheless the triggering off of so many dismissals was very painful indeed, both for me and for the other company executives who were involved in the decisions. Fortunately most of those who left have done well in the more 'normal' climate of companies that operate under more moderate conditions of stress.

I have said that the most common fault was that many staff men had been appointed to line jobs and were simply not capable of making things happen. At lunch with Henry Ford II, I pulled his leg about the Ford Motor Company's contribution to British Leyland's problems:

> Your company has excellent staff men in staff jobs. A number of them have aspirations to run factories and manage large departments. British Leyland, seeing Ford's success, seduced many of them into line jobs, at which a large proportion predictably failed. Ford lost good staff men, and British Leyland gained inadequate line men. No one benefited.

He readily agreed, for during the late 1960s and early 1970s, large numbers of Ford men were recruited into British Leyland, in a vain attempt to halt its inexorable decline. With some notable exceptions Ford men did not transplant well. They were fine managers in the orderly environment of Ford, with its established disciplines and product-led growth. BL, on the other hand, has required the pioneer rather than the regular administrator. In the event, the few real line men in BL with Ford experience, 'the notable exceptions', have come through to the top. The two Group chief executives who took over my executive functions both once worked for Ford.

Replacing senior executives during those months was done by promoting those whose track record was good, whose psychological assessment confirmed their potential, and who had years of energy and drive ahead of them. In short, we pushed good young men into top jobs. At the same time we recruited from outside the company, in order to accelerate a change of attitude. The mix of external recruits and the best of those who had worked in the company, produced a heady mixture of determined people. But not everyone could be won over – our success rate in recruiting those we actually approached was only one in two: had we been more successful our recovery would be further along the road today. On the other hand, this forced us to take some risks with younger internal people, and by and large these have been successful.

My colleagues involved in this work of recruitment shared some anxious moments (and many international phone calls) while we fought, and lost, and sometimes fought and won. There were various reasons why, sometimes after months of time and effort, we failed to attract people. The obvious reason was the sheer risk involved, for the company seemed about to 'go under'. The less obvious reason was that their own companies hung on to them like limpets. The motor industry is very competitive, and good men are scarce. I have no doubt that many of the key people we approached and failed to get, came out of the episode better paid and with better prospects than when we first approached them!

Helped by a steady stream of good men from outside, who joined their beleaguered colleagues, we set about getting the business under control. Many hundreds of senior managers left the company, for you cannot reduce employees by more than 90,000 without management bearing its full share of the pain. I have no doubt that some good men were lost in the process because we needed to cut costs drastically and quickly, but on balance we found ourselves with a much stronger, younger and more effective team 18 months after the process started. As we tackled crisis after crisis managers were quickly put to the test and showed their courage and dedication. Had we not used thorough techniques to recruit top flight people, the managers already in the company would soon have rebelled at the 'foreign invasion'. Just as the body tends to reject a transplant so the corporate rejection mechanisms would quickly have been at work! Only the excellence of the recruits made this a feasible way to strengthen the teams and accelerate changes in attitude, for it is far more difficult to establish a mediocre man from outside the company than from inside. A good man will quickly win his colleagues over, even if he is a 'foreigner'.

This major concern – how to get the right people into the key jobs, and how to 'top up' a management that had been depleted by a host of factors, over the years – meant spending many hours of debate at my home over weekends. First informally and later meeting formally as the Management Resources Panel, we battled with the problem of deploying the talent we had to best advantage; meeting prospective recruits and trying to persuade them that the company had a future. Some, who shied away at the time, have since conceded that they regret not having been tempted. Others might have been relieved to be spared some of the stresses and strains, in which case they would not have been right for us.

The Management Resources Panel took up a great deal of executive time of the most senior people in the company. I had found at Chloride that the only way to make sure of discipline and control over the vital business of placing people was to set up an appointments panel at the highest level, and then let it function, and be known to function, so that people quickly learned to take it seriously. For most of the five years the Panel, chaired by me, consisted of David Andrews, Ray Horrocks and Pat Lowry — the latter succeeded by the Personnel and Organisation Director, Berry Wilson. While David Abell was with the company, he, too, was a member. Throughout this period, Sheila Witts was its secretary, and contributed to the debate.

Candidate after candidate was rejected in the early days, until the message went home: standards had to be raised significantly. People within the company were not used to seeing this sort of control working systematically — still less taking up many hours a week of three or four of the most senior men in the company, as it did for the first two to three years. During this period we devoted hours to people and organisation; people had to be persuaded to accept both organisational changes and job moves. This together with the periodic crises that cropped up, meant anything up to a hundred phone calls over a weekend, and additional telephones were installed at my home for the purpose. I am sure none of us regrets that those days have now gone.

By the end of the first few weeks the top team — or the nucleus of it, those likely to stay on — were becoming clearer about the way things should go, although none of us was aware at that stage of just how much 'surgery' there would have to be. Slowly but with increasing momentum, morale at the senior levels was rebuilt and this paved the way for regaining control of the business.

Within six weeks of stepping into British Leyland I found myself back at the NEB — this time on the other side of the board table, for I had resigned immediately on taking the BL job. There I listed a long catalogue of deep and strategic problems, with a tentative set of remedies which we all knew fell far short of what would be needed.

It was clear that the 1978 Corporate Plan formulated by the former management was completely unattainable and with it went any last lingering hopes that the Ryder blueprint could work. The product range was inadequate, particularly in cars. Some models were basically good but suffered from detailed defects and there were serious gaps in the range. As a result, earlier estimates of the British market share had to be revised downwards to below 24%; and we applied a contingency for an even lower figure for it would be 1980 and 1983 before fundamentally new models could be launched, in the small- and medium-car markets. We were losing a great deal of money in Continental Europe and it would be necessary to withdraw from some countries even though export prices were helped by the then low rate of sterling. Elsewhere in the world there were similar problems, and some of our overseas subsidiaries were losing money, particularly in Australia and South Africa. Too many of our products were neither up to date nor reliable.

I remember making the point to the NEB that the long held view within British Leyland that the continuous loss of market share was merely due to lack of production output would now be put to the test. Harry Urwin, of the TGWU, and an NEB member, had always countered the company's criticism of the unions by asserting that while models were not up to date sales would suffer so that 'better behaviour' by employees would not of itself solve the problem. Even at sharply reduced levels of production there was to be a build-up of stocks over the coming months, and Harry Urwin's point of view began to be borne out.

I said that we had no magic wand to produce new models out of a hat, and furthermore we weren't going to solve our problems simply by making more vehicles. Fixed costs had to be cut by at least £100 million a year and over-manning in the factories would have to be dealt with, which meant that many thousands of jobs would be lost across the company. There was no other way. Although the precise figures had not been worked out it was thought likely that job losses would be of the order of 15,000 people in Cars and 2,000 in Commercial Vehicles. However, even this level of de-manning would only bring jobs into line with the reduced scale of operations. It would not tackle the fundamental problem of poor productivity. That would be a task for later years.

The management structure was totally inappropriate to the task in hand and we did not have people with the strength to make things happen at the operational end: our factories were not being adequately managed. Also, there was a critical shortage of senior engineers capable of managing the engineering effort. If sufficient managers could be recruited into the engineering area, it seemed likely that the perceived shortage of 1,500 engineers, which the company had said was a major cause of many design, manufacturing and quality problems, might in fact disappear. Efficient management of the 5,000 we already had could work wonders.

The prospect for earlier introduction of future models was not good. As it was, all new car and truck programmes were well behind schedule, and there was considerable doubt about the viability of the new small car project, the Mini replacement. This in turn had a serious impact on the whole product strategy which involved capital investment programmes running into hundreds of millions of pounds.

In all my report to the NEB was comprehensive and very discouraging. The situation was not only a serious one for British Leyland, it would be a considerable embarrassment for the Government; for the Ryder Plan had been approved by them and was the basis of £1,000 million worth of public funding agreed in 1975. As the Ryder Plan was no longer remotely credible, it was our duty to say so to the NEB and to the Government.

The only tit-bit of encouraging news I could give the NEB that day was that Mike Carver, the Business Strategy Director who had moved to the company from the NEB, was rapidly developing a strategic planning base, as well as chairing two study groups to get to grips with the model programme. The low standard of planning and other documentation that had emanated from the company had been a source of grave concern, and Mike Carver would add some very much needed expertise. At least we should be able to table some credible product plans before too long.

When I had finished there was silence. Leslie Murphy looked around the room. Everyone was thoughtful. I was half expecting an unfavourable reaction from our union colleagues. Slowly it emerged that no one was surprised; no one disagreed with the broad assessment, for they had suspected the worst.

Lord Scanlon, the ex-AUEW leader, and Harry Urwin were plainly shocked at the implications of our getting to grips with the over-manning and over-capacity. But their view was that the NEB, like everyone else, would have to face up to the situation. Of course, none of us appreciated in those early days what the ultimate extent of the de-manning was to be. Lord Scanlon made the point that Cars' employees had just agreed by ballot to accept centralised bargaining and he hoped that the fundamental rethinking would not mean that this 'step of progress' in industrial relations would be thrown away. We really had no option but to go along with this. We would honour the commitment both on bargaining and on pay parity (the same pay for the same job in each factory). But in my heart of hearts I knew that had the new Board become involved earlier we would not lightly have undertaken to introduce central bargaining at a time when so much else was wrong with the company. Furthermore, there was a real doubt in my mind about the wisdom of centralising pay bargaining, when there was every intention of decentralising the organisation. But the ballot in support of this had been concluded on the 1st November, 1977, the day I walked through the door, so there was nothing I could do about it without causing an immediate confrontation. The cost of parity was to be a very big burden but we were inextricably committed to find the tens of millions of pounds that would be needed to honour the agreement.

As I returned from the NEB and drove down Piccadilly to Nuffield House, I thought about the challenge that lay ahead. That factories would have to close, that people would lose their jobs, was abundantly clear, but it would take many months to work through the permutations. In the meanwhile, a Corporate Plan had to be submitted quickly to secure funds from Parliament for 1978. The first Plan was a poor thing from a professional point of view but it was our own.

The new 1978 Plan was the result of a series of executive meetings held in November and December culminating in a crucial meeting of the Advisory Board at the Post House Hotel in Beaconsfield four days before Christmas 1977. It was the result of a searching review of our whole business, and it sought £450 million from the Government to see us through 1978. Not for the first time we were to meet at an hotel – off-site, and away from the hurly-burly and the frenetic activity that characterised BL in those early days. We found it impossible to have strategic debates in the day-to-day atmosphere of crisis and the inevitable interruptions that went with any meeting held on a company location!

At this meeting, the top executives, many of whom had conflicting views, prejudices and convictions had to come up with a coherent strategy for the company. The strategy had to settle items such as new products for the next five years which alone had investment implications of many hundreds of millions of pounds, and which had to be credible to a Government which was being asked to hand out the £450 million as an act of faith. Because of the size and enormity of the task at hand – and the depth of unreconciled opinions – there was great tension around the table. Over the months tensions were to ease as we built a top team that was on the same wavelength, but this was not so at Beaconsfield in December 1977.

The future of the new small car, code-named ADO 88, was a big issue that day, but there were others. After 30 years of short supply the expansion of the Land Rover factories was still unresolved and was still being debated: there were truck models that needed approval; Jaguar plans were still uncertain; the future of sports cars was in doubt, especially as a review of the TR7 factory at Speke had been dragged to the Board table to the dismay of many managers. All these problems faced a disparate group of people – some were in the company and had a future, while others were on their way out, and knew it.

My most vivid memory of that day was the way the new and the old, those who knew they had a place in the sun, and those who knew, or thought, they did not, all pulled together, and unbelievable as it was to me at the time, committed themselves to the new strategy. My respect for Alex Park and his colleagues grew appreciably. Eight hours later we left the room having achieved the first product strategy for some years on which the company's top management had reached agreement. In fact there was complete unanimity, and this partly explains why the press subsequently found it so difficult to persuade ex-BL people to criticise the new team or its strategy. For these senior men who left the company were a party to it, and indeed they played a valuable role in shaping it; they knew the business backwards, and many of us did not. It was a great step forward. At last there was a broad consensus and possible solutions were also beginning to crystallise on aspects that could not be settled immediately.

The Land Rover expansion project had to go forward urgently before other manufacturers took over world markets, but it would be at a less ambitious level of expenditure. A drastic rethink of the small-car programme was agreed to be essential but this could not delay the building of the modern £200 million plant at Longbridge. The building would have to go up while we thought about what we were going to build inside it! Objectives for quality, reliability and productivity were set; short-term 'face lifts' of existing models were essential if market share was not to evaporate. Market share was under pressure, because of the appalling image the company was presenting to the world. The whole of the company's weaknesses were painfully exposed by the Advisory Board – the failure to command adequate European market share on both Cars and Commercial Vehicles; the profusion of overlapping models and engines; the need for new single-decker and double-decker buses; pressing problems in several parts of the world for in some countries we were losing millions of pounds every year. Closures would cost money, but would have to be faced. All these programmes and others required in the region of £1,000 million for restructuring and investment; we were making decisions in that hotel room (which would later go to the BL Board) at the rate of about £125 million every hour.

One of the actions decided upon was to establish a test track and technology centre. Unlike other major manufacturers British Leyland did not have its own but had to hire these facilities. No wonder the company's reputation for poor development work had filtered through to the public at large. Spen King, then Director of Engineering at Leyland Cars and one of Britain's most talented engineers, had had to resort to testing new vehicles at night on public roads.

We set off home from Beaconsfield, tired but relieved at the rapport, some of us ready to relax for the couple of days over Christmas. Others of us, on the other hand, had such a mass of paper to read and problems to consider that Christmas 1977 – and indeed others to come – would pass almost unnoticed.

It was sad that the Advisory Board was to have a limited life span, but this was inevitable because as we decentralised authority to Leyland, Land Rover, Jaguar, Austin Rover and Unipart so Boards were established and operational authority was passed to them from the Advisory Board.

Meanwhile, to the outside world little had seemed to change; strikes and disputes continued. Even as we were weighing up the case for closing the Speke factory, we observed that the message had not sunk in – for the men at Speke were in the eighth week of their unofficial strike, a strike that contributed to the closure and sowed the seeds for the ultimate termination of the Triumph TR7 sports car. So in January 1978 Pat Lowry advised me to spell out the state of the company to national union officials, shop stewards and employee representatives. Over 700 were to meet at Kenilworth on the 1st February, 1978. I readily agreed to do it, for two reasons. First, I have always believed in involving employees in issues that affect their livelihood, and second, it was important to start as we meant to continue, by emphasising the impact on the company, and therefore on employment, if wildcat strikes and the many unacceptable practices, which had dragged down not just British Leyland but much of post-war industrial Britain, were to continue for much longer.

My speech lasted for just over an hour, far too long in any normal situation, but this was abnormal in the extreme. I had to convey a sense of purpose and a flavour of the decisions and strategies which had evolved over the previous few weeks. Much of it was unpalatable; the loss of at least 12,500 jobs and a warning that there would be factory closures to bring capacity into line with demand. Leyland Cars had had a theoretical capacity to produce close to 1.2 million vehicles, but were not achieving anything like that total. Market projections suggested that 819,000 vehicles for 1978 was a far more realistic figure.

Other issues produced a guarded but positive response; the fact that we intended to re-establish the company's main marques – the famous names of Austin, Morris, Triumph, Rover and Jaguar for cars, and give back the Leyland name to trucks, where it belonged – was welcomed. Loyalty and identity had to be built on recognisable foundations. Despite efforts to impose the 'Leyland' image across the company during the previous ten years, Longbridge employees still regarded themselves as working 'at the Austin' and this sense of local loyalty applied throughout the company. Sublimating proud names, loyalties and traditions to an artificial corporate identity struck me as being a great disincentive and therefore commercially unsound.

I reaffirmed that it was not the intention to throw away the seven years of work by both management and unions to achieve central bargaining, and I used a rather stupid employee relations dispute which happened the previous week to highlight the basic problem. Somehow management and unions at the then brand new, showpiece Rover car factory at Solihull had got themselves into a tangle over the issue of clean overalls and production had been affected. The new Rover saloon and the factory – then the most modern in Europe – had cost some £90 million, but there had been appalling production and employee relations problems from the start and this was the latest manifestation.

I asked the meeting:

> If your objectives are the same as mine then how can it be that hundreds of vehicles can be lost in one week because managers and workforce find themselves unable to agree on overalls, while the business goes to ruin? This seems to me to be utter madness. We just can't afford to go on tearing ourselves apart while the traditional BL customers drive cars from American, Continental and Japanese stables.
>
> I tell you quite seriously that unless we can have active and positive support and commitment at all levels of the company there is no point in attempting to persuade anyone that it is worth putting another pound into British Leyland.

I ended by evoking a not very original but nevertheless apt comparison with the dinosaur; British Leyland was lumbering around making a lot of noise, but not making a lot of headway, and it was not seeing the need for change. Unless there was change the company would certainly go the same way as the prehistoric animal.

When I had finished, there was a thoughtful hush, and indeed during the full 60 minutes there was little noise apart from the occasional shuffle of a chair. No one who was present doubted that I was speaking with absolute conviction, and that I was speaking with the Board and top management behind me. Later one union official, Ray Edwards, went further. He stood up and told the meeting not to imagine that Labour MPs were of a mind to 'bail us out again'. The previous week, when he had spent time at the House of Commons, the mood of MPs was so 'anti Leyland' (as he put it) that withholding funds was a real possibility.

On the previous evening I had mulled over and refined the

speech, and I knew it was comprehensive and fair. But something must have been on my mind, for I woke at about 5.00 am and could not get back to sleep again. Suddenly I knew what the problem was – our plan for Kenilworth had a major defect. Even if we were able to persuade the stewards, how would we know, how would the 197,300 other company employees know, that the meeting was in fact 'on side'? Indeed, would the militants, most of whom were among the 500 stewards present, deny that there had in fact been a good rapport? There probably wouldn't be any clapping – it wasn't that sort of meeting. My speech was frankly more like an oration at a funeral. How to extract some kind of a commitment? A plan came to me.

Later that morning, when I arrived at the Chesford Grange Hotel in Kenilworth, all but 25 of the 720 delegates were packed like sardines into a hall designed for 500. I joined the 25 key people, national union officials and shop stewards, who were having coffee in the back room together with a few top managers. With minutes to go I lobbed my brick into the pond.

'By the way, when I've finished speaking, I want Pat Lowry, as chairman of the meeting to say that after the debate, he will be calling for a vote of confidence. We will take the vote only after people from the floor have asked questions or addressed the meeting, to give everyone the opportunity of opposing the confidence vote.'

There was a shocked silence for five seconds – but what could they do about it? Clearly, it was our meeting, and it was also our risk. The stewards put a brave face on it, and so we went into the meeting with only a few of us knowing that this was more than a casual address; the company was looking for a commitment, which would become public in a couple of hours.

When I finished speaking two extreme militants argued against the company position – triggered off by Pat Lowry's statement that a vote would follow. I feared the worst, but then a string of union officials and stewards supported what I had said, and the gamble looked less dicey. And then came the vote – 715 in favour and 5 against. It was just the commitment we needed to start to offset the damaging image the company had shown to the public for years.

As the men poured out into the winter sunshine the positive atmosphere of the meeting was conveyed to the journalists, surrounding the hall. For the first time in years the company had a sympathetic press as the inkling of a tentative unity between the workforce and management became apparent.

The uplift was to continue two days later at a meeting in the Wembley Conference Centre of some 2,000 of our dealers and distributors. Their morale had reached rock bottom; many of them were wondering if the sensible thing would be to turn their back on British Leyland and accept one of the many offers being held out by European and Japanese manufacturers who were eager to increase their own British networks. I remember that about this time Renault had chartered planes to take selected British Leyland dealers for a few days in France. But such was their loyalty that there were few takers, even though they, too, lived with the possibility of the company closing and, with it, their own businesses; some were family concerns built up over 80 years or more.

The dealers had to be retained. In due course, as new models were introduced and volume started to increase – hopefully in 1983 and 1984 – the British and European networks would be crucial. A mass exodus of dealers would have been as disastrous as a major strike and would have pushed the company over the precipice.

Understandably, before the Wembley meeting started, there was an air of 'We've seen it all before'. They had been let down time and again with successive management teams in the so-called driving seat. Why should this one be any different or any more successful? Why should we end up in the seat rather than under the front wheels? History was against us.

We were able to tell them of the vote of confidence at Kenilworth and we outlined the decentralisation plans. The fact that Austin, Jaguar, and other marques were to come back to prominence was greeted ecstatically. The response confirmed that we were on the right lines, and that employees and dealers had had their fill of centralisation. Wembley that day was an experience, for I doubt whether any of the management team had ever before harangued and encouraged 2,000 people, all in one vast hall.

While giving them the sort of news they wanted to hear and believe, I also reminded them that their own shortcomings, particularly in servicing customers' cars, were doing nothing to help the company's image. This was a source of irritation to me throughout my period at BL; the company had been a sitting duck for any harassed dealer, or his employee, seeking to shift the blame for poor service. 'It's the factory's fault,' is heard far too often in the motor retail trade, and certainly in the climate of British Leyland bashing of 1977/78 a customer was likely to accept it unquestioningly as yet another instance of the company's failure. Whatever they may have thought of the criticism, they responded strongly and positively to the main issues, and after Ray Horrocks and his senior sales team had taken them through the product programme, it was a very motivated and quite emotional audience which pledged full support and commitment to the company's survival at the end of that three-hour meeting. I have seldom heard such enthusiasm; it gave us great encouragement. A continuing feature of the three years before the introduction of Metro, was the sheer faith which kept these dealers loyal.

We had taken the first positive steps in public, just a few days apart. The media speculation which had reached almost hysteria levels over the future of the company between November 1977 and February 1978 had subsided in the face of the plans we had announced and which had been generally well received. Over 700 shop stewards, union officials and key managers had committed themselves to our general strategy, and the dealer network had thrown its weight behind us too.

However there were still major obstacles to overcome before anyone could begin to see a way through the minefield. One of them, the closure of Speke, came within a few days of the Wembley meeting.

The future of the plant had been periodically under review for many years; it was one of those misguided efforts by successive governments to impose their will on the motor industry – to create new factories and jobs in areas of high unemployment and away from the traditional motor manufacturing centres; away from the centre of gravity from a competitive cost standpoint. The Triumph Motor Company acquired an old safe-making factory on Merseyside in 1959 to set up satellite vehicle production, and then they expanded operations to take in a purpose-built assembly plant on a 103-acre site on Speke Industrial Estate nine years later.

The decision to close the Speke No. 2 assembly factory was the first test of the new Board's resolve, for there was no enthusiasm for closing it among the veterans in the management team. The decision was not taken solely because of the factory's industrial relations record. There was massive overcapacity in production facilities throughout the Cars operations and all locations were under review. Closures were clearly essential, but there was a complex web of inter-dependence between many of them, particularly in the Midlands, which was still the heart of the business. It was obviously not cost-effective to transport the many thousands of components needed to build a car – from washers to engines – from Coventry, Birmingham and other locations to Liverpool.

On any commercial consideration the Speke Plant had to be a prime candidate for closure, and the Board decided that it would have to close, and that production of the TR7 would be transferred to the Canley Plant in Coventry, where other Triumph cars were built. Yet the decision was bitterly opposed inside and outside the company, not necessarily because it was felt to be wrong. Many managers were simply convinced that the closure could not be delivered, that the Labour Government or the unions would make it impossible to implement. These doubts were also shared by some influential public people.

Shortly after the decision was announced in mid-February, 1978, Michael Heseltine, the Opposition spokesman on the Environment, came to see me and before he sat down he said, 'You'll never close Speke.' I imagine his objective was to test our resolve, but the purpose of his visit never really emerged. I made it clear to him that the Board would stand or fall on the issue. To keep uneconomical factories in business would be no way to deal with the mammoth and complex problems facing the company. His doubt about our will to drive through the closure was echoed by Bernard Levin in his column in *The Times* of the 22nd February, 1978. He wrote:

> I . . . will believe in the closure of Speke only when it happens and will not be in the least surprised if it does not. . . . I do not suppose that anybody in the Speke Plant believes that it really is going to be shut down for good . . .
>
> Of course there are people weevilling away in Leyland, as elsewhere in British industry, whose purpose is the destruction of the firm and of the jobs it provides, because they believe that their political aims can be furthered by damaging the economy and increasing poverty and resentment. And greater fleas have little fleas upon their backs to bite 'em . . . there is no lack of candidates for the

role of villain in this piece. But there is a much greater villain than the most villainous fomenter of discontent, the most obtuse and selfish shop steward, the most incompetent and selfish manager: and that, of course, is the philosophy so well, and tersely, stated by Timon of Athens: "'Tis not enough to help the feeble up, but to support him after."

British Leyland – and in this British Leyland is only a symbol of so much of Britain – is infected with the corrupting knowledge that others will make good its own deficiencies, and so long as that remains true, the deficiencies will not abate, but on the contrary will increase.

The main burden of his article was that Speke would not close, and he spoke for thousands who thought likewise.

Before the public announcement of the Speke closure we advised the Department of Industry through the NEB. Subsequently, the Prime Minister, James Callaghan, asked me to see him together with the Industry Secretary, Eric Varley and Sir Leslie Murphy, representing the NEB. We did not require the Government's approval for the closure, but we felt we should fully explain the logic of the decision, particularly as this was the first major car factory closure in Britain for many years.

There was intense speculation about Speke and the unions were understandably concerned. Press interest was frenetic, so to avoid too much excitement, I was taken through the Whitehall entrance to the Cabinet Office and into Number 10 and the Cabinet Room by the 'back door'. For half an hour I was closely questioned by the Prime Minister, who was extremely well briefed on Speke. Then he asked a question which made it clear to me that our case was won. It turned out to be a prophetic doubt: 'You have said that your new Board will always act in a business-like way and will make no decisions that are not commercially sound. Surely on that basis the TR7 sports car should be scrapped and not transferred elsewhere?'

Now he may have said this with tongue in cheek, but as things turned out, he was absolutely right. I argued the case for keeping the car in production on the grounds that stopping it would effectively ruin our export business to the United States of America – our major sports car market. Provided TR7 became *less* of a loss maker, the transfer of production back to the Midlands was justified to protect our distribution network in North America. But TR7 never did make a profit and when the dollar/sterling relationship moved heavily against us in 1979/1980, both the TR7 and MG sports car models became a serious drain on profitability and had to go. MG losses amounted to £26 million in its last year. The currency shift painfully exposed how unprofitable both TR7 and MG were to make as each model has so many unique components that it was impossible to achieve economic scale of manufacture.

In the event the predictions of doom and all-out warfare over Speke proved groundless. The workforce voted to accept the closure terms and managers who had warned the Board that plant and equipment would not be allowed through picketing mobs, watched the equipment being loaded and transferred peacefully and quickly to Canley and elsewhere. The Speke closure was a test of the new Board's determination to carry through difficult and painful actions, and from that point onwards it dawned on employees and public that there was a positive determination to get the business into shape.

It was at this time that we decided to rename the company and to bury British Leyland Limited. The company needed silence while it gathered strength and got its house in order. So long as we were British Leyland the media focus would be on the total business; the good things going on in parts of the company would not emerge, while at the slightest rumble in Longbridge or Cowley the press would attack the whole business. It was vital to get people's attention focused on Jaguar, Austin, Rover, on Leyland for trucks, on Land Rover and on Unipart. The only way to do this seemed to be to provide the holding company with a low profile uninteresting title, and so BL was born – not a popular move with the media.

The Government and the NEB had been mulling over our 1978 Corporate Plan for some weeks and it was with some relief that I learned our assessment of the business and its future had been accepted, and that the Government was prepared to provide the required £450 million in the form of equity; that is cash paid for shares in the business.

The announcement was made by Eric Varley in a written reply to the House of Commons on Monday, 3rd April, 1978, and to the outside world it set the seal on the glimmerings of a recovery.

5

Hearts, Minds and Militants

The period from early 1978 to the summer of 1979 was frustrating because progress was not always apparent. Tangible results came later. We entered the period with a massive staff redeployment programme, appointing some managers to new positions; confirming others in their old jobs within the evolving organisation structure; and encouraging others to look for jobs elsewhere. It took all of 1978 and 1979 to bed down. Business is about people and it was only at the end of this exercise of getting enough of the right men in key jobs that we began to take a real grip on the business. Nevertheless, while we were doing so, we formulated objectives, and none were more urgent than those which would lead to a workable employee relations strategy.

Some of my colleagues describe this 15 months as an illusion of progress. Although it was an apparent hiatus, a metamorphosis was in fact occurring beneath the surface, without which we could not have moved forward. The real problem was that management was still striving to get into the driving seat, having been out of it for many years. Some constructive things were happening on an *ad hoc* basis, but the major problem of employee relations was not being resolved in a strategic way. That shop stewards were ostensibly committed to the company's recovery, following the February 1978 Kenilworth meeting; that the dealers were enthusiastically behind the product and other potential changes we had outlined at the Wembley Conference that month; that Parliament had approved our request for £450 million (without a division of the House of Commons) were all encouraging signs. Customers saw that the Government and Britain were willing BL to succeed, but none of this was enough. We had to win the hearts and minds of the workforce. It was all a question of deciding on the right objectives and having agreed upon a strategy, then sticking to it.

We beavered away at key objectives through the summer of

1978. We needed to improve productivity by something like 150% over a very few years; we needed not only to reduce unit labour costs, but also the cost of components bought from other companies. There was evidence that a Ford Fiesta cost little more to produce than a Mini, partly because of more up-to-date design engineering – and therefore simpler manufacturing methods – but also because Ford's purchasing policies and procedures were far more professionally thought out. This was a direct indictment of BL management. Quality and consistency of production had to be improved immeasurably, and this meant that the number of disputes had to be cut to something like one fifth of what had become the norm in our 34 car plants. There is nothing like a production stoppage for ruining quality. Cutting disputes and improving purchasing techniques would also make for far more reliable deliveries and, of course, a better public image.

It followed from this that we needed to re-establish management authority, both outside the company, where our management of material purchasing was lacking in discipline, and inside the company where our 198,000 employees were relatively leaderless. To regain the management role would mean counteracting shop steward power, which had got out of hand to the point where national union leaders, local union officials, and certainly management, were being treated in a cavalier fashion by some 200 militant stewards who had filled the vacuum left by management. Not to put too fine a point on it, we needed to take on the militants. To do this meant improving communications, and going direct to the shop floor, while keeping national union officials in close touch with our problems and plans. We could no longer allow the militants to be the conduit to the shop floor and to Transport House, with the management view going by default. Everyone needed to know the facts in plain terms.

The objective was not to destroy or weaken the unions. On the contrary, it was to rebalance the whole order of things so that together with management national union officials would be able to play a proper role without finding their authority eroded by strong stewards, weak management, and a lack of understanding of what management was trying to achieve. This mixture had led to chaos in the past.

By any standards this was an ambitious programme; it required patience and persistence, and above all consistency. Giving way on principles that mattered would quickly conjure up the idea that 'the bad old days are coming back.' It couldn't all be done in a day, but we didn't have ten years either. We had to do what was right and then hang on.

What was important was to recognise that we were only nibbling at the edge of the problem. When I say that employee relations issues were not being resolved in a strategic way, I mean that we were still fire-fighting, running from dispute to dispute without tackling the root of the problem: which was that employees simply did not believe that the new management had a level of commitment, a determination that was fundamentally different. Years of vacillation had taken its toll, and managers had little credibility in the eyes of the shop floor. Indeed at that stage even quite senior managers did not appreciate how different they were expected to be, that new and higher standards of performance were being demanded, so it was not only a question of educating the mass of employees, but of changing the attitudes of managers who had grown up in an atmosphere of compromise and conciliation. This also applied to the personnel and employee relations area, where past experience led managers to a certain knowledge that they would not be supported at the crunch. They had learned that there were soft centres at the top of the company, and woe betide anyone who went out on a limb, for it would surely be cut off. During this period some people continued to sleep on nightshift, to clock off early, to refuse to work overtime and production time lost through disputes was still running at five times the subsequent 1981 and 1982 levels. Managers tackled some of these problems in a spasmodic way but there was not a general resoluteness, although courage was shown in isolated instances. Taking the company as a whole discipline was lax, and bad practices were widely in evidence and too often readily tolerated.

A watershed came in the autumn of 1978. A shop steward at Leyland's truck factory in Bathgate, near Edinburgh (where some 1,800 machinists were on unofficial strike over working new machine tools to standard performance) made some unwise comments in about the fifth week of the strike, which were reported to the press as, 'Stay out lads. They've given way before – and they'll give way again.' The strike being unofficial meant that it did not have the backing of the union; in this instance the union was working actively against the strikers, for they had no moral, procedural or constitutional justification for downing tools.

This attitude shocked me; particularly as I had gone to Bathgate a few months earlier for an Advisory Board meeting, and to meet management and senior shop stewards. We had been very explicit about the need to eliminate disruption and to achieve continuity of production if Bathgate was to stay in business. We had received assurances which rang true at the time.

Bathgate as a factory was regularly under review. Like Speke, it was another legacy of the geographical dispersal policies of the past, for it was far from the centre of the company's commercial vehicle activity, which was at Leyland in Lancashire. Everyone at Bathgate knew that it was vulnerable to cutback or closure, and this made the strike even more inexplicable – reinforcing my conviction that despite strong words, the new people at the top of the company were simply not being taken at face value by the stewards or the workforce. Indeed when eventually we were believed – perhaps by the early summer of 1979 – it was the employees who cottoned on; the stewards were the last to learn, a long time after their members and their own national union leaders.

What made the Scottish dispute particularly galling was that it was sparked off because the company had invested heavily in new equipment as part of a £22 million modernisation programme. Instead of welcoming the opportunity, the men wanted to be paid a premium for working the new machinery. While we saw this investment as providing tangible evidence that we were prepared to give Bathgate a future, a section of the workforce saw it simply as a bargaining counter for more money. If we were going to run into this sort of problem over £22 million of investment in one factory, how could we contemplate a wholescale modernisation and new product programme across BL, running into hundreds of millions of pounds in dozens of locations? Positive action to save the company was apparently creating even more attitude problems than those with which we had started! The workforce still seemed to be suffering from a euphoric post-Ryder sense of security.

The announcement of the company's results for the first six months of 1978 was due within a few days and we were expecting the usual intense media interest. This seemed to be the right moment to try, once again, to get across the message that management would not give way to disorderly industrial action, for the Bathgate situation provided a prime example of a *destructive* wildcat dispute.

When I went on the ITV and BBC lunch-time news programmes with Peter Sissons and then with Ian Ross, I was very angry and didn't try to hide the fact. I said that losses during the six-week strike had cost £30 million and the shortage of components was threatening to shut down other parts of the commercial vehicle operations. This was unacceptable.

I also said we were absolutely determined that management control and authority would be restored, and that the Board would rather see the factory closed for six months or more than give way on a matter of principle. Mindful of the shop steward's comments, I added:

> If we say we will not meet the demands of the strikers because we cannot, and should not, we mean it. Furthermore, I tell you now that investment at Bathgate will be reduced by the amount of cash flow we have lost due to the strike. We simply can't pay twice. I mean what I say. We will not cry wolf.

I was intrigued – and impressed – when I received two particular messages that afternoon, apart from general messages of endorsement from the BL Board. The one from Eric Varley, the Secretary of State for Industry, was explicit. He said how much he supported what I had said and that a strike in defiance of the union needed to be roundly condemned. He had seen the lunch-time television interviews with Peter Sissons and Ian Ross – in short, 'Well done.'

I had a less explicit but nevertheless encouraging message from the Prime Minister, James Callaghan. It left me in no doubt that for all his low-key posture, here was a man who could be relied upon not to let us down as we entered the grim battle for control of BL; a battle that stared us in the face, and could not be shirked.

We had tried the palliatives – increased investment, complex participation structures, and increasing egalitarianism in our pay structures. None of this, nor all of these, had done the trick. Five days after I appeared on television, the 1,800 workers were still on strike, but the shop stewards asked to meet the Commercial Vehicle management. Was it true that investment was to be cancelled? Yes. It was confirmed that a further £32 million of investment due at Bathgate would not go ahead and would be diverted to other parts of the business. At this the strikers were persuaded to return to work by their union leaders, with no concessions whatever from management. Nothing had been gained by the stewards or the employees and a great deal had been lost by each side, both in terms of business and jobs, for the longer term. But one important achievement had been gained: people were beginning to believe us.

The AUEW Executive Council member responsible for Bathgate at the time, Gavin Laird, is a man of strong character – firm but fair. I believe he had been a victim of local management vacillation in the recent past, and this was another good reason for standing firm when the strike occurred shortly after. His feelings about BL management were probably unprintable. It is symptomatic of those days that it never occurred to him to ask Terry Duffy, his union's President, to take the matter up with me; it wouldn't have occurred to any of them that if management actions had undermined his position I would be just as angry as they were. The fact is that the unions had come to expect BL to behave that way and to give in; and so had Britain. The militants were firmly in charge. As far as I was concerned the business was out of control, and something would have to be done about it.

Bathgate was a particularly serious dispute; but it was symptomatic of an attitude of mind that took disputes for granted – some were petty and lasted only a few hours, others were prolonged and damaging – this had gone on for years and it continued throughout 1978 and into 1979. When the employee relations record for the first six months of 1978 was collated it showed an appalling situation. Although disputes were well down on 1977, there were nevertheless 346 disputes which had disrupted the flow of production. The overwhelming majority were wildcat strikes – unofficial strikes which embarrassed the more responsible union officials who knew their own authority, as well as management's, was being challenged.

On one particular day, the 30th August, with Bathgate on strike, I analysed the figures and found that out of 13 major interruptions to production, 12 involved a total of only 160 people out of a total workforce of some 190,000. Less than 1% of employees were causing widespread disruption and damage to the business, flying in the face not just of management but of their own unions. All the disputes on that day were unofficial and unconstitutional. In fact, during my five years at BL, only a handful of disputes were either official, that is backed by national unions, or constitutional, which means within recognised rules and procedures.

The following day I was to speak at a meeting of the Guild of Motoring Writers, at the RAC Club in Pall Mall, supposedly on the general topic of BL. They were somewhat taken aback, I think, when I launched an attack on the militant extremist minority within BL who were putting the recovery of the company in real danger. It had never been spelled out before. How the militants over the years must have wondered at this reticence of management to bring the problem out into the open! One had only to listen to the vocal and strident interviews with militants on the early morning 'Today' programme on Radio 4 to realise how management's case was going by default.

It was clear to me that somehow the majority of BL employees and the leaders of unions, at shop floor, regional and national level had to become much more involved in defeating the disruptive minority. I knew that we couldn't join forces in an obtrusive way, but we could and should work in the same direction without necessarily being too explicit about it. There was no doubt in my mind that responsible union leaders would welcome a positive strategy from BL management, provided it emerged in the form of a pattern of actions, rather than an explicit statement of intent. We could hardly say to the many responsible union leaders we had come to know, 'We will take on the militant shop stewards; this will help you to restore your authority and stature – therefore, please help us.' But the new top team was conscious of the damage that had been done, unwittingly over many years, by turning the other cheek – damage that had been caused to moderate union leaders by backing down, having insisted we would not, and thus giving strength to the militant stewards who invariably resisted the realistic solutions worked out with local or national officers of the union concerned.

I often point out that 60 of the top 300 managers were brought in from outside; while several hundred managers had to leave. In other words the turnover of managers was a crucial factor in putting more backbone into the management hierarchy. Yet colleagues have pointed out to me that many hundreds of key managers, who perform very effectively today, were in BL in the early days when managers gave in, compromised and vacillated. Of course, this is true, and it strengthens my conviction that everything flows from the top. It was only when these people were given a lead from the top six executives, were repeatedly backed by the Board and encouraged, whenever they took a stand – and sharply rapped when they did not – that they were given a climate in which they could manage differently and effectively.

For all these reasons I took the opportunity when speaking to the Guild of Motoring Writers to initiate a deliberate strategy. We would either regain control of the company, or in the event of failure, concede that closure was the only viable option. This explains why I was so vehement in my condemnation of the 1% of employees who were prejudicing the 99%. It was to lead to unwelcome personalisation by the media – mainly around me – but it had to be done. The strategy had the full backing of the Board, and of the handful of key executives. Managers at every level were to join in, and at my frequent informal meetings with small groups among the top 300 of them I mounted a major assault on the problem:

> Act firmly, put some backbone into it – and you will be
> backed. Repercussions? Yes, of course there will be, but I
> give you my word, you will not be let down. The old ways
> are out – your job is to manage your part of the business.

Slowly the message filtered down the line.

Had the Government or NEB tried to soften our approach – or intervened as they had done so often before November 1977 – the Board would have been prepared to resign, to a man. But they didn't. My respect for James Callaghan, Eric Varley and Sir Leslie Murphy grew each time we were involved in a tussle with the militants, for they quite properly let us get on with it. Although there was some barking from junior TGWU officials, particularly from Oxford, our tough line with the militants was never really challenged by the union leaders. And if they remonstrated with us publicly, they were more understanding face to face, for on virtually every occasion we chose our ground carefully. There were isolated instances of bullying and unfairness; when these incidents occurred we dealt firmly with the perpetrators. The corollary of a firm management style is that it should be fair. Fairness is probably one of the major factors in leadership, along with the golden rule: never be petty – not always easy for any of us to achieve.

But despite the strategy I have described here, and probably dating from the heat of that summer speech to the Guild of

Motoring Writers in 1978, the media and the public regrettably saw the problems of BL's employee relations as a case of management and unions continually being at one another's throats. In 99 times out of 100 this was not the case; management was faced with countless cases where union authority over their own members had broken down and our dealings with the militants were to have the effect of strengthening the union structure in an unprecedented way. The problem could no longer be swept under the carpet when there was a very small minority of people who had both the company and the union leadership by the ears. The strike had been transformed from an effective and legitimate weapon to be used by trade unions to advance the cause of their members when all else failed to an immediate response used indiscriminately to further political and inter-union objectives; this invariably hurt other workers and the company. But workers were now beginning to become restless about this, showing far more awareness than before.

A case in point was a strike of 32 employees at the SU Fuels factory at Castle Bromwich, near Birmingham, also in August 1978. The men, who were toolmakers, were as much in dispute with their union, the AUEW, as they were with the company, over the right to have pay parity with other factories in advance of other employees. The union instructed them to return to work, and they refused. The strike dragged on for 13 weeks until threats of expulsion from the union finally brought it to an end. Had it been effective the dispute would have crippled virtually all our car production as the factory was BL's major source of carburettors. Production was unaffected throughout the strike because of cooperation by the management, the AUEW, and above all the workforce, who kept supplies moving by hook or by crook. They used the most ingenious means to keep machines going – more in keeping with *Alice in Wonderland* than with a Midlands carburettor factory.

One hot Sunday afternoon that August I was working at home when the telephone rang. The call, 'John McKay for Dad', rang through the house, as it did many times a day over the weekends, during those first four years of frenetic activity. In those early days, the Communications Director was synonymous with crisis, although he took it all calmly and philosophically.

'Those women at SU – they really are doing an excellent job – could you spare a day next week to visit the plant?'

'Not a hope; the only potentially free time is the first part of Monday morning when I have a routine meeting – with you as it happens. But why don't we meet on the M1 motorway, say at 7.00 am, and have our routine meeting in the car driving up to Birmingham?'

John McKay agreed. 'I suggest we keep this to ourselves and I'll telephone Ken Edwards, the General Manager, at 6.30 am, before you set off to meet me, and ask him to expect us but not to tell a soul.'

We arrived at 9.15 am and were let in to the factory by an astonished security guard. Past practice had been that the Chairman gave several weeks of advance warning before a factory visit during which time, the stewards claimed, vast sums were spent getting everything shipshape. Ken Edwards briefed us on the current situation, and confirmed our hunch that what was needed was a quick morale-boosting visit covering every corner of the factory.

What a din! As the message spread ahead of us, the ladies of SU banged every piece of metal at hand, converting the visit into the biggest cacophony of metallic sound imaginable. Appreciation of the visit poured out. The theme was 'every carburettor is one less Japanese car shipped from Tokyo', for at that time British factories were unable to keep up with market demand due to strikes. I recall that Ford also had several hundred disputes that year, and importers of French, German and Italian cars were exploiting the situation with telling effect.

I must have shaken hands and talked to hundreds of those determined women, who were defying the pickets each day and insisting on keeping their plant and the rest of BL going. They were the 'good fairies' who mended machines by Heath Robinson means, to keep production going; they used the most remarkable improvisation not only to keep the carburettors flowing but to do so at near-normal levels of production.

The *Birmingham Evening Mail* described the visit:

CHEERS AT SU AS BL BOSS DROPS IN

Cheers greeted BL Cars chairman Michael Edwardes when he paid a surprise visit to the strike-hit SU Fuel Systems factory in Birmingham.

There were shop-floor smiles as he appeared out of the

blue to give workers a pat on the back for keeping production going throughout the seven-week strike.

He told them:

'Every carburettor you make helps to keep another Japanese import from coming in the door.'

He spent more than an hour talking to groups of workers – including shop steward Mrs Sheila Conway, who a few days ago made a personal back-to-work plea to the 32 striking toolmakers.

'Everyone was surprised when they saw him,' she said later. 'It cheered us all up tremendously.'

Again and again our managers have shown how important it is to see people on the shop floor, to exchange views with them, and to show that they do care. The SU visit was typical of the factory-floor meetings I had with employees throughout the five years at BL. It would be hard to overstate just how much encouragement came from these frequent expressions of support and understanding shown by so many employees in so many of our factories. They wanted the company to succeed as desperately as management did, and they were as sick and tired of militant and minority disruption as we were. But it took a firm stand over Speke, Bathgate, at SU Fuel Systems, and over numerous other unconstitutional disputes before we began to get the message of management determination across both internally, where it was crucial, and externally, where it was helpful. On the surface, this was not a creative period, but it was a watershed in attitude terms.

There were occasions when firm management action did not in the event precipitate a strike although one might have expected it to do so. One example was the remarkable 'working' habits at Drews Lane, a factory producing transmission components in Birmingham. Activities there forced us to assert our authority as we were to do progressively in other parts of the company. At a meeting with Ray Horrocks in late 1978 he said:

We talk of regaining management control and applying proper disciplines. But at Drews Lane we still have an extraordinary situation. There is a long-standing tradition known as stint and finish. This means that employees can complete their daily stint, or work quota, and then go

home at any time from 3.00 pm onwards, but still be paid
up to the end of the shift.

Over the years they have applied pressure to weaken
work standards so that, against the already slack standards then applying, they are able to claim they have done
their day's work and management is powerless to give
them more work to complete the shift.

I told Ray that by chance, quite recently, I had been talking about
this to Eric Varley. It was an aspect of our peculiar affairs that I felt
should be brought to his attention – something that clearly had to be
faced at an opportune moment. It certainly could not be allowed to
continue. 'What do you plan to do?' I asked. 'Well, Drews Lane is
the key to overall production at our major assembly plants. An
all-out strike there would cripple us, yet we can't let it go on.'

A week before the BL Cars executives acted we advised the BL
Board that there could be a potentially disastrous chain reaction,
once the powder keg was lit at Drews Lane. They did not hesitate to
support the initiative. The day before, Eric Varley's office was
informed that we were about to reform the Drews Lane eccen-
tricities by enforcing normal working disciplines with a full day's
work for a full day's pay. In practice it went smoothly.

Drews Lane was only one example of many disorderly arrangements. In some plants there were negotiated 'deals' that made it
impossible to search employees, even when the flow outwards
extended from spark plugs to whole engines! In other plants
managers and particularly industrial engineers, were not welcome
on the shop floor.

Bringing a modicum of discipline in bit by bit was virtually
impossible. The inertia that protected these practices was too
powerful to be eroded gradually. After the Drews Lane episode we
realised that what was needed was a fundamental, far-reaching
change, and that is what the situation eventually attracted, with the
introduction of new working practices which swept away generations of extraordinary arrangements which ensured inefficiency.
But it took two years of progressive tightening up – preparing the
ground – before we could act in a comprehensive manner, right
across the board.

The year 1978 was not without encouraging events. The much
needed investment in the advanced engine test facility at Leyland,

was approved. Speke was closed and the TR7 transferred from there to Canley, in Coventry, on time to the day. Production of the Rover saloon car, which had been dogged by poor quality and manufacturing performance since its launch in June 1976, started to come through strongly at double the previous production level. The new 'O' series car engine of 1.7- and 2.0-litre capacity gave a new lease of life to the Princess and Sherpa models. And to brighten a lack lustre year, just before Christmas, the 96,000 hourly paid employees in the Cars operations voted 2 to 1 in favour of a pay package consisting of a general 5% increase, and a scheme to equalise rates of pay for similar jobs across the Cars factories by reaching very modest levels of productivity.

This happy outcome was short-lived, however, because by February 1979, when the question of parity payments arose, a combination of our own poor production performance and external strikes – particularly the Road Haulage drivers' dispute – had put paid to any hope of even a modest productivity improvement. This meant that the parity payments not being self-financing could therefore not be paid. As the payments were to be backdated to the previous November, we laid ourselves wide open to the accusation that we had misled the men at the time of the wage deal. In fact, what the shop stewards were really after – and based on past experience probably felt entitled to expect – was that we should pay the increase regardless of the fact that it had not been earned. That was the way things had been done in BL and elsewhere.

Some managers were indeed tempted to find an easy route around the problem; there were plenty of examples of 'give away' pay awards, thinly and unashamedly veiled as productivity deals, being concluded in Britain at that time. But the Board and senior management were agreed that we had to reverse the decline in output per man. To retain credibility and to emphasise our determination to achieve these genuine productivity improvements, we had no alternative but to withhold the increases. These might have amounted to £10 a week, had performance gone according to plan. Our approach could well mean precipitating a complete shut down of the 34 car factories, but this was a risk we had to take.

As the *Economist* magazine put it in February 1979, 'Nobody was required to bust a gut to qualify for these payments.' The benchmark was the dismal 1977 output figure of 5.77 cars per man a year. An increase in output of less than half a car per man a year between November 1978 and April 1979 would have triggered the first increase, but the strike at the Drews Lane factory over the parity issue had stopped virtually all car production and current performance dropped to less than five cars per man. Once again, mindless action by militants in one plant deprived employees generally of a proper reward for work they were prepared to do – but couldn't.

On the 2nd February, 1979, the company met union leaders and employee representatives on the Cars Joint Negotiating Council to tell them that the productivity part of the pay agreement could not be paid; employees would receive the basic 5% rise, and no more.

The following week employees gathered at factory mass meetings to decide what action to take. At Longbridge the convenor, Derek Robinson, erroneously claimed that work targets had in fact either been met or missed by a whisker, but that management had chosen to renege on the agreement. The media published his statement, and it received much more coverage than the management's refuting of it. At that time management's skill in putting across the facts direct to employees had not been developed, and the true position went by default for a day or two. A day or two was, unfortunately, all the militants needed.

There followed a particularly virulent campaign by stewards at Longbridge. The convenor repeated the erroneous statement of the day before, to the effect that production had in fact increased and that the men were being cheated and the entire 20,000-strong workforce went on immediate strike, after a mass meeting, without waiting to learn the outcome of voting in the rest of the plants. The Drews Lane Plant, which was instrumental in causing the original problem, also voted for strike action.

At Longbridge the convenor had 'talked' the men out before management really knew a strike was imminent. My estimate is that 80% of those men actually understood the issue and did not back the strike, but they were too frightened to reject the 'out of the gates' call. And they were more frightened when they tried to get back into work. Militant hoodlums had put barbed wire across the main gate at Longbridge, and had got away with it. Television cameras picked this up, and we lost more customers in a week than we would normally hope to gain in a year. 'There they go again . . .' rang through Britain, and some of it sadly found its way abroad. Few of the men at Longbridge – as opposed to the militant minority – supported this extremism, but I know that many of the moderates blamed management for tolerating this sort of behaviour; as indeed we had done for far too long. We deserved censure.

To add weight to the management's case, Longbridge and Drews Lane found themselves largely isolated from the rest of the workforce within two days of their precipitate strike action. When the plant votes were tallied only 6 out of 34 factories supported strike action and the numerical voting was 2 to 1 against. At last the facts had percolated through to the employees who came to understand that they really had not earned the right to the payments and, most important, that here was a management that would not pay out cash unless it was truly earned.

The overwhelming majority of the 250 stewards went along with the vote of the shop floor and called off a company-wide strike which, had it taken place, would certainly have put an end to the volume car operations.

Prominent among those stewards who would not heed the majority vote was the Longbridge convenor. But, although he misled the men, by distorting the facts behind the parity issue, and tried to keep Longbridge out, he was unable to carry the men with him, and Longbridge also returned to work three days later. But we did take one important step – we issued a formal warning to this steward for misleading so many of his members.

The strike at Longbridge and Drews Lane had cost the company dearly, both in production and in further damaging the company's public image, for BL was still perceived as being a business at war with itself. The parity saga was in fact to drag on for several months, until eventually it was implemented on a factory basis. As each plant reached the required threshold of productivity, it received the extra money.

These events brought home to us the need to set up direct communications between management and the shop floor. There was no other way to win the hearts and minds of the men at all levels. Politically motivated shop stewards could not be relied upon to present a balanced view to employees: they had a vested interest in the outcome, which was independent from and usually in conflict with the interests of the business and its employees.

From that time onwards we made sure that on each occasion when an important issue was at stake the company view was communicated directly to employees as well as through normal union channels. This often meant sending letters to employees' homes (where they could calmly and deliberately consider the situation with their families), the issuing of factory briefing sheets, and posters. When we felt a particular issue had wider significance we used newspaper advertisements and they seemed to be effective, for the militants invariably called 'foul'. These actions were supplemented by meetings on the shop floor, face to face with managers and I well remember Ray Horrocks and Harold Musgrove, then the Manufacturing Director of Austin Morris, turning up at Drews Lane Plant where shop stewards were holding a meeting. They sought and obtained entry to the meeting, stood on the platform, and put the management case direct to the stewards. This did not sway the militant group who dominated the meeting, but afterwards what my colleagues said spread to other employees like wildfire and the moderate view eventually won the day.

On many occasions we were accused of peddling propaganda and 'going over the heads' of the shop stewards. In reality, our new policy was only a threat to those stewards who had something to

'I hope you all realise that without Comrade Robinson's influence, we are faced with the threat of months and months of normal, regular, uninterrupted work!'

By courtesy of the *Daily Mail*

hide, for a balanced and fair account of the issues defeated their purpose. These were the people who had often exploited differences and who had caused widespread damage throughout the company in the past, simply because they were given a clear field. So management initiatives were starting to change the scene and slowly managers, throughout the company, started to climb back into the driving seat for the first time in 20 years.

The benefits of direct and effective communication with employees became apparent within two months of the parity dispute, when in April 1979 the toolmakers again took on both the company and their union, the AUEW, to press for separate wage negotiations for skilled workers.

I indicated earlier that I had some sympathy with the philosophy expressed by their leader, Roy Fraser, who worked as a toolmaker at the Cowley Plant. His aspirations for higher relative pay to recognise skills were music to my ears, and indeed I am sure that Terry Duffy sympathised with his philosophical objectives too; unfortunately like us he could not support further fragmentation of pay bargaining. Roy Fraser seemed to be honest and straightforward; unlike some others I knew, he did not seem to be politically motivated. However, it was quite impracticable to change the negotiating structure. There were bigger issues that required our time and effort. We could not concede for although his mission was right, his means were not.

The motor industry as a whole needed fewer and stronger unions, not a further division as Roy Fraser proposed. To have agreed to recognise his United Craft Organisation would have been to open the flood gates to other pressure groups, and we would have reverted to the sectional negotiation which had caused so many employee relations problems in the early 1970s. Decentralisation of bargaining rights might well have made sense, but this had to be done by product company and profit centre, not by proliferating craft and other unions. Furthermore, we were already thinking of the coming wage round in November when we planned to table a two-tier proposal; 5% for the majority of employees and 10% for the skilled minority. As a major move away from the egalitarianism of the past, this would prove hard to sell to the dominant union, the TGWU, whose membership was in the lower semi-skilled and production grades; but we were prepared to try. Had it been possible to tell Roy Fraser this, he might well have backed down before 'his' strike actually started. As it was, we had no option but to risk the possibility that he might succeed.

The unofficial toolroom strike was called for the 6th April, 1979, and between 3,000 and 4,000 skilled workers stopped work – far fewer than the 8,000 hoped for by the strike leaders. In a few days the numbers of strikers dwindled as more and more returned to work and people 'covered' for the men on strike. Within two weeks it was over and the company had not lost a single car through the action, in stark contrast to the 50,000 cars lost during the earlier toolmakers' strike in 1977. Why was the earlier strike damaging, and this one not? Because both immediately before and during the strike 100 senior managers spent considerable time on the shop floor – walking and talking in all 34 factories to explain the company's position; why the demands could not be met and the dangers to the business as a whole if production was disrupted.

The company was slowly overcoming employee relations obstacles, but the price in public esteem and market share for our products was very high, for each and every showdown reverberated around the world. At the Annual General Meeting in May 1979, I was able to tell shareholders that, at last, the employee relations nettle had been firmly grasped. But standing firm against unconstitutional and unofficial strikes had cost BL production of 110,000 vehicles over the previous 12 months, and some £200 million in lost sales. It was cold comfort to compare this with the 250,000 vehicles lost the previous year. Yet slowly we saw signs that attitudes were changing, and managers who had once seemed weak were exhibiting courage and determination as they began to believe that they would be backed and to feel confident that they could, in fact, manage. Ray Horrocks has a picture in his office of two seagulls in flight, and the inscription from Virgil reads, 'They can because they think they can.' This was the new situation in which our managers found themselves.

During this time there were powerful external influences which kept faith with BL. Government's and Parliament's support for the company remained generously high, and the private sector banks, both in Britain and North America were generally very supportive. The British banks had filled the funding vacuum when the new Board took over and, in the early part of 1979, both they and a group of overseas banks had been sufficiently impressed by our progress to agree to a £115 million loan at normal commercial rates.

It always fascinated me when our bankers, particularly in the United States of America, expressed more interest in our determination to deal with our employee relations problems firmly and unequivocally than in our short-term trading prospects. They knew that unless we – and indeed British industry – restored management control, there would be no hope. Therefore, they were prepared to share in the risks involved in facing up to the militants. Indeed had we not faced up to the militants I am in no doubt that they would have channelled their funds away from the problem-ridden company. Their help was enormous and with the Government equity injection of £150 million for 1979, the balance sheet was looking a lot stronger than many of our competitors' – although our capital investment needs were immense and we were not generating money ourselves.

I said earlier that colleagues have described this period (mid-1978 to mid-1979) as an illusion of progress, and so it was in the sense that ageing products and a rising cost base were about to catch up with us – exacerbated by a strong pound. Nevertheless, this was the time when we built up management resolution and started to firm up attitudes for what was to come – the storms, resulting from both internal and external forces; the crises, which were to put the whole company at perilous risk on no less than seven occasions over the next two and a half years. We were recognising the need to stand up to extremist tactics and we were learning how best to do so. The company had been at great risk through the Bathgate strike, the deferment of parity payments, the disruptive militant leadership at Longbridge, and Roy Fraser's attempt to force us to recognise his elite craft union. But in none of these instances did the company compromise on principle. It mattered greatly that no concessions were contemplated or made and this did not go unnoticed. I drew this point to the attention of the two 'Ronnies' who generously offered to review the nature of their 'Leyland' jokes, so that we heard less about workers clocking on by signing the visitors' book! My personal involvement in this was an indication of how much our poor public image damaged our sales.

But overshadowing all these things was the General Election, due in May 1979 – would there be a change of government, and what would be its impact on us, if there was?

6

Riding the Storms

There was indeed a change of government, and it had an immediate effect upon BL. After the political hiatus leading up to the change we looked forward to a period of stability. The company needed stability, whichever party won the election, but we didn't get it, because the Conservative victory had an accelerating effect on the strength of the pound, which had already edged up in anticipation of the election result. The impact this made on BL was fundamental. It brought us to our knees.

I don't want to imply that the fault lay entirely with government economic policy. We were brought to our knees because we were weak, because out cost base was just too high, and any major obstacle would have had the same effect. It so happened that it was the pound that nearly took us over the brink; it exacerbated problems which already permeated the company. But if there has been one issue on which the Conservative Cabinet has been widely doubted by many of its supporters, and censured by even the most moderate of their opponents, it has been the handling of exchange rates. Some said there was no policy, others said that there was an informal policy to 'steer' the rates to a predetermined target. Allowing free market forces to operate is a non-interventionist doctrine, and perhaps that is what we were being subjected to from mid-1979 until the end of 1981. Perhaps there was a broad strategy to tighten interest rates, and strengthen the pound, but my own conviction is that there really was no specific exchange rate target, until early 1982; one day when the facts are released from the archives, I may stand to be corrected. As to policy, the decision to have no policy is itself a policy.

The fact is that the pound took off – it took off for three reasons: because Margaret Thatcher was Prime Minister and her firm and unbending style quickly made its impact on our foreign trading partners, and on their perception of Britain and the value of the pound; because the North Sea oil resources were being reviewed and revalued by economists and it was being tacitly admitted that their impact on Britain's balance of payments – especially at higher oil prices – would be greater than earlier envisaged; and finally because the Government used interest rates as a lever. I believe it would be wrong to say that any one of these three factors caused the pound to reach such heights; it was a combination, for all three factors were at play. If these things had not conspired to strengthen the pound, or if public expenditure had been cut back sharply,

SID, PULL YOURSELF TOGETHER
– SHE MIGHT NOT GET IN

interest rates might have eased, the pound might have softened, there would have been less downturn in the economy, we would have exported more, and had less unemployment – but done less to streamline industry by reducing over-manning and changing un-acceptable work practices. Of course, none of these counteracting events happened so that particular scenario is hypothetical. What-ever the reason for the rise in the pound, it certainly forced many managers in Britain to take firm action!

The dollar strengthened at the end of 1980, despite the pound's "progress". This was mainly due to the United States outdoing Britain in many of the same stringent policies – but failing, like Britain, to reduce the national bureaucratic overhead. This failure to cut public sector employment and bureaucracy in Britain places a heavy burden on industry, particularly as more and more govern-ment employees are dependent for wealth creation on fewer and fewer productive workers. In the 20 years since 1961 the number of 'market sector' employees has dropped by 13% but government employment has risen by 46%, over the same period. The failure to cut public sector employment meant that the Government's funding requirement increased, and, in turn, this drove interest rates even higher. Both the pound and the dollar went on up to levels which made British and American products extremely uncompetitive compared with German, French, Japanese, Spanish and Italian equivalents.

Imports were sucked in to the United States and Britain, and the car industry in both countries suffered. In BL's case, despite the quick response, leading to the Recovery Plan, losses mounted, reaching some £500 million in 1980 and 1981. But funding these losses actually added to the public expenditure burden – precisely what the Government did not want!

There is a general misunderstanding about what a 'strong' currency does to a country's manufacturing industry, particularly to major exporters like BL – which aims to earn about £1,000 million each year from direct export business. The pound's strength against currencies other than the dollar had (and as I write it continues to have) two fundamental effects on BL. It meant that in overseas markets we got less sterling revenue for a given selling price and in our home market the opposite happened to importers. They received a currency windfall when pounds were converted into yens, francs, and Deutschmarks. So our competitive position was hit twice – through less overseas revenue and tougher competition in Britain.

This distortion in currency relationships makes goods in foreign countries seem cheaper, and goods in Britain become more expensive. Yet the general assumption, fostered by the media in such terms as 'the pound had a good day, it strengthened against other currencies . . .' is that we need a strong currency. When is 'strong' in reality over-valued, and 'weak' under-valued? Perhaps the answer differs by company – a strong manufacturing company can stand strong local currency, and a weak one cannot.

Twenty months later the pound was to go to a trade weighted average of 105, before easing back to the (still high) 1982 level of about 92. Even then, to be competitive with its 1975 level would have required a massive but unrealistic drop to about 76! The trade weighted average is the value of a group of foreign currencies (pro rata to the trade between countries) compared with a similar package some years earlier. The 105 related to a base of 100 in 1975, but of course, Britain's inflation in the interim was much higher than, for example, that of Japan, Germany and the United States of America, and so our competitiveness suffered by the difference.

Once again, largely due to our own inefficiencies but also due to these external factors, BL's future was in the balance. There was much burning of midnight oil in June 1979, and eventually we worked out a plan that would offset this new nightmare. And so we initiated 'CORE' – the Coordination of Resources programme. CORE was a far-reaching and meaningful term – it meant shrinking the business to a level beyond which we believed it was not safe to go. Arriving at this programme, known publicly as the 'Recovery Plan', was no easy matter. The fact was that the Recovery Plan, which was projected to cost money for restructuring in 1980 and 1981, and start to repay the initial outlay in 1982 and 1983, had to be imaginative and it had to be right. It had to convince the ascetic but sensitive Secretary of State for Industry, Sir Keith Joseph, and the somewhat doctrinaire Cabinet. The strategy for the recovery programme was probably the most extensive restructuring of a major company that has ever been done in a very short period of time. It was hammered out over several months, stretching over a number of Advisory Board meetings; many hours of thought and effort were put into the planning and the decision-making process.

We had the opportunity to present the outline of the problem to Sir Keith Joseph when he came, by helicopter, to the BL Technology Proving Ground and Research Centre at Gaydon, in Warwickshire, to meet the full Board on the 9th July of that year. He and his phalanx of officials sat on one side of a great square table, and our six-man Board sat on the other.

We told him that the remarkable appreciation of the pound since January, which accelerated when his party was returned to government in May, had had traumatic consequences for BL. Conventional wisdom stated that the competitive effect of strong sterling would be offset by cheaper imports of raw materials. But *our* raw materials were indigenous, and more than 90% of our components manufactured in Britain. It wasn't feasible to have a more indigenous product, with the possible exception of whisky. We were the archetypal case; a strong pound could only make our exports more expensive, and our competitors' imports a lot cheaper. We couldn't win.

Britain exports 33% of her gross national product, so there has always been pressure on successive governments to ease sterling when exports and employment have come under pressure. But this Government wouldn't budge. Any discussion on the subject met with a stonewalling response. Nevertheless, the Minister saw the implications, 'What will it cost you?' he asked. We replied:

At present projections – if the pound doesn't go still higher – the whole of our mid-car sector programme over four years will have to go. In other words, the whole of the LC10 programme – LM10, LM11, LM14 and LM15 – will have to go by the board, unless the Government provides additional funds *and* we take very drastic action; it is that action that will cost much of the additional money, for it involves restructuring, intensification of the de-manning process, and more factory closures. The redundancy cost will be horrific. Management is doing its damnedest to deal with the problems. However much we achieve with the unions – and much remains to be done – cost reductions will take time. All we can do is ratchet back what has been lost over the years. If the Government insists on looking at BL as a problem to be resolved quickly, then the Board's view is let it be 'packed up' now.

Without the new mid-car range the business has no future.

We continued:

> Our present plans are vulnerable, in the light of currency changes. They are now too ambitious, and the 1980 Plan will have to be less so; we would prefer to go in with a cautious Plan, and then beat it in essentials like productivity. There certainly is scope in that area but it will take another 12 months to implement closures, load the key factories, implement far-reaching changes in working reforms, get the new Metro, Land Rover, and Leyland, Lancashire, investments off the ground, and start to deliver productivity.
>
> The gaps from where we are now in the summer of 1979 to 1983 will be painful and costly. Market share will be under great pressure. We have a gap in the range from Mini through Allegro and Marina, to Princess. Until the small-car, the medium-car and trucks ranges have been renewed, we can't possibly generate the cash flow. BL has no option but to battle through the barren years, and trust the Government to fund us.

Thus we expounded the backcloth to the 1980 Plan – covering 1980 to 1984 – which would be on his desk in some four months' time and present yet another difficult problem for the Secretary of State to reconcile with his highly developed political conscience! In the meantime he gave no indication of how his mind was working. We were left to speculate on how the Government would eventually respond to the real issue; should BL be closed or funded?

Within a few weeks of the meeting with Sir Keith Joseph, the Advisory Board met at Ye Olde Bell at Hurley near Henley to make detailed decisions on how to restructure the business to achieve competitiveness. I stated that the purpose of the meeting was to agree the CORE action needed to put the company back on the road to viability at the new exchange rates, and to agree how this action should be communicated and implemented. There were two main challenges: to drive through the fixed expense action, and to drive through the more comprehensive recovery programme as a whole.

Peter Regnier, the Corporate Controller, stated the crux of the problem. 'Revenue in recent years has grown by 3.5 times, while fixed expenses have grown by 4.5 times.'

Mike Carver, Director of Business Strategy, stressed – not for the first time – that what was needed was performance by managers. He foresaw the need to go much further in all parts of BL, and he was right. All the line executives underestimated the task ahead, and so while the Recovery Plan was drastic and took some selling, in the event it wasn't nearly drastic enough.

But the meeting carried us a great step forward. To deal with the reduction in volumes, and the resultant over-capacity, and to live within the amount of money which we thought might be available, required a simpler product and facility programme. That objective, 'a simpler product and facility programme' is only six words, yet to achieve it on the scale we believed necessary would have profound consequences on the people within BL and on our manufacturing capabilities.

After each executive had outlined what he planned to do to meet the objective for his part of the business, the magnitude of the task ahead became apparent. In manpower terms a further 25,000 jobs would have to go to reduce manning levels and production capacity to a tolerable level. Triumph car assembly at Canley would have to cease. The MG models produced at Abingdon, near Oxford, would have to be discontinued. These models were uneconomic and were piling up losses which in turn were exacerbated by the shift in currency as the pound strengthened against the dollar. The United States had traditionally been BL's major market for sports cars and luxury cars like Jaguar. All was well with our exports to the United States as long as the dollar/pound exchange rate stayed at an unduly favourable level. This to some extent masked the uncompetitiveness of producing unique models like the MG for a specific market. As soon as the currency advantage was lost then our losses began piling up. We calculated that in the summer of 1979 we were losing something like £900 on every MG we sold in the United States. We could not stand that kind of drain on our resources and the age and uniqueness of the MG range offered us no alternative but to cease production.

Our capacity to produce car bodies far exceeded our needs, and so the large press shops at Castle Bromwich and Liverpool would have to close. Foundry operations would have to be drastically cut back. In total, some 13 factories would either have to be closed or severely cut back and the future of every one of the remaining car plants would have to be under searching review.

These measures were almost exclusively directed at the Cars operations, as the management of the Commercial Vehicles operations said that things were not so bad in their patch and they didn't want to be closely associated with a major upheaval in Cars. David Abell argued that massive action has already been taken to reduce overheads in Leyland Vehicles; that there had been a manpower reduction of 3,500 over the last nine months alone; and that they were forecasting a volume increase of 15% to 45,000 vehicles, despite the reduction in manpower. Nevertheless, the closure of Park Royal Vehicles, a London bus factory, was agreed due to its very poor productivity record.

Land Rover contributed to the need to conserve cash by cutting back the scale of its investment programme – more than £100 million was cut from its budget.

Yet when I summed up at the end of the meeting I doubt that I was popular for saying that I did not feel that we were going far enough. If BL was to seek the additional funds it needed, it had to cut back realistically. It was necessary to act immediately to cut fixed expenses. Managers would need to be prepared to carry out the tough actions that were necessary. We also required a period of low pay awards and a comprehensive overhaul of working practices in addition to the Plan itself. It was, however, difficult to pinpoint what more we could do.

The statement outlining these actions to the unions, and the public, could not afford to be either soft or negative. Our public stance must assume we would get the cash to support the Plan, otherwise we would lose our banks, our dealers, and other constituents. It was vital to keep our product programme going at full tilt. The announcement would be made on the 10th September, when BL's first half results for 1979 were due to be made public, and when a press conference would be expected. Before then Pat Lowry and I put the most senior union leaders in the picture, and none of them seemed surprised at the proposed actions – draconian though they were – and we were left with the feeling there would be no orchestrated resistance to the Plan.

The Advisory Board decided that the 10th September statement would be a mixture of decisions which were fixed and those which were for debate. It would be stated that before a final view was taken and before the Board put its proposals to the Government, there would be a period of discussion during which the views of all employees would be sought in a consultative process, for the reduction in the workforce of about 25,000 over the next two and a half years would affect those plants remaining open as well as those which would be closed.

John McKay thought that there was a high risk of a leak before the 10th September, but it was agreed that no statement whatsoever would be made prior to the official announcement. He was right; there was a leak. On the 2nd September a national Sunday news-paper often excessively critical of BL, but generally on the ball when it comes to digging out the facts, carried the headline: 'Leyland's £500 million shock for Joseph'. Its source became clear from the second paragraph of the text:

> British Leyland Chairman Sir Michael Edwardes is about to present Sir Keith Joseph with the Government's worst problem yet. In effect he is saying: give us an extra £500 million or I will resign, the company will be wound up and Britain will soon have no car industry of its own. The effect on unemployment would be catastrophic.
> *From Blackpool where trade union delegates are gather-ing this weekend* there were leaks of the major shake-up which Edwardes plans as a quid pro quo for asking for the extra cash.
> Edwardes wants to lose at least 25,000 and possibly up to 50,000 jobs from the company's 165,000 workforce. He is preparing what is called 'a very serious review' of the company's entire vehicle production facilities which will probably mean the end of the TR7, the Dolomite and the Spitfire. Hardly a model will be unaffected by the biggest pruning programme in the company's history.

Apart from the resignation threat, the article was largely accurate and on the 10th September we met a large group of national union officials and shop stewards at Leyland House, in Marylebone Road – itself under the axe – and we spelled out much of what the newspaper had gleaned from the most senior union leaders at the Blackpool Conference.

That same afternoon Ray Horrocks and his colleagues gave the same message to the Cars Council, the body of senior shop stewards inherited under the unwieldy system of employee participation set up following the Ryder Report. Both gatherings took it calmly but there was a general air of shocked resignation. It was made abundantly clear that the unhappy things we had to do could not be afforded without government help – closing plants and reducing manpower is far more expensive in Britain than say in the United States of America. This wasn't massive BL/Government collusion to cut the size of the motor industry – on the contrary, it was a Plan which might never receive government support, for it involved hundreds of millions of pounds of extra public funding. Indeed it was the antithesis of Tory policy: it sought cash to restructure, whereas their instinct was to let an unprofitable enterprise founder, naturally, in its own way, without let or hindrance.

The debate continued all that day – would we give them until the end of September to consider our plans, and respond? Yes – but we must make our thoughts public later that same day; which we did, meeting the press in the Piccadilly showrooms and sending letters to employees. Most employees were not at work as at the time all the Cars operations hourly graded workers were on strike in support of a dispute over pay and hours between the Confederation of Ship-building and Engineering Unions and the Engineering Employers' Federation. This was an issue totally beyond our control but devastating in its financial effect.

As the full implications sank in with the unions, meeting after meeting took place, in the days that followed, until the TGWU finally rejected the Recovery Plan on the 21st September, 1979. On the 1st October a management team travelled to Brighton to try to save the situation – we met the Confederation of Shipbuilding and Engineering Unions' executive en masse at Hove, comprising all the unions involved at BL. Hours of inconclusive debate followed during which the unions suggested we should avoid the painful actions by seeking from the Government £500 million *more* than we had in mind, in conjunction with import controls.

We said that unless we streamlined the company so that it could ultimately become profitable, we could not justify further funds. The BL Board would only be persuaded to go for further funds if there was a clear demonstration that the workforce was committed to streamlining. It was at that point that I asked, 'Are you sure that the Confederation [the CSEU] are reflecting the views of all employees in rejecting our proposals? If you are, then we will recommend to the Board on the 10th October that we seek no further funds at all. If on the other hand the CSEU feel able to support me, I'm prepared to fight like hell for the funds – and the BL Board will back the fight. If the Government says no, then it is the end of the road for BL – even with firm support for the new Plan, the odds in favour of getting the funds are no better than 50:50.'

Alex Ferry, the CSEU Secretary asked what would happen if there were no further funds – we said we would have to declare the company insolvent. We built on an earlier point, and stressed that if 'all of us did not deliver' then a right-wing government would feel justified in 'pulling the rug' because the company would make it obvious that it was not capable of acting to save itself. However, if the unions supported a ballot and the verdict was favourable, then it might be possible to get a sceptical BL Chairman and a sceptical BL Board to go to the Government for approval of the Plan. We would then try to get public goodwill behind us. As the £1,000 million was morally agreed, all that was needed was unity to get BL to the stage where any Government would find it difficult to resist the groundswell of supporting public opinion.

Thus the seed was sown for a ballot – but Ken Baker as Chairman of the CSEU reacted against it: 'There is no question of holding one.' They still felt that the Government might bail the company out by a massive injection of funds. The quicker they saw the Government the better, for this unrealistic thinking was clouding the issue, and it was left that the unions would seek a meeting with Sir Keith Joseph on the 5th October, with a view to responding by the time the BL Board met on the 10th October. The absolute deadline was to be the 17th October, when an emergency reserve Board meeting had already been scheduled in case of failure to agree by the 10th.

The CSEU Executive meeting with Sir Keith Joseph was a somewhat chilling experience – so they told us that afternoon of the 5th October, when the whole Executive trooped into Nuffield House to continue the talks with our management team.

As we met for a cup of coffee at the start of the meeting, there was some recrimination: one of the union delegates at the Hove meeting had handed the *Birmingham Post* a full account of what was, by common consent, a private meeting. I had written to Ken Baker, saying that the leak of information from the Hove meeting was the most cynical action I had experienced in 30 years in business, and that it would have a marked effect on what information BL would risk making available in the future. He was genuinely upset about the breach of confidence, as was his colleague Alex Ferry. I believe they knew who had done it, but it would have been impossible to prove.

Pat Lowry chaired the union/management meeting – a role he always performed with impartiality and skill, and not a little patience – leaving me free to lead the debate with Ken Baker and his colleagues, supported by senior BL executives.

Ken Baker told us that Sir Keith Joseph had kicked their import control proposals into touch with the argument: 'BL is itself a major exporter.' On additional funds, his appraisal was equally uncompromising: 'My role is to look after the electorate, not the motor industry.' He implied that he would consider proposals from the BL Board, but assumed we would not go forward with positive recommendations without the full support of the shop floor. It was what we hoped he would say, for there was no point whatever in giving the unions any false hope. After some hours of debate I said, 'There is not one iota of change in your position since our Hove meeting. I will now withdraw the Recovery Plan at the BL Board on the 10th October and recommend we seek no further funds.' We had already given the CSEU a BL draft press statement indicating this action; this would be released at the end of the meeting, in the event of a failure to resolve the problem. The meeting adjourned. On reconvening, Ken Baker proposed that we should seek the Government cash first, and then ask for workforce support. This we rejected. We would only go to the Government with employee support already committed, not before. It was clear that the second Board meeting would be needed as we would not complete the discussion process before the 17th October.

Despite the agreement with the CSEU to cool matters in advance of their consultations, and our further get-together before the deadline of the 17th October, a march was organised for the 19th October – independently of the CSEU – by the TGWU. It was to go past Leyland House, for the purpose of demonstrating against the Recovery Plan and handing a letter to me. (They seemed not to know that I had never moved into Leyland House.) We decided to pre-empt the TGWU. I spent an hour with John McKay drafting a letter 'from the heart', and when Tod Sullivan of the TGWU's clerical section handed over his letter to our people, they handed over mine to him and to the press. I wrote:

> Your march today is symptomatic of the reluctance to face facts and to be realistic about the ability of the British Motor Industry to survive in its present shape and size.
>
> How can we persuade a Conservative Government – any Government – to give us funds to secure our recovery when responsible union officials seem to be bent on thwarting our plans?
>
> We do not want to go over your heads to test where employee support really lies. We want you to cooperate with us to justify the funds we need.

My allusion to 'not wanting' to go over their heads indicated how our minds were working. The BL Board had taken the decision in principle to go forward with the Recovery Plan if we could find ways and means of securing the support of our employees. We made specific commitments to reduced manning levels, reduced production capacity, tighter productivity targets and new work practices. We would put this to a ballot of the workforce, and then sink or swim on the outcome. We would try to secure CSEU support for a joint ballot, to avoid a union inspired boycott. But if we could not secure support for the ballot, we would consider going it alone, and balloting over their heads.

A few days earlier we had taken a crucial management initiative which appealed to the non-executive directors. We brought the top 120 managers together, from all parts of BL, and proposed that we should put the future of the company on the line: if we earned the support of more than 75% of the vote of those employees throughout BL who voted, we would go ahead and seek funds from the Government; if we achieved over 70%, but less than 75%, the BL Board would weigh up the situation in the light of the size of the overall poll and other factors; a vote of less than 70% in favour, and we all agreed that we could not deliver the Recovery Plan. In that event we would immediately recommend to the BL Board that no further funds should be sought and we would set about dismantling the company.

This position was arrived at after senior executives and I had briefly addressed our colleagues. Various managers from the floor spontaneously expressed their views in support of the specific proposition: 'that it was up to all of us to persuade the mass of BL employees, at all levels, that as painful as it may be, the Recovery Plan was the only sensible course for the company. If we failed, so be it.' The view of those present was that the shop stewards would reject the Plan again, when they reconvened – but what mattered was the way our employees as a whole voted in the ballot. The issue would be decided by 150,000 employees, not 250 shop stewards. When this thinking was put to the management meeting the vote was 120 to 0; everyone there knew that his job was on the line if the ballot result went the wrong way, that a vote by all employees and managers in BL would determine the future of us all.

Then in mid-October came the crucial day of decision, beyond which we were not prepared to continue the debate. The CSEU started by meeting our management team in the morning. Later in the day the Chairman and the Secretary of the CSEU, having failed to find a solution in the management meeting downstairs, were invited to join the BL Board on the fifth floor, at about 3.00 pm. We told them that we intended to ballot all employees, with or without union cooperation; that if we did not achieve a substantial vote in favour we would not proceed to seek further funds. We admitted that without their involvement in the ballot, which would be under the supervision of the Electoral Reform Society, we had little hope of achieving an adequate poll. In this event closure was inevitable. Even with their involvement, the workforce might well vote against, or support our proposals in a half-hearted way – in either event we would still opt for calling it a day. We then told them for the first time of the outcome of our meeting with our top 120 managers, and that these men were philosophical about the outcome, despite the impact it might have on their own jobs.

Some pertinent questions were asked by the CSEU officials, and the members of the BL Board made some incisive and convincing remarks about the issues at stake. I knew that it would not take much for the Board to be persuaded that the whole exercise was a waste of time – that we had come to the end of the road. We all knew that only the overwhelming support of the workforce would ensure the success of the Recovery Plan. I said this coldly and starkly, so that the CSEU officials would be in no doubt what was at stake. Only a positive decision from them to cooperate in the ballot – and preferably to support the proposal – would give us a fighting chance of securing the substantial majority we required. Anything less would be like playing Russian roulette – not an inappropriate simile in the circumstances!

The CSEU team withdrew, and an hour later were working with our people to draft a statement supporting the Plan! We had won their support despite the powerful TGWU opposition. Not only were the CSEU prepared, after weeks of intense debate, consultation, and soul-searching, to cooperate in the ballot – but for them to go to the lengths of actually *supporting* the Plan was more than any of us had dared hope for. I had great admiration for the Confederation Chairman and Secretary, who had been under tremendous pressure from all sides, but who opted finally for what was best for their members – our employees. We were in with a chance, but the cost in inter-union relationships was very high – the TGWU were not amused!

On the 1st November, 1979, nearly two months after the Recovery Plan was laid bare at the meeting at Leyland House, the result of the ballot was made known by the Electoral Reform Society: 80% of employees voted. Of those voting 87.2% – over 106,000 employees – voted in favour of the motion:

Do you give your support to BL's Recovery Plan?

We all knew that this was not the end of our problems, but the beginning, and that what the vote gave us was a fighting chance of securing further government funds; a fighting chance of driving through the changes in work practices, and everything else implicit in the ballot paper. Nothing could be taken for granted.

Our letter to employees, recording the vote in some detail, included the following comments:

> The positive attitude expressed by employees voting privately at home has to be quickly translated into a new sense of collective responsibility at work, otherwise the ballot and what it means will have been a waste of time and effort.
> To agree individually that productivity must be improved and then to resist it collectively or to vote for continuous production and then to become involved in wildcat strikes would mean that we can never achieve the Plan. The company would not deserve to survive.
> Now that a big majority of employees has voted to support the Recovery Plan it is up to each and every one

of us to work for the survival of BL and by our actions show there is no further interest in obstruction, disruption or inefficiency.

It is by the behaviour and performance of each and every one of us in the coming weeks and months that BL will be judged. We have voted 'YES': we have given our word. But, it will be our actions that will count.

By courtesy of the *Birmingham Evening Mail*

"YOUR VOTING FORM DID
COME, I'VE DEALT WITH IT . . .
YOU VOTED 'YES'!"

The letter did not end the matter, for we were to have considerable further opposition from Derek Robinson and a handful of influential stewards.

When the Recovery Plan was originally explained to union officials and stewards on the 10th September, there was no strong reaction to it at first, but opposition grew steadily about a week later, and it was certainly orchestrated. What really surprised us was that it continued unabated after the outcome of the secret ballot demonstrated that we had overwhelming support for the Plan.

Early in November, soon after the ballot result was made known, we learned the answer; a copy of Minutes of what purported to be a meeting between Communist Party officials and BL shop stewards, came into our possession anonymously through the mail. The meeting and the Minutes were dated the 11th September, the day after we announced the Recovery Plan; the whole agenda was devoted to the Recovery Plan, and how best to thwart it. Because we had no way of proving its authenticity, we kept the Minutes at Nuffield House and did not make them known to management in other parts of the company.

The Minutes listed a number of well-known shop stewards, and a handful of nationally known Communist Party leaders, and were quite explicit as to strategy – plant and equipment would not be allowed out of factories due for closure, and reference was made to emulating sit-ins that had been successfully enacted in other industries. The meeting was alleged to have been held at an address near the Austin factory at Longbridge with some 17 people in attendance. (Derek Robinson was not listed as being present.) Shortly after we received this document, we learned that a pamphlet was being circulated and we were struck by the similarity between the Minutes of what was ostensibly a strategy meeting, and the pamphlet which espoused the same cause and followed the same 'anti-Edwardes Plan' theme. It was this pamphlet that led to Derek Robinson's dismissal.

At the time of the alleged meeting on the 11th September, the views of our employees were not known, for that was several weeks before the ballot result was published. The pamphlet, on the other hand, was published and distributed despite the known wishes of the workforce, and signed by four shop stewards whose role was to represent their fellow workers. The strategy seemed to be that if the

Recovery Plan could be undermined, management would be forced to revert to the earlier strategy of heady expansion and the Conservative Government would come up with £2,000 million to fund a 'no redundancy', 'no closure', 'no change in work practices fought for over the years' approach.

Because of our experiences in the preceding months, and the way disputes were being orchestrated, those few of us who had read the Minutes believed them to be genuine. Our interpretation was that here was the Communist Party, an electorally bankrupt political organisation, determined to replace the existing structure of society in Britain by using every means at its disposal and with a number of our shop stewards as their willing instruments. We saw the attempt to sabotage the 'Edwardes Plan' as an opportunistic gamble to cause disruption, which could well lead to total and final closure. Just the fluid situation required by the Party planners.

But we could not prove it so we said nothing about all this to executives at Austin Morris, who were wrestling with the problem of the pamphlet. Would they come up with a do-nothing decision, a warning, or a dismissal? Although employees in other parts of our car and truck business were signatories to the pamphlet, the key signatory was the Longbridge senior convenor of shop stewards, Derek Robinson. There was a speedy response. Within two days Ray Horrocks asked me to endorse a recommendation from Austin Morris to dismiss one steward and to give a formal warning to the other three. The Austin Morris executives concerned were simply exercising their operational roles in determining disciplinary action and were quite unaware of the apparent involvement of the Communist Party. They were of course aware that Communist Party members were among the signatories, which was no surprise to any of us.

I had no hesitation in endorsing the decision, for apart from the obvious merit of their case, Derek Robinson, the one dismissed, had kept Longbridge in ferment and upheaval for 30 months.

Following the earlier disciplinary warning for his distortion of the facts in the parity strike earlier in the year, he was now a signatory to the pamphlet – determined (as the pamphlet said) to resist the Recovery Plan:

All our efforts and resources must be mobilised to change the policy of closures and contraction . . . The Leyland Combine Committee's policy of refusing to accept the transfer of work from one plant to another, unless the parent plant agrees must be fully supported . . . in other industries like Upper Clyde Shipbuilders work-ins and occupations have been necessary to prevent closure. If necessary we shall have to do the same.

These words lined up with the Minutes of the 11th September, but we shall never know the full truth.

The sad thing was that having won the overwhelming support of the workforce for the Recovery Plan we now faced another battle – a battle to implement our employees' vote! And the supreme irony was that the AUEW, the great protagonist of secret ballots, would find itself obliged to support its least loved lay officer and so, willy nilly, take BL back to the brink again. For Derek Robinson's fellow thinkers had powerful connections, and insidious influence, and this was to make the fight for his reinstatement drawn-out, hard, and very damaging in the market place. This created great uncertainty, and whether he won or lost, Derek Robinson's backers would gain from the disruption and upheaval – which is their food and drink. With the Metro launch one year away, this must have seemed to them to be the last opportunity to bring the company to its knees. From the point of view of Austin Morris, it was the last chance of gaining manageability of Longbridge – they simply could not afford to go into preproduction of the Metro in a continuing state of master-minded anarchy, for we had to show what mammoth new investment, a new model, and far-reaching changes in work practices could achieve. We were looking for an increase in productivity of 100% at Longbridge, and that could not be done in the environment of the 1970s. We simply had to change all that in 1980, and the Communist challenge to the Recovery Plan could not therefore go unanswered.

And so on the 19th November, Derek Robinson was invited by Stan Mullet, the Longbridge plant director, in the presence of the AUEW District Secretary, to withdraw his name from the pamphlet. He refused, at the same time making it clear that ballot or no ballot he opposed the plan. He was dismissed.

The immediate reaction to his dismissal was a partial walkout at

Longbridge with some show of support in other factories. While Jeff Rooker, a left-wing MP, told Britain on the 'Jimmy Young' programme that the dismissal was a management error – which he was quite entitled to do – 1,000 men, including one of Derek Robinson's brothers, pushed their way into the factory through the pickets at Longbridge for the express purpose of working normally. They must have wondered what the world had come to for they had just endorsed the Recovery Plan and now they were being asked to stop work to show solidarity for the man who led the opposition to it! Many refused; nevertheless with intense picketing we clearly faced a damaging strike, and we only had three options for dealing with it. These were to reinstate Derek Robinson, in some compromise way; to let the strike run its course; to insist on an immediate return to work. I phoned the non-executive members of the Board, and said that with their support management would opt for the third course, because we could not afford to fund a three-week strike – and on past performance that is what we were in for.

The Board supported our taking an initiative. We had nothing to lose, for if we did not take the risk of trying to bring the strike to a head quickly, it would kill us in the market place, and it would make it very difficult to obtain funds from Parliament. So we decided to insist on a return to work, and those who did not respond would be deemed to have terminated their contract of employment with the company. A letter was drafted which put the whole matter beyond any doubt, and in extremis this would be mailed to all employees. But first, we decided to appeal to the AUEW to get the men back to work; and so on the 22nd November, 1980, Pat Lowry sent a letter to Sir John Boyd of the AUEW:

> As to the future, those of BL's employees who are now on strike must make up their minds – and quickly – where they stand. They return to work (leaving the AUEW, if it so desires, to pursue the case of Mr Robinson through normal procedural channels): alternatively, they put at risk the company and their own future in it.

If this broke the strike we would re-employ most of those on strike; if it didn't then we would have to pick up the pieces which were left, for there would be no ongoing volume car business.

On the 27th November the matter came to a head. The AUEW President, Terry Duffy, asked for an urgent meeting. 'Our AUEW

Executive is meeting at Peckham – we are discussing Pat Lowry's letter to John Boyd, and we need to meet you urgently. The press are all over the place down here – can we meet somewhere privately?' I suggested we should meet at the Stafford Hotel, off Piccadilly, in about an hour's time.

We met in a private dining room on the ground floor, at 11.15 am. With me were David Andrews, Ray Horrocks and Pat Lowry. Because we knew what a penchant the unions have for 'adjournments', we also set ourselves up in another room – a suite converted into an office, on the second floor – and John McKay held the fort there, to be joined later by Harold Musgrove, then Managing Director of Austin Morris, and Geoff Armstrong, Employee Relations Director for our Cars business.

The meeting started off quite amicably – the early discussion focussed on the TGWU who were thought to have acted precipitately in declaring the strike official for the dismissed Longbridge convenor was not even a member of their union. He was a long-standing member of the AUEW, although it was generally agreed that he was closer to the TGWU on a number of philosophical matters. When we made it clear that we had no intention of reinstating the convenor, the debate hotted up. At one stage we suggested to Terry Duffy and his colleagues that this was all academic anyway for the TGWU had already taken the initiative. Terry Duffy phoned Moss Evans in front of us and told him that he would be making the running; it was an AUEW matter, and the TGWU was to back off. 'Leave it to us Moss – this is an AUEW matter and we know how to handle it.' He was furious at the TGWU making the strike official; but as soon as the phone was back on the hook, the heat was back on us.

The AUEW had various ideas, none of which we could accept, ranging from 'Reinstate him and the whole fuss will die down,' to 'Keep him on your payroll.' While this debate was going on, and unknown to us, journalists were gathering in strength outside the hotel and inside the lobby.

What had happened was simple. A city editor, having drinks before lunch at the Stafford, made a call from the public call box opposite the private dining room. The waiter happened to open the door of our room to deliver yet another trolley load of coffee, and to the journalist's astonishment and delight he saw some well-known faces – the secret was out. From that moment on, the whole tempo changed, and we were all under pressure. To get from the private dining room, which had become the 'union room', to our 'management room', at the other end of the hotel on the second floor, was likely to prove something of a feat, for as the word spread so journalists headed for the Stafford Hotel.

The hotel manager responded with his usual briskness, and quickly pioneered a route so that we could continue with our adjournments without running into the press. We had to go into the next private dining room, down a passage, down one flight of back stairs to the kitchens, across the hotel at basement level, up the flight of back stairs on the other side of the building, and into our 'operations' room. Each time the union team had completed their adjournment, they would phone us, and we would retrace our steps, single file, and find our way through the maze of pots and pans, the flour and dough, and zabaglione – studiously avoiding the media who were to sit in wait for a further three hours.

The AUEW argument went on; 'If management persist with the dismissal there will be an all-out strike – the TGWU has already pre-empted the situation – and the company will have weeks of official strike action to face.' I countered by saying that the union had misunderstood our intentions:

> We've fired a man, who if he had been a manager, would have gone quietly and there would have been no influence or pressure for his reinstatement. This man is trying to wreck the company; so he goes just like anyone else would in the same situation. He cannot be protected merely because he is well known.
>
> His objectives are synonymous with closing the company, for even if the Board were to support his wild idea of funding the company at the one million vehicle level the Government would say 'enough is enough', and closure would be inevitable.
>
> If against that background, the men respond to your · all-out strike plea, as some already have to the TGWU initiative – that is, if all the men, or a large part of them, are out on Tuesday, we will write to tell them that they have in effect dismissed themselves. They will have broken their contracts of employment. We will never engage them again.

The AUEW team was astounded. Whatever the difference between us, I trusted that particular group of men on the other side of the table, and I believe they trusted us. They knew we were not bluffing; of that I am sure. Terry Duffy, Sir John Boyd, Gavin Laird, Ken Cure, John Weakley, Jack Wyman and Gerry Russell – not one of them wanted to see BL come to an end, of that I was equally sure.

'But surely you couldn't do that? What if the bulk of them don't report for work?'

'The doors will be open for work, on the 4th December, and if most of them stay out – even if all 50,000 do so – then they will have dismissed themselves. We will then recruit people, or failing that, close the doors once and for all. In no circumstances will the disciplinary action be reversed.'

The AUEW team considered the point and asked: 'Could you give us some time to think about this?'

'By all means. All we ask you to do is to delay making the strike official, in which case it will peter out by next Thursday. If you make it official, we will have no hope of getting the men back in – but you think about it.'

Back through the labyrinth we went, for the fourth time; down the stairs, through the scullery, the kitchen, the pantries, and up the back stairs to our colleagues in the 'ops' room. Harold Musgrove, John McKay and Geoff Armstrong were on tenterhooks to know the score.

'We've told them our intentions. Clearly with the whole of Fleet Street now outside and inside the hotel, we will never get away without a statement. We'd better draw one up on the basis of our ultimatum, for the pressure on them could still force them to go ahead with a strike call. And where is the draft of the letter to employees? – it would help to let them know that we really are ready to trigger it off.'

One of my colleagues at this stage said, 'I was watching them closely when you told them of our intentions. They believe you.'

'Nevertheless,' I replied, 'the more evidence they have the better they will be able to convince their colleagues who are not at the meeting.'

The phone rang – only minutes after we had left them – could we rejoin them? Back we went – down the stairs, through the pantries and the bustling kitchens. And when a few minutes later, we appeared in the 'union' room we found seven worried men. They were even more worried when we showed them the letter to be sent to employees on strike, which warned of dismissal and breach of contract.

'We believe you mean this – will you make one concession; will you agree to keep him on the payroll? He needn't appear on the premises.'

We looked at each other. As keen as we were to find a fair but firm solution, and recognising that Terry Duffy, with his enthusiastic outlook, even in extremis, and Sir John Boyd really were in difficulty, we all knew we couldn't agree to this. Our credibility would be ruined, and two years of progressive tightening up would be out of the window. Yet we realised that they felt they were making a major concession themselves.

'Do you want to withdraw?' They hoped a few minutes of private debate and we might settle for their proposal.

'No need – let's explore your suggestion. Perhaps if we build on it we might get nearer to a solution. It isn't on as it stands.' We sat in silence for a full minute.

It was Sir John Boyd who came up with the thought that led to a workable answer. The AUEW would set up a Committee of Inquiry, under the chairmanship of Gerry Russell, who was the Executive member perhaps most perturbed by the whole episode, as one of his 'local' stewards, about to become a local official at Leyland, was the subject of one of the warnings. He couldn't believe the fellow was culpable, and indeed we subsequently found that he had lent his name, sight unseen, to the pamphlet as a result of pressure from Longbridge. The Committee would report 'in a matter of weeks', and meanwhile the AUEW would instruct their members to return to work!

The company, for its part, would make weekly ex-gratia payments equivalent to Derek Robinson's normal wage while the Inquiry was held. This avoided reinstatement or suspension – he stayed fired. Terry Duffy and his colleagues argued long and hard to persuade us to categorise it as a suspension, but we couldn't agree to this. Our payments were to end on the day the report was submitted. If their Committee found that dismissal was not in their view justified, and management refused to reinstate the man, they would again consider the question of an official strike.

'Okay, Terry, that's a fair deal, but can you guarantee you will get Longbridge back to work?'

'One call to Moss – I'll tell him our decision. The Transport and General could not possibly carry a strike over one of our members if we don't support it, and anyway what matters is that we are setting up the Committee of Inquiry to investigate the circumstances leading to the dismissal. If we come to the view that you are in the wrong, then as I've already said, you can ignore our findings if you wish, but we'll press for reinstatement.'

No one could argue about that as a way forward, he said, but he was wrong. Their ex-steward was livid and made it abundantly clear in public that he considered that his union had let him down in his moment of crisis – nothing but an all-out strike for him.

The men returned to work, time marched on, and so did the political left, who marched through Birmingham in support of their man, under the banner of the 'International Union Movement' – a generic term the ex-steward attributed to his diehard supporters who met in Birmingham to bring the wrath of the world Labour movement onto the heads of BL management. His particular world hummed with activity, while the real world remained surprisingly calm, including the people who mattered most – the men at Longbridge. This despite the fact that Pat Lowry, who was inter-viewed at the end of the Stafford Hotel meeting, had made it clear that their convenor had not been reinstated; was not on the company's payroll; that the dismissal would stand. One might have expected this to provoke some reaction but it didn't.

A few days after these events, Ray Horrocks and I decided to weigh up the atmosphere at Longbridge for ourselves. We kept the fact of the visit quiet, until the moment we entered the gates, when, of course, the news spread quickly through the factories that make up the 375-acre site. For the hour and a half that Ray and I were walking Longbridge, relieved at the warmth of the reception, the Works Committee was drinking tea in the boardroom, preparatory to meeting 'Management' – they weren't quite sure who it would be. When eventually we walked through the door they were very surprised. 'Where do you think we've been?' I asked, as we sat down at the Board table. No one was in a mood to be drawn. 'We've been through the bulk of the plant, including the car assembly buildings (traditionally the most militant) and what do you think we found? Excellent morale throughout.'

The Works Committee was not amused, and I can't say that the meeting with them achieved anything constructive except that we made our point – there was far less heat being generated internally than by the non-BL people like Leslie Huckfield MP, Geoffrey Robinson MP (an ex-employee who had fallen foul of the Ryder scythe) and one or two others who felt that the whole union system was at risk because we had treated a convenor 'as though he was an employee'. Which indeed he was, for we paid his wages, although he was allowed to give all his time to union business, as were far too many others at the time.

On the 30th January, 1980, I went on television to give the facts on Derek Robinson's 30-month stewardship at Longbridge – 523 disputes, with the loss of 62,000 cars and 113,000 engines, worth £200 million.

The AUEW Committee of Inquiry duly reached its conclusion after volumes of evidence had been taken with full management cooperation. I had not been called, for it emerged clearly during the evidence that the decision had been taken at local level. Only the media speculated that I had personally agonised over the decision.

During the first week of February, before publication of the Inquiry report Terry Duffy phoned, again from one of his regular Executive meetings. 'Can we meet you? Our people have completed their investigations, and we need a private, unpublicised meeting, to explain the outcome of the report.'

The report was highly critical of Derek Robinson and spoke of his 'serious failings and lack of responsibility' as the AUEW convenor, but pressed the company to reinstate him because the inquiry team concluded that we had not followed the correct disciplinary procedure!

We met a day or two later in London, at about 7.00 pm. As midnight approached, we were still 'noting their point of view,' and declining to reinstate the steward. We issued a joint statement late that night:

> Mr Terry Duffy, President of the AUEW advised the company, and subsequently announced publicly, that the union supported the claim for the reinstatement of Mr Robinson and was prepared to embark upon official strike action to achieve that objective.
>
> The company has cooperated in providing information to the Inquiry Team, although it was made clear at the

outset of the Inquiry that it was essentially an AUEW internal investigation.

The company has now studied the report and has concluded that it is not prepared to reinstate Mr Robinson. His disruptive behaviour and damaging influence, as shown by the events in February and November 1979, make this impossible and a strike will not change that decision.

The private meeting was inconclusive and Ray Horrocks wrote to Terry Duffy in these terms:

We have reached two main conclusions on the Report:

1. The inquiry has brought to light no new facts.

2. The report deals almost exclusively with *the procedures* that were applied in the disciplining of Mr Robinson. We have searched in vain for any views as to whether the company was justified by the facts of the case in taking disciplinary action.

I think it is common ground that if BL Cars is to survive (and we are determined it will) management and employees must work constructively together. It is our view that Mr Robinson's conduct over the past two years has proved convincingly that he is not prepared to work constructively either with the company or, indeed, with your union. As evidence of that statement, I would remind you of the following:

1. He campaigned (and continues to campaign) against the Recovery Plan, this despite a 7 to 1 employee vote in its favour.

2. Your own Inquiry Team reported on the way in which Mr Robinson has conducted himself as a AUEW convenor. (Mr Robinson's statements yesterday to the media that the report 'completely exonerated' him were typical of his tendency to mislead and misrepresent.)

3. The miserable record of disputes and lost time at Longbridge since Mr Robinson became convenor. This included 523 internal disputes in some three

years at a cost to production of 113,000 engines and 62,000 cars. These figures exclude the CSEU/EEF dispute and all other external issues.

Given the problems that BL Cars have to overcome and the responsibility we owe to hundreds of thousands of people who depend on the company for their livelihood, we are not prepared to comply with the demand of your union that Mr Robinson be reinstated. I have to admit to a feeling of surprise that given the whole series of public statements made by Mr Robinson over recent months he would wish to be employed by the company.

Finally, I would like to comment on the suggestions made on television last night that Mr Robinson should be re-engaged as an employee on the basis that he would be de-barred from holding union office. Mr Robinson has apparently rejected that suggestion himself. I have to say to you that, based on his track record at this time, he is a person who is not suitable for re-employment by the company.

Significantly, Ray Horrocks pleaded for a ballot before strike action was triggered off:

I urge upon you and your colleagues to consider once more the appalling consequences that could flow from your decision to back official strike action in support of Mr Robinson's reinstatement. In addition to the 20,000 employees at Longbridge upwards of 30,000 employees elsewhere in BL Cars would need to be laid off almost immediately.

If you are determined to go ahead, then we press you to do so only when you are certain that the majority of your members at Longbridge are prepared to back the strike. This can only be ascertained by a properly conducted ballot, as indeed is your practice in electing your own union officers.

This frank letter did not of itself cause the strike to be postponed: what did was a 2,000-name petition against the strike, spontaneously put together at Longbridge on the 8th February. This caused the strike call to be deferred while the AUEW tried to sound out the views of their members; and we went through fire and brimstone for 12 days.

The *Sunday Times* of the 17th February, 1980, described the five working days from the 11th to the 15th as: 'Five days that shook the car world.' The article reminds one that the 1979/80 pay talks – nothing whatever to do with the Robinson affair – actually broke down on the 15th February, thus leading people, including influential commentators, to the erroneous conclusion that the mood of the men was to vote for a strike over Derek Robinson. The two issues were in fact quite different, but John Fryer of the *Sunday Times* was not alone in assuming that rejection of the pay offer spelled support for Derek Robinson.

The following extracts point up the drama:

> Tomorrow shop stewards at British Leyland's Long-bridge plant are expected to declare a strike in support of sacked convenor Derek (Red Robbo) Robinson.
> Twelve weeks ago, when Robinson was sensationally dismissed, a stoppage would have been damaging, even cataclysmic, for BL's redoubtable chairman, Sir Michael Edwardes. Now, although it will be a blow, Edwardes – burdened by far wider and more intractable problems – may well view any walkout as just a little local difficulty.

and:

> Tuesday's ballot result, showing a 3-2 majority against Edwardes's 5%-10% pay and conditions package, merely exacerbated Leyland's crisis. Edwardes says there is little hope of the company becoming viable, let alone profitable, without the improved productivity the pay deal is supposed to generate . . .
> The real question is whether Edwardes can sustain Leyland on a January-level market share. Even with the £300m of state funds recently dispensed by Industry Secretary, Sir Keith Joseph, Edwardes cannot afford to keep men employed if he is not selling cars, hence the lay-offs.

As I lay in bed that morning, reading the Sunday newspapers, I wondered whether BL really was doomed, and I reminded myself how the men at Longbridge had seemed relaxed about the dismissal when Ray Horrocks and I had visited the site in December – only days after the event. No, the press must be wrong. Of course the stewards were vocal – they were pressing for strike action. But they had done this before, and they had lost. The stewards had called a mass meeting for the following Wednesday, at Longbridge's Cofton Park. This would determine whether our employees would back their stewards and finish off Austin Morris. I reread the Fryer article – fair, but he hadn't shaken hands with those fellows at Longbridge, and heard the encouraging comments about what we were doing. I also noted that Adam Raphael in the *Observer* claimed that Sir Keith Joseph had told the Cabinet privately that BL's chances of survival were five to one against! He summed up:

> What are the Government's options? The chairman of BL, Sir Michael Edwardes, has pledged that his board will abandon the State-funded recovery plan 'if there is a significant shortfall in cash flow' through whatever cause. That point must now be near – it will clearly be breached if there is a strike over pay or sacked convenor Derek Robinson.
>
> If that happens and the plan had to be abandoned, 'all bets,' in the words of one Minister 'would be off.' Sir Michael and his board might well resign and the Government would be left with a mess on its hands.

The previous Monday's *Times* leader was equally pessimistic

> British Leyland now promises to become the most serious industrial crisis facing this country since the war. It will also be a test of fire for the industrial policies of the Government in general, and of Sir Keith Joeseph in particular. On the face of it the current corporate plan, with its conditional commitment of public money, is as good as dead. The BL request for government funds was based on the assumption that there would be no significant shortfall in the company's cash flow for whatever reason, whether internal or external. Events of the past week or so, including the revelation of the company's serious drop in its share of the domestic car market, have now reached the point where it must be clear to all concerned that a significant deterioration has taken

place in the basic assumptions on which that corporate plan was based.

At present, therefore, British Leyland is in some kind of limbo. The headline-catching items of news, like the problem with Mr Robinson, or the pay ballot, have been overtaken by the more fundamental issue of whether British Leyland as the group we know today has any future at all.

and:

> . . . Its problems of thin management, poor labour relations, inadequate product range and the rest have been seriously worsened as a result of the Government's overall economic strategy, which has led to a high exchange rate for sterling. Whatever benefits such a steep upward revaluation of sterling may have in helping to contain domestic inflationary pressures, the fact is that vulnerable industries are unable to survive under it. In the long term such discipline through the exchange markets may produce healthier industries. In the short term the performance of sterling must have contributed substantially to the company's financial problems.

I agreed with most of the *Times* leader, and I strongly agreed with the last sentence! I had been pleading for a moderate pound for many months. I did not, however, agree with the implication that sparked off the leader; that there would be a strike.

I spent the Sunday working on a major spech – I was to address the Birmingham Chamber of Commerce and Industry at a luncheon on the following Wednesday. What an accident of timing, but fortuitous for the Chamber! I wrote a main speech, and an alternative one; the main speech heralded a new and better outlook – for it assumed that Derek Robinson's colleagues had overwhelmingly voted him out on that very morning. The alternative speech conceded defeat, and the impending closure of Austin Morris – prudent, but hopefully not necessary.

My colleagues and I consulted on the telephone. The outlook was rather bleak, on that Sunday in February, but clearly last ditch efforts on the shop floor should be directed at persuading the workforce to vote for 'no strike and no reinstatement' at their mass meeting on Wednesday, 20th February; and on the back of that, to get the pay deal put to bed, but without making concessions and without provoking strike action. A tall order, but how else to save the company? Unless we were able to pull both chestnuts out of the fire, it would be the end of the road – our market share would slump further, and the funds needed from the Government would not be forthcoming.

On 20th February, only an hour before my speech to the Birmingham Chamber of Commerce, the final showdown with Derek Robinson was to be enacted at Longbridge. My meeting had been set up months before; the meeting of Longbridge employees, called a couple of days earlier, must have been 'in the stars' for these two events to fall together in this way.

An hour before I left the Metropole Hotel at the National Exhibition Centre outside Birmingham, I speculated on the outcome of the Longbridge meeting with John McKay and other colleagues who were to be at the luncheon. My close colleagues still had a feeling, but not a conviction, that the men would refuse to strike over Derek Robinson's reinstatement. I had been convinced since my musings on the Sunday that the mood at Longbridge could not be in favour of him, for nothing had happened to induce a change of heart since we took soundings there after the dismissal. I explained to my colleagues that I had prepared two speeches – one prophesied the end of Austin Morris if the men went out, which I was sure I wouldn't need. The other anticipated the further evidence of realism that we had rightly come to expect from our workforce – the (as yet undelivered) overwhelming rejection of strike action.

A quarter of an hour before we left, John McKay received the call. 'It's okay, they've voted overwhelmingly against reinstatement. Its over. They say the vote was 14,000 to 600.' I tore the unpalatable alternative draft into shreds, and we set off for the Birmingham luncheon. Doug Towers, my chauffeur, was as excited as the rest of us, and we lost our way to the hall.

You need all your concentration to negotiate the Birmingham road system, and for once the chauffeur missed an exit on the ring road and we found ourselves in a commercial district well off the beaten track. He pulled up at the offices of a small company to ask the way to the Top Rank Suite, where the lunch was being held. On spotting me, the gentleman in the office insisted on jumping into the Rover and personally conducting us across Birmingham. As we turned the final corner we were faced with a wall of reporters and photographers, spreading right across the road.

The last thing I wanted was to have to give snap, off-the-cuff remarks – we were late enough as it was, so we drove up a loading bay behind a parade of shops and then found a back way to the adjoining multi-storey car park. We hoped to slip through to the Top Rank venue from there. However, our escape route had been spotted and a stream of journalists poured up the ramp, and pursued us wildly from ground floor to top floor and then down again, while we tried to figure out how to reach our objective! In the end, we drove out over the 'in' lane ramp of the car park (in the process testing the Rover's 'bottom' construction to the full). I dashed across the pavement into the hall, leaving my chauffeur to take our guide back to his place of work who apparently sat in contemplative silence for a while and then asked, 'Is it always like that with Sir Michael?'

Inside the Top Rank Suite, the atmosphere was charged; the 300-strong audience were predominantly people from the engineering industry and many were from the motor components industry. Their livelihoods depended upon BL, and like us, they had been on a knife edge. The welcome was very generous; I followed the President into the hall as it exploded into a table-thumping, arm-waving welcome, tinged with relief. I began my speech with the words: 'There is no audience I would sooner address this day on BL's problems than members and guests of the Birmingham Chamber of Industry and Commerce. I am grateful, Mr President, for this opportunity to do so and I compliment you on your remarkable sense of timing.'

My theme was that BL had come a long way since 1977 but no one should have any illusions as there was still much to be done, and even if it could be done, we had to persuade the Government, suppliers, dealers and the general public that we could make it. We were at the crossroads – and it seemed appropriate to spell out to that audience that euphoria was not appropriate and there were still many problems to overcome. The key passage of the speech read:

> I have said all along that BL would reach its moment of truth during 1980. This is the year of make or break, and the next few months are the most critical of all.
> So where do we stand now?

Obviously we could trip over our feet and fall flat on our face. But equally we stand ready to reap the rewards of three years of slogging, determined hard work, of vast investment about to reach fruition, of repaying 'support beyond the call of duty' to suppliers; and our dealers and some of the British public have been very loyal indeed. The major factor that stands between BL and success or failure is uncertainty. Uncertainty as to whether the company can resolve its strategic problems. Uncertainty in the minds of customers about whether it is wise to buy BL products at this time. Uncertainty about the attitude and mood of BL employees.

But there was no uncertainty this morning about our Longbridge employees' determination to stay at work! However, the 93 days it took to reach a conclusion caused incalculable harm to our market share – 93 most damaging days. Make no mistake, the mood of the market was dead right! Had there been an extended strike at Longbridge today Austin Morris would not have continued in business.

What we said to the AUEW Executive last November was only the truth – and I say to you now that the BL Board has not bluffed and will not bluff. If I have one plea to make to the unions it is that they should believe the scale of BL's problems and they should never say 'I thought they were bluffing.'

And so BL had been dragged screaming but alive into early 1980, and on the 8th April, we introduced the new work practices. This initiative, following months of fruitless negotiation, was arguably the most important industrial relations move since the war. At the same time we implemented the new wage deal, which had also dragged on and on. Neither were welcomed with open arms by the unions, but significantly neither action provoked a strike.

The new work practices were tabled for the consideration of a disbelieving group of stewards immediately after the Recovery Plan ballot result was announced and just before Derek Robinson's dismissal. As they were to change the habits of two business lifetimes, the stewards were entitled to wonder whether our proposals would ever get beyond that table. From management's point of view, we knew that the Recovery Plan had no hope of being delivered without a massive change in the way people were prepared to do their day-to-day work: not in terms of energy expended, but in terms of net output.

At the heart of the 92-page document outlining the changes we needed was the challenge to 'mutuality' – the proposition that every change, no matter how minor, was not to be implemented until there had been an exhaustive process of consultation and negotiation – and then acceptance. This concept held almost sacrosanct by the unions for generations could take months to complete, if indeed agreement was ever reached. In the past the introduction of new models and new facilities had been the signal for marathon negotiating sessions with shop stewards who knew that the longer the talks went on, the more desperate management became, as the launch date approached – with the almost inevitable consequences that managers would either 'buy out' practices or take the line of least resistance. The alternative was to see model launch times slipping past.

Two of the key areas of change we needed were: first, the ability to move workers from one job to another (particularly to cover absenteeism at the start of shifts), which meant introducing flexibility in the use of skills, so that, for instance, maintenance did not require four people from four different unions to carry out repairs. The second was the end of anomalous cash buy-outs for 'practices and customs' which were widespread and had been negotiated on a factory-by-factory basis – practices which could not be retained if the company was to recoup its lost competitiveness.

The stewards should not have had any difficulty understanding the company's need to reform these out-of-date habits, and the national union officials were in even less doubt about the rationale. The problem was power. The type of bargaining process that enabled the stewards to spin out the transfer of one Mini line so that it took weeks before it was in normal production provided the stewards with considerable leverage, and they were reluctant to lose the bargaining power. The very act of shortening these laborious processes, by writing into the agreement management's right to change working methods, would have a profound effect on the stewards. They had lost the ballot on the Recovery Plan; they had to win the work practices issue. And indeed they held all the cards, for while the principle of these changes was an implicit part of the

Recovery Plan ballot, the actual detailed changes could still, in practice, be a matter for laborious negotiation and agreement.

All in all, directly and indirectly, several hundred hours were spent by management and stewards arguing and debating through November and December and into early 1980, the aim being to effect the changes by mutual agreement. Minor concessions were made by management, but all the meaningful parts were kept intact – which was why the package was still not acceptable to the stewards.

After 16 exhaustive meetings, some stretching over many days at a time within the Joint Negotiation machinery, the Cars management came to the view that the changes could not be won by intellectual argument. There was too wide a divergence of objectives. And so eventually, with the national union officials understanding the need for the fundamental changes, and the stewards showing no signs of conceding, we came to the view that employees had voted on the principle (which they had) and that the stewards would continue to frustrate its implementation, however long the debate continued. In discussions during February and March, we decided to implement the new work practices, regardless of opposition. We did so by announcing on Tuesday, 25th March, that anyone who reported to work on the 8th and 9th April (after a holiday period) was deemed to have accepted the change in employment conditions. Managers were carefully briefed to be tactful in actual implementation, and indeed when Metro was launched six months later, there were still isolated instances where some of the clauses of the document had not been fully implemented.

To everyone's relief, what the stewards called 'imposition' and the management called 'implementation', went ahead without a major hiccough, and on those two days, Tuesday, 8th April and Wednesday, 9th April, 1980, 30 years of management concessions (which had made it impossible to manufacture cars competitively) were thrown out of the window, and our car factories found themselves with a fighting chance of becoming competitive. The results were not long in coming through; productivity, which had declined steadily over the years, leapt up. In 1980 Longbridge produced seven cars a man. With the new working practices progressively introduced alongside the new Metro facility, productivity in 1981 rose to nearly 17 cars a man and continued through to 1982 when it exceeded 25 cars a man. Bonus incentive payments also increased. Of course, the productivity take-off has transpired since, but back in the first half of 1980, we only dreamed of these things; we planned; but we had no hard evidence that it could be done.

Production was going well and we were six months away from the Metro launch – but the new LM10 mid-car model was too far away for comfort. We knew we were in for a difficult time commercially, until March 1983, for we did not have the full range of products. We would inevitably be hounded by the press, who never really understood that until the medium-range cars arrived on the scene, we would inevitably be living in a state of market share anxiety.

We had just been through two storms with some success, but there was another looming ahead which would take all our imagination and ingenuity, and some boldness, for the only way forward, faced by the new currency rates, was to cut deeper than we had ever thought feasible. Problems always seem to come in threes. I remember in the earlier headlong take-off of the pound, Leslie Murphy, David Andrews and I met Gordon Richardson, the Governor of the Bank of England. I told him that if the Government persisted in these policies, 50,000 of our people would lose their jobs. He didn't contest the figures – and when 50,000 had been 'planned' out of the establishment, the pound took off again, and we were to look for the next 30,000; and then in 1982 for, hopefully, the last 10,000.

Against this background of material improvement within the company, the external environment worsened. The pound was moving inexorably upwards, and we would have to find some way to fund the hundreds of millions of pounds in extra cash needed, or slim the business still further. It was infuriating. Just as we got the business into a semblance of shape and order there would be another surge in the pound which yet again threw us off course.

The culmination of our planning to meet the currency threat was on American Independence Day, at that very English institution on the banks of the Thames, the Compleat Angler at Marlow. We met in the Walton room with the weir just outside the window – the weir used by canoeists to test their ability in 'rapids' and therefore so noisy with its rushing water that it makes London traffic seem like a whisper! But its atmosphere is particularly convivial with its history and its Sir Izaak Walton memories – and so it was apt that what we debated that day became known within the company as the 'Marlow Concept'.

The group included David Andrews and Ray Horrocks, Mike Carver, Percy Plant, Frank Fitzpatrick and Peter Regnier. The notes were taken by Roger Holmes, recently seconded from the Department of Industry. Marlow gave him a fascinating insight into our problems, for the day was spent in a far-reaching review of our car business. Decisions were made then, and later endorsed by the BL Board, that would transform BL's car business – and have a major impact on Britain's motor industry. The purpose of the meeting was to build up, from a zero base, a product and facility profile for BL Cars which would be fully competitive with the major European manufacturers, and would enable profitability to be restored in the later part of the 1981 Plan period against the new currency projections; and to consider what changes were needed to enable this profile to be achieved.

The assumptions we made and the conclusions we drew were to have some interesting sequels. In riding this third storm in less than two years we would be obliged to do some revolutionary things. First, we would have to halve, as a percentage of sales, the fixed expenses in BL Cars, in order to match the profile we had before us – that of the most efficient European manufacturer. Warranty costs would have to come down by 66% and that was to mean very reliable Jaguars! On this basis we could make the business viable even with the new projections for the pound, and with an overall production of about 600,000 vehicles a year. Wage cost increases would have to be mainly paid for out of productivity – and productivity would have to increase dramatically. (As indeed it subsequently did in 1981 and 1982.)

There was just one snag; if the new projections for the pound turned out to be correct, we would need hundreds of millions of pounds more than was originally planned, and this from a government which had just given us £300 million! Also we would need a willing and committed management and a cooperative workforce, who must be getting just a little weary of our coming back time and again for more far-reaching sacrifices.

The objective at Marlow was to agree upon a concept that could be sold to the management team, and then to the BL Board. If so far so good, we would start discussions with the unions, while feeding in the new actions as we built up the 1981 Plan. This would have to be done quickly, for work on the 1981 Plan had started at the operating companies level, and the whole complex document would have to be made to hang together by the time it came up for approval at the BL Board three and a half months later. Right now, how far would my colleagues at the Compleat Angler go? What Peter Regnier had worked out looked virtually impossible to achieve, and yet all the figures showed that if we did not bring about a miracle in cost reduction terms, our car business could not become competitive against European competition – still less against Japan. In all this, the pound was the driving force.

One reads a lot of nonsense in the press about relative prices of cars across Europe. If the value of the pound goes up by say 33⅓% against the Deutschmark, British car prices go up (potentially) in the export market's currency by 33⅓%, enabling that country's prices in Britain to be reduced by 25% in sterling terms and at no cost whatever to the manufacturer in Germany. Nothing changes except the calculation! Yet the media imply that British manufacturers are causing these mammoth differences between countries – what can we do about it, when we have no influence whatever on the currency relativity at any given moment in time? We can only do two things: cut out costs so that over a period price increases can be moderated, to reduce the differential prices across Europe, and complain privately and publicly that the Government's currency policy is crucifying us. The former action is unpopular with the unions, for it adds to unemployment; the latter with the Government, for it puts pressure on the credibility of their policies. BL isn't a place for people who need to feel popular.

I had opened the Marlow debate:

> There is no point in soldiering on unless we can show that BL Cars can be profitable by 1983/4. It is no good using soft economic assumptions in testing its viability – all that will happen is we'll be back here trying to cut our way out of the jungle again in 12 months' time. If the 'Marlow Concept' (based on a reasonable estimate of what Government might be prepared to give in additional funding) doesn't enable us to produce the LC10 mid-car family in 1983 and beyond, then our volume car business has no future – probably only Land Rover and Jaguar will then survive.

If we cannot fund LC10 (and even if we can, if we can't demonstrate viability by 1984) then I would not be prepared to put a case to the Board or the Government for further funds. Therefore BL Cars is effectively under sentence of death until we can show that a further slimming down – a mammoth cut in fixed expenses – is achievable, without cutting into the vital organs of the company.

We must agree here, today, on how far we are prepared to go, and can afford to go, in cutting out models, facilities, and people. In short, we must emerge from Marlow with an agreed 'Marlow Concept' as the basis for the 1981 Plan – a sort of Recovery Plan 'plus'.

I went on to say that the real skill would lie in making the business profitable with fewer cash consuming models, and therefore with lower overall volumes than previously thought possible.

The question to ask is – if we did not already have a Cars business, would we be justified in starting from scratch in making and marketing a selected range of models, to be made in an ideal configuration of factories – as Ray Horrocks always says: 'no carting of bodies across Britain'. And if the answer is yes, then we must set it all out *ab initio*, and convert our present Cars business so that it matches this profile.

Clearly this would be a very expensive exercise. Carving new structures out of the old British Leyland, much of which was Dickensian, would be a complex and costly thing to do and the sums would have to add up and be justified in the Board's and the Government's view. And it would also have to make sense to the workforce – for a business is people.

The debate at Marlow went on for many hours, some of it technical, and much of it confidential even now, for it presaged the whole product strategy of Austin Rover and Jaguar. What matters is that the team who were there worked out a profile that showed we could compete with the best European manufacturer – even at the new currency projections – while replacing the whole model range by 1986. The axe would fall on a number of plants, but we would still be left with sensible surplus capacity, after reaching our target of 600,000 cars a year. Solihull and the remaining Liverpool factory would probably have to close, and so the surgery would have to work through, cutting out a further one in four staff, and reducing overall BL manpower towards the 100,000 mark.

All this was in profile, but we all agreed that if it stood up in the final analysis, and became part of the 1981 Plan, we had the will to accomplish it. A further major revolution in our business was under way.

Once the decision was taken in principle that day, the cost-cutting elements could go ahead immediately, without waiting for the Plan to be approved. I spoke for the Board – we must get fixed expenses down fast. When the meeting ended, the Marlow Concept was already under way.

As we moved towards the year end, when the dice would be cast, we grappled with more earthy things. We launched the V8 Land Rover, and the new Commercial Vehicle Engineering Test Centre was opened by Sir Keith Joseph, at Leyland, Lancashire. The BL Board approved the investment for the LC10 mid-car family, and the Corporate Plan itself, which would cause the dice to roll later in the year when the Cabinet came to consider our funding require-ment, was finally agreed. Approval of the funds, amounting to £990 million, did not come easily, and in pressing for the money we left no one in the Government in any doubt, there were risks attached, both internal and external.

We had come through three storms in 12 months: could we surmount the obstacles that lay ahead? For each time we rode one storm, the next would loom up – and the next one was already on the horizon, eight months out; this time it would be about pay.

7

'Not a Penny More'

To become competitive we had to reduce costs. One of the crucial ways of achieving this was to keep wage settlements at a realistic level. This contrasted sharply with the historic expectations of the motor industry worker who had grown used to seeing his income rise sharply throughout the 1960s and early 1970s, until he was at the top of the manufacturing 'league table'. He was determined to stay there.

The Government's pay policies in the mid-1970s limited the room for manoeuvre on the part of both management and unions but eventually there was general pressure to concede inflationary wage settlements. BL had to set its face against this, with basic annual settlements in its Car operations amounting to 5% in 1979 and in 1980, 6.8% in 1981, 3.8% in 1982, and an unprecedented two-year agreement of around 5.6% for 1983 and a similar amount for 1984.

The need for low wage settlements led to militancy among shop stewards as in each succeeding year the settlements remained in their terms miserly, and in our terms realistic and the most we could afford. The way to reward the workforce had to be by offering generous bonus incentives, related to performance, for this way our unit labour cost could be reduced, and employees would still improve their earnings. This happened in practice, for the average wage right across BL's car factories rose by 43% between the time the productivity scheme was introduced in 1979 and the end of 1982.

The two most difficult years were 1980 and 1981 when on each occasion the company teetered on the brink over pay for the following year. In the face of all-out strike threats over pay, management responded that strikes would close the factories for good. In both years the outcome was far too close for comfort, but each time the good sense of the majority of employees outweighed the wild and militant minority, and the employees pulled back from the precipice.

In 1980 the run up to the Cars wage negotiations – which are normally started in late September as the pay year runs from November each year – began when the stewards submitted a claim for a 20% wage increase in August. This claim was in stark contrast to the profile we had sketched at our internal management meeting at Marlow a month earlier. The 'Marlow Concept' required cut-backs, significant increases in productivity, and low wage settle-ments. Out of that Marlow meeting came a determination not to settle either the wage deal or component purchasing contracts on an inflationary basis; a determination to reduce the labour cost per vehicle, and to hold or reduce the material cost: in short, to become competitive.

Management exposed this thinking at a meeting of the Joint Negotiating Committee on the 30th September when the pay talks started. Despite a comprehensive review, not just of BL's own financial position but also the wider effects of recession on all Western motor manufacturers, the management's offer of 6.8% left the unions unmoved. Their claim for three times that amount would have cost more then £90 million and would have had a disastrous effect on cash flow and profitability.

The meeting broke up and weeks later the debate was still raging. Feelings were running high, and when it was learned that Prince Charles was to open the new Metro factory, the *Socialist Organiser* newsheet commented:

> Not content with fobbing us off with their miserly 6.8% offer, the bosses want to rub our noses in it as well. On Wednesday they'll be parading Prince Charles round Longbridge, and expecting us all to polish our shoes and comb our hair just in case the next King of England wants to have a word with the wonderful workers who make his favourite little toys.

In fact when Prince Charles visited Longbridge, right in the middle of the wage issue, he was extremely well received, and morale in the new Metro Works could not have been higher. The vocal militant really is in a minority, and when faced with events head on, he's not so vocal. There was nothing but enthusiasm for the Royal visitor.

The shop stewards continued the battle. The Longbridge Works Committee reported to employees in the following terms:

> We are told that we are privileged to have the new technology and investment, privileged to be associated with the Metro, privileged to have a winner. What we need is to be privileged enough to be able to buy one.
>
> In short, we recognise that we are going through a period of recession, with unemployment topping the two million mark, but we also recognise that continuing to accept low wages and cuts in living standards will not help but only worsen the depressed market.
>
> BL will not be turned round on the back of continual sacrifice of the workforce. Our members have had less recognition than the West Works Robots.
>
> *Think again Leyland management: we need a decent living wage not sweet talk.*

The 'sweet talk' alluded to the bonus incentive scheme. They were suspicious of it, because unlike earlier incentive schemes it was not within the aegis of the stewards – they could not control it.

It was clear that the intellectual and emotional gap was too great. It could not be bridged – and so once again we went to the brink. An all-out strike was called for Tuesday, 11th November.

The crisis was so serious that we brought our major suppliers together two days before the strike was due to take place, to warn them that we had decided not to back down over the strike. We did the same with our Dealer Council. We explained that anything above the 6.8% on offer would add to our unit labour costs and erode our competitiveness; there would be no point in going forward with further investment on that basis. The discussions with the suppliers and the Dealer Council were friendly, and they were supportive, but, of course, our colleagues were greatly concerned at the way things were developing – and no doubt bemused at the lack of any assurance that 'everything will be all right.' In fact, we took the opposite position: unless the unions or the shop stewards could be persuaded to accept the wage offer – our final offer – then only the employees' decision would stand between us and final closure of the business. We encouraged them to make their own employees aware of our thinking.

The pay talks culminated in a meeting at the Tavistock Hotel in London in early November 1980 between senior management and national union officials. The Tavistock was chosen because it was close to Euston Station, where many of the regional union officials arrived from the Midlands.

That the meeting occurred at all, was in no small part due to AUEW commonsense. At their Executive Committee meeting on the 4th November, 1980, they pressed for a top level meeting between the company and the union leadership. There was of course no question of involving ministers, which is what the unions would have liked, but we readily agreed to meet the General Secretaries of the unions involved in the dispute.

I have seldom spoken to the media during negotiations, or during major differences of opinion, partly because other executives usually represent the company at the sharp end, and anyway it isn't helpful to fuel the fire by commenting publicly. On this occasion I was closely involved. As I went into the Tavistock to meet the General Secretaries I was tempted to say just one thing, lest there be any doubt about our determination. I must have sounded as I felt – tightlipped and tense. In answer to a barrage of media questions on the hotel doorstep, I said, 'Not a penny more.'

We pushed through the mass of reporters and cameramen, and headed for the meeting. On this occasion I had asked our non-executive Deputy Chairman, Sir Austin Bide, to accompany Ray Horrocks, David Andrews, Pat Lowry, Geoff Armstrong and me. It was important that the non-executive directors should be represented for I felt that the future of BL, and arguably that of the British Motor Industry, really was at stake, and I opened the meeting by saying just that. I went on to remind the General Secretaries that the mass meetings at which strike action had been agreed were 'split' – even the stewards who initiated the action were not united about it – and that given the catastrophic consequences of a strike, there was not a sufficient mandate for going ahead. I continued:

> There is no money available to increase the pay offer, which is the maximum we can pay without reducing our already thin margins. The offer is final, and we have never bluffed. The incentive scheme provides a genuine basis for increasing earnings in return for improved produc-

tivity. The combination of higher volumes, with de-manning, makes productivity incentive bonuses achievable.

I went on to explain that heavy trading losses could not be eliminated until 1983 and that over and above the massive funds to come from the Government, we also needed funds from the banks. A strike would put paid to both sources of funding. The financial position was so tight that BL Cars could not stand a strike for more than a few days. Not being a profitable company, we could not afford to buy peace. A day or two before, I had written to the Secretary of State for Industry to say that if a damaging strike occurred we would seek no further funds from the Government and that this would mean closing plants which would not reopen after the end of the strike, thus throwing tens of thousands of people out of work without redundancy pay and with little prospect of jobs elsewhere. We would make this clear to our employees and I said:

> All this could be happening not next year, not even next month but in the middle of next week. We have the letters ready to be mailed to employees at 2.00 pm today. Copies are available if you wish to see them.

I said that I sensed a feeling on the part of the stewards that the Government would intervene:

> They will not; the Prime Minister made it clear in the Commons on Tuesday that negotiations were a matter for the management. It will be hard enough to persuade them to provide the £990 million we need – of which £800 million is for the Cars business – even on the basis of a 6.8% settlement. But to ask for still more funds to finance a higher settlement would be a waste of time, even if we were prepared to do it. We are not in fact prepared to seek further funds.

We explained that the standing of the union side of the Joint Negotiating Committee was at stake. In a public campaign we would have to persuade our employees to ignore the strike call and we believed we could succeed in doing so. This would further erode the credibility of the shop stewards; but if we failed, then the stewards were on a hiding to nothing, for if this Board had come to the end of the road, it would be idle for anyone to suppose that there would be new management, or indeed, new owners, waiting in the wings. Thus far my statement was listened to in grim silence – someone, I think it was Ken Gill of TASS, the engineering union staff section, commented that all we were offering was gloom and doom. I countered by saying:

> We are not; we now have Metro, and the new Triumph Acclaim is around the corner. Given funds we will have an exciting new mid-car in early 1983 and if we can get fixed expenses reduced further, as we must, then we can approach a profit before tax and interest in 1983. It isn't by any means a gloomy outlook, if you can persuade your colleagues to be patient in this wage deal. Our performance is improving – we were free of disputes for 98.2% of working hours this year. Production on Metro is climbing steadily.

> Many of us and many of you have worked hard to save BL. I don't have any ambition in life except that BL should be saved. But one must be a realist – if the workforce are in fact prepared to follow the irresponsible guidance of their shop steward representatives, then BL Cars will close, and that will be one dream gone up in smoke. Nothing will save the factories, and that includes Metro, for BL Cars currently lose £4 million a week even when we are not on strike.

I remember looking at the sea of faces in front of me – from Ken Gill, looking cynical, to Terry Duffy and David Basnett, who believed what I was saying and knew that failure to settle the wage deal would inevitably bring disaster. I went on:

> If you want to take your members over the brink, in the face of these opportunities – new models and new investment – it will be on your conscience. You face a heavy responsibility, bearing in mind the hundreds of thousands of jobs which are dependent on BL Cars, quite apart from the horrendous cost in union funds.

I finally said that if the discussions were not concluded by lunchtime, it would be necessary to mail letters, giving the management position, to the homes of all 50,000 BL Cars' hourly-paid employees, to give them time to consider the matter before the Tuesday strike deadline. If the General Secretaries were prepared to defer the strike, while talks continued, then the letters would likewise be deferred. The important thing was to keep the men at work on and after the 11th November. I threw the issue back to them. 'We have no money – you have us over a barrel. The decision is yours – you'd better make up your own minds.'

The negotiations started an hour later, after the General Secretaries had gone into private session to debate my statement; after Alex Kitson had arrived, very late, from another TGWU meeting to join Terry Duffy and Gren Hawley – the latter having represented the TGWU in Alex Kitson's absence. Alex Kitson was, in turn, standing in for the TGWU General Secretary, Moss Evans, who had been ill for some time. The BL management were not inclined to stand on ceremony, but we did want Alex Kitson present before we would get into serious discussion. Gren Hawley, as the leader of the union negotiating side, was too involved in the specifics of the BL wage negotiations to speak for the TGWU as a whole. It would have been incongruous, for we would have found ourselves in debate with one of the very officials who had already failed to persuade the stewards of the dire consequences of their actions.

Alex Kitson can be refreshingly direct. He asked point blank, 'Will the company improve on its offer of the 17th October, 1980?' I said 'No.' In fact, after the 17th October we had offered to guarantee an element of the productivity bonus for twelve weeks commencing the 1st November, 1980 – this had not been accepted, and it had immediately been withdrawn. As we sat around the table, on the 6th November, Ray Horrocks confirmed that it was no longer on offer. Alex Kitson asked me to elaborate on our decision to offer nothing further – the journalists still patiently waiting downstairs had fed back to the General Secretaries my pavement comment, 'Not a penny more.' There was some joking about this, but it was read correctly as our final company position on the basic offer. I explained that the 6.8% on offer could not be improved upon, because our cost structure could not stand a higher element of give-away cost, but any imaginative adjustment of the bonus incentive scheme was acceptable, provided – a big qualification this – the per vehicle cost to the company did not increase. Ray Horrocks put it more succinctly:

If you are seeking a form of words to settle the issue, we can provide one. There can be no settlement which materially increases the cost of the offer; the offer of the 17th October is all we can stand.

Alex Kitson said that he would convey this to his colleagues and join us in due course.

The union leaders returned a couple of hours later, complete with a suggested draft announcement which would take the steam out of the situation, but Alex Kitson came up with a very big but. 'If you agree to this, we will put it to the lads [the shop stewards were also waiting downstairs in a different part of the hotel] and see whether they like it.' I said something like: 'How can they like it, when it amounts to their capitulation?' We wrestled with the draft, and persuaded them to accept the following wording:

> Both parties acknowledge their unique responsibility for the success and competitiveness of the sole major British car manufacturer. And they accept that BL Cars cannot impair its competitiveness. Both parties agreed that the matter would be referred back to the JNC and the Cars management for meaningful negotiations and a timely final settlement effective from the 1st November 1980.
> On this basis the national union officials recommend that the strike planned for Tuesday, 11th November, will not now go ahead.

Alex Kitson and his colleagues took the draft, and went downstairs to face the music. He later told me that he hadn't tried to persuade the men to accept the proposal. He had reiterated what I had said to the General Secretaries, given his view that the management team were adamant, would really and truly not go further than the offer on the table; and he had put it to a simple vote. But he must have been convincing, for the vote went our way, the strike was shelved, and no concessions were made, or needed to be made. On the 10th November the Joint Negotiating Committee duly met the company. The earlier offers on the bonus scheme were again tabled, and this time they were accepted – effective from the 1st November.

On the 11th November, therefore, everyone in BL worked normally, and another major storm cloud evaporated under pressure. Alex Kitson's leadership was a major factor in his advocacy at shop steward level, but the influences on him, the pressures that caused him to use his undoubted persuasiveness with the shop stewards, came from some very responsible General Secretaries. The following year, he acted quite differently.

The 'not a penny more' episode was over, but it was a close run thing, and none of us enjoyed the strain of those ten hours at the Tavistock Hotel. But we were all relieved to be able to scrap the elaborate communications programme. The printed letters signed by Ray Horrocks had already been loaded in vans which were sitting outside postal sorting offices in Oxford and Birmingham, ready to be posted within minutes if the Tavistock meeting had failed. But it did not fail, and the national union leaders were as relieved as we were. There were many jobs at stake.

The next major crisis came almost a year later.

We had been having a good year in 1981, with a minimal incidence of disputes when suddenly all hell broke loose. At the very first negotiating meeting on the Cars operations pay claim, the shop stewards cut short the normally exhaustive negotiations, and marched out with threats of strike action. They were simply not prepared to talk at all unless we agreed, there and then, to raise the wage offer of a 3.8% general increase. For our part we were only prepared to pay more on top of that through the bonus incentive scheme. From the first moment the negotiating machinery had reached an impasse. This state of affairs left me determined that this time we would not go through the long ritual of meetings extending over weeks, with damaging speculation about strikes, while all the time customers at home and overseas walked away from us. We had conducted market research which clearly showed that every industrial dispute lost us thousands of customers.

It was for these reasons I felt we had to put the position squarely to employees and spell out the consequences of strike action. So on the 14th October, a few days after the stewards summarily broke off talks, all 50,000 hourly-paid employees in the Cars operation received a letter warning of dismissals and possible liquidation of the company if no agreement was reached, and a damaging strike took place. The letter was the result of a great deal of thought and debate over the previous weekend. On the Friday, 9th October, Ray Horrocks had told me where he stood on the wages offer. He and his colleagues were totally logical in their approach to the wage deal:

This is what we can afford. If we pay more we prejudice
the Plan, and we dare not provide the cash by cutting the
model programme. It is obvious that we must improve
earnings mainly out of productivity. The top 'give-away'
figure is 3.8%.

There was no need to ask whether I supported his stand. And I
didn't need to ask the Board, for our determination to make no
concessions to employees or suppliers, if these would prejudice the
recovery, represented a Board position and resolve that needed no
reiteration. How could we deliver one of the most ambitious
recoveries ever attempted in any industry, if we 'gave' on fundamental parts of the strategy – if we committed funds we didn't
have, and had no right to expect from any Government? And so I
said to Ray Horrocks:

I'm with you all the way. I agree with your conclusions
and I agree with your strategy. But we need one further
thing. I want a letter to go to employees now, in mid-
October, saying what we will otherwise be saying in early
November, if by then we haven't resolved the wage
negotiation. I know that this will be seen as provocative,
as a crude threat. The fact is, it isn't a threat – for you and
I know that dismissal and closure will be inevitable if the
men don't believe us, and they finally challenge our pay
offer. Therefore, we owe it to all our employees to get the
facts on the table now, before their attitudes harden.
They must be told that their jobs and the business are at
stake.

I am often criticised for the harshness of the words – certainly, I
remember them well, for I wrote them in my study at home on
Sunday the 11th October, surrounded by birthday presents, and I
read them to each member of the Board in turn. The reception
accorded the letter varied from a conviction that it was the only
obvious thing to do to the belief, that far from pre-empting the more
extreme steward's efforts, it could well inflame the situation and do
their work for them. That was David Andrews's opinion, and I had
no difficulty in following his reasoning. Once more I went over the
pros and cons of sending the letter.

David Andrews had summarised the cons, and John McKay,

who was not against the concept, had nevertheless added another dimension to David Andrews's very real concern: that the media, the world at large, would inevitably see the letter as a threat. The more responsible journalists would know why we were doing it – that it was being done so that we might act responsibly towards our workforce. But apart from the *Financial Times*, *The Times* and the *Daily Mirror*, there was not a deep understanding among the national newspapers of what we were trying to do, particularly on the employee relations front. I believe they at least knew how sincere we were in our determination to put BL on a sound footing. The public relations risk, and David Andrews's conviction that the men would react badly to it, added to the formidable argument. Of course the letter would be dangerous, but here we were, once again in this inexorable cycle.

I cast my mind forward two or three weeks and I plotted the critical path on a scrap pad – in no time at all we would be at a crisis point. The stewards were meeting in a few days' time formally to turn down the offer; they would never admit that they had avoided hearing out the full offer and that because of this our offer was incomplete. The men would be stirred up by militants, 'look at the sacrifices you have made, look at the increase in productivity – look at Edwardes's own salary increase.' The situation would be orchestrated to create the climate needed. In no time we would be into yet another 'Leyland Strike' – the two words we dreaded, for they would then reverberate around the world, and our annual £1,000 million of potential exports would be at risk yet again and our home market share would plummet. At that point, as ritual would have it, BL management would say:

> If you don't come back on Monday, or Tuesday, or Wednesday – you will have dismissed yourself. The company cannot stand a strike of more than five days and we all face closure etc., etc.

No, I couldn't see how we could allow ourselves to get into this cycle of apocalypse again without telling employees right at the start what the consequences would be, as seen by the Board. Honesty may not always be the best policy but it was the one rule we had adhered to, and it had kept us in business so far. Despite the risk, the letter had to go.

The offending lines of the letter were:

Gemini, the *Birmingham Post*

IF WE DO CLOSE, PRIME MINISTER, I HOPE
YOU'LL KEEP YOUR PROMISE TO HELP
THE SMALL BUSINESSMAN

If a widespread and damaging strike does take place the
company will have no option but to take the following
action:

Hold those on strike to be in breach of their contracts of
employment. Their employment would subsequently be
terminated and in these circumstances striking employees
would not be entitled to any redundancy payments or
payment in lieu of notice.

The Board would consult the Government on the steps
which would be needed to liquidate those parts of the
business within the Cars bargaining unit which are on
strike or prevented from working.

As employees you must be in no doubt that a vote for
strike action in support of a pay claim which the company
is in no position to meet, will have the effect of placing
your jobs and thousands of other people in the components industry in the greatest possible danger. These are
the simple facts.

We had never spoken of liquidation of parts of the company before
and it required careful consultation with Board and executive
colleagues. I spoke first to Sir Austin Bide:

The issue is simple, do we tell the men now that we won't
give way, that what we have on offer, plus the yet to be
negotiated incentive scheme, is all we can afford? Or do

we let them learn the hard way, when it may well be too late to stop the momentum building up to industrial action? There is a point of view that we may provoke the stewards to prosecute the strike, and unwittingly provide them with the language that they need to carry the men with them. Such a risk exists. The other way to look at it is that the stewards will vote heavily for a strike at their meeting in Birmingham on Friday, regardless of our letter. After all, for them to break off negotiations which should have taken days, after only a few hours, on day one, makes it clear that they want a showdown. Having made that decision, they don't need our letter to press the men to take up a strike posture. We'll be criticised either way, but I would gamble that we could well appeal to another and stronger force if we take the risk: their families. The letter will go to employees' homes, it will be read, and while it may annoy and irritate and even provoke a strong initial reaction, the penny will drop over the next 20 or so days, that a strike will accomplish nothing. That is the best argument of all.

I say that I recited all these arguments to Sir Austin Bide. It would be more accurate to say that we tossed them to and fro, and after the Deputy Chairman had given his unqualified support, I debated the pros and cons with the other non-executive directors. They took the same view. By Sunday evening I was sure that the letter had to go, that it was our duty to send it, and that the risk had to be taken. I have not often been involved in such a calculated risk, for we were doing at the beginning what most of our critics might readily have accepted 20 days hence in the heat of the battle, when these strong words would assume a greater respectability. The reaction to our doing it in cold blood could be unhelpful, but it was the right course of action.

On Monday, we talked at greater length to the experts. Geoff Armstrong counselled that we should moderate the letter and he made some helpful changes; by then my colleagues were resigned to the fact that the letter would be mailed. The letter went two days later with the support of the full Board. Collective responsibility was the order of the day, and once again I was to admire the strength of character of my colleagues – even those who were not quite sure whether we were wise to spell it out so crudely and so early on, lived with the decision and hung on, as we went through the inevitable and irrevocable trauma that followed.

That it gave the militants some ammunition and some credibility I do not doubt; and as we anticipated, it offended the more liberal minded, but alas naive, among the media. They argued that the BL Board had provoked the workforce. The fact is that all the things that happened would have happened anyway. That was my hunch on the 11th October.

So the letter was sent, and the atmosphere became highly charged over the next fortnight, with the spectre of closure hanging over our 34 car factories and 50,000 of our employees. By Friday, 30th October, 1981, things looked grim. The press had not been favourable, although there were signs that they were beginning to understand our predicament.

We had explored most of the avenues in trying to avert the strike but we hadn't involved the Labour Party. I knew that Stan Orme, Shadow Spokesman for Industry, had the future of the company very much at heart, and that if he felt the company was in real danger, he would be bound to help. On the 20th October, Ray Horrocks and Geoff Armstrong, gave Stan Orme a comprehensive briefing on the dispute. Geoff Armstrong was the BL executive shot in the legs while delivering a lecture at Trinity College in Dublin. A man of strong character, he must take a great deal of the credit for having established management credibility with the unions. At 35 years of age, he was taken very seriously indeed by management, unions and shop stewards. Stan Orme understood the need for pay restraint, and did not contest the level of the offer. But he took issue with us on the style adopted – he thought that our attitude was unbending, our public stance was no better, and he was genuinely shocked at the lengths we were prepared to go to drive through our objectives. He thought our style of negotiation, and in particular our determination to dismiss employees on strike, was unacceptable, and he was appalled that we were prepared to liquidate the business if the men did not in fact return to work. The BL Board and senior management had come to the view that if this was the end of the road, so be it. It was important to get across to the Opposition that the problems associated with recovery remained formidable, that unit labour cost was a key factor and that we needed the full support of the workforce to make the battle for survival worthwhile. If the workforce were bent on suicide, there was no point in soldiering on. There was complete agreement on this among my Board colleagues and I therefore felt justified in involving the Opposition. At 10.30 am on Friday morning, 30th October, I phoned Tom McCaffrey, Michael Foot's Press Secretary, and sought an urgent meeting with the Leader of the Opposition and Stan Orme. Half an hour later, Ray Horrocks, David Andrews, Geoff Armstrong, John McKay and I were at the House of Commons.

Michael Foot and Stan Orme were in the Leader of the Opposition's small office, at the east end of the Commons; it takes both time and knowledge to find it; very effective in protecting its occupant from casual interruptions! Stan Orme had obviously briefed his senior colleague, and it became clear that one or two phone calls had already been made to union officials – certainly Alex Kitson had been consulted on the nature and extent of the crisis. (At that time Moss Evans, General Secretary of the TGWU was still on sick leave, but was happily well on the road to recovery.)

The Labour team looked very despondent; did we really mean to terminate by constructive dismissal the employment of those on strike and then close those factories that were not at work? Yes. We would take this action; the Board had decided that it was the only thing we could do in the unhappy circumstances. We were still not fully competitive, even with the 30% average increase in productivity achieved so far in 1981. Any increase in cost over and above the 3.8% wage offer we had made would be unacceptable. We simply couldn't give the men the increase the shop stewards were demanding, and at the same time deliver the 1981 five-year plan. If we did not achieve the plan, then the business was doomed anyway. We were not surprised when the Leader of the Opposition proposed a compromise solution:

> You want us to help you to save the company. This means
> you must moderate your unbending stance – epitomised
> by your aggressive letter to the workforce. If you with-
> draw the intention to dismiss the men on strike, and the
> threat of liquidation – and we accept that these are not
> idle threats – we may be able to help persuade the unions
> to secure a return to work. If you then increase the offer
> from 3.8% to 4% and consolidate some of the bonus
> payments, you could well settle the whole thing.

His proposal seemed so reasonable on the face of it that I could well understand his being puzzled at our rigid attitude. But in Britain we have had 30 years of management not meaning what it says; of government intervening in major strikes, and so undermining the management of public sector companies; of militant stewards justifying a harsh and aggressive line by pointing to a history of last minute concessions by weak and indecisive management. There comes a time when reason is no longer the way forward, particularly when those who have initiated strike action have other objectives – objectives of a political nature. These people want to change society at any price, rather than pursue the proper interests of their members. Not for the first time, these thoughts flashed through my mind on that Friday morning.

I much appreciate your genuine desire to find a solution, Mr Foot. You and Stan Orme have been helpful in talking to Alex Kitson and others, but I'm afraid we can't solve the problem by making concessions at this late stage. If you would be good enough to do two things, I would be very grateful. First assure the unions that we will readily meet them at the Advisory Conciliation and Arbitration Service, or anywhere else. We are prepared to spend the whole of Saturday talking to the General Secretaries concerned.

There seems to be a feeling that we won't meet and talk. On the contrary, we do have things we want to explain to the union leaders, in particular our determination to improve employee involvement. To do this we need to resolve the 16-month-old impasse between the unions. I think you know that the TGWU are still insisting on having a majority vote on the union side of the BL Cars Negotiating Committee while at the same time having the right to appoint one of its men as chairman. Until this is resolved to the satisfaction of the other unions, we will continue to have a vacuum. How can we negotiate with our workforce when for 16 months the unions have been unable to agree upon their representation for negotiating with BL Cars? Here we are in this dangerous situation, and in all this time we have had no union line up with whom to talk. We really do want to talk, and anything you or Stan Orme can do to get this across would be appreciated, but it will have to be about style or cooperation, not cash.

The second thing is this: some militant stewards believe that we mean what we say about closing the relevant factories next week – given the men don't return to work. This would not go amiss, as far as they are concerned, for it will cause the sort of confusion they seem to want. But the vast majority of employees, and many of the stewards, genuinely want to resolve this problem, get back to work, and save the company. These are the people who need to know that we really are at the end of the road; if you could reinforce this by making it clear, publicly, how serious the situation is, I would value it greatly.

Michael Foot listened with his usual courtesy and attention and in the space of the next 48 hours he delivered both messages very effectively.

When we left the office, Tom McCaffrey accompanied us to the Central Lobby, where we were to speak to lobby correspondents. I told him what we planned to say – merely an objective statement about our discussions, without implying in any way that Michael Foot or Stan Orme agreed with us; just that they noted our point of view, and would use their influence to get the parties around the table. He thought it fair and reasonable, and at my invitation he stayed to hear it said. His presence added weight to the veracity of our statement. As we arrived at the St Stephen's entrance of the House, the pair of usually tolerant, good-natured policemen on duty were having a problem and they were very angry indeed. The entrance to the Commons was jammed with journalists, cameramen, and television cameras. They had got wind of my meeting with the Leader of the Opposition. The two policemen were blocking their entry as they pushed forward. John McKay said, 'put your head down and make for the car. Only say the one or two key things you want to put across – don't try to answer questions, or you'll be swamped.' I did just that, followed by Messrs Andrews, Horrocks, Armstrong and McKay. Head down, I entered the mêlée. I remember saying, 'This is like a bloody rugby scrum.' I also said something like, 'We can't pay money we haven't got. Mr Foot was helpful with constructive advice. Of course we are prepared to meet the General

Secretaries.' (I saw the incident on television later that day, and it confirmed my impression of a rugby scrum.)

Things then started to happen. When I walked into the BL headquarters at Portman Square 35 minutes later, the Press Association tapes were already typing out the basic content of the Lobby meeting. And the phone was ringing from the Department of Industry.

Immediately after we had left Michael Foot's office, the impasse was broken and the fact that he had activated the General Secretaries of the negotiating unions was confirmed within the hour. Michael Foot had persuaded Alex Kitson to meet the BL management on Saturday morning, under the auspices of ACAS. But Alex Kitson had made a shrewd move: he had immediately phoned Patrick Jenkin, the Secretary of State at the Department of Industry, and had persuaded him to see the trade union delegation after 'a meeting which we are having with Michael Edwardes and his colleagues at ACAS tomorrow.' I was horrified and immediately telephoned Patrick Jenkin. I explained that if he saw Alex Kitson and his colleagues after our meeting he would nullify the negotiating process. The unions would revert to the old game of 'listening' to management, but 'settling' with the Government.

> Unfortunately, you are committed to seeing them, and I can't ask you to retract that commitment. But insist that they see you first thing in the morning – not after our meeting – otherwise you will emasculate us. Our meeting will have no standing – they will quote their meeting with you as the definitive meeting. You will enable them to put us over a barrel.

Patrick Jenkin readily agreed – he fully accepted our point of view; telephoned Alex Kitson and reversed the timing arrangements. The ACAS meeting was postponed until 11.00 am to enable the Secretary of State and the unions to meet first.

As we entered the ACAS offices on that Saturday morning, we knew that Alex Kitson and his colleagues were with Patrick Jenkin. This added to the occasion, for anything might happen there. What were the odds in favour of a satisfactory outcome? I was not sanguine. Some days earlier, when the General Secretary of the TUC, Len Murray, together with Sir John Boyd and Alex Kitson had joined the full BL Board for a review of the situation, we had made it clear to them that we could not in any circumstances pay a wage increase that would increase our unit costs. The meeting had helped to explain our position, but strike action loomed no less alarmingly. The quickest way to ensure the inexorable decline of BL was to give in. The level of our pay offer just about enabled us to hold the unit labour cost of our products; it was just about economically possible to pay the increase without sliding further into the abyss, provided of course we also held down the cost of bought-in components. There was nothing brave or bold about our strategy; it was commonsense and we had no other option. If we acted differently we would be written off by the banks, by our major shareholder, the Government, and by the public – already both an unwilling taxpayer and a shareholder, they might become an even more unwilling customer. And in this latter role they had full discretion, for there is, quite rightly, no law against buying German Fords or French Talbots. So the key union leaders should now know where we stood, but I was nevertheless apprehensive about how events would unfold. In our strategy lay great risk; union leaders might well stake everything on saving face; challenge our 'final offer' – and final it was – and decide to go down fighting. We would then be out of business in short order.

Yet again we were to learn that even final crunches can be spun out. We had initially resisted an ACAS involvement because we had little or nothing to offer by way of compromise. We felt there was a danger that the unions might assume we would pull a solution out of the corporate purse, rather like the proverbial rabbit out of the hat. Indeed, when Pat Lowry telephoned me a few days before the end of October, suggesting a meeting, I had discouraged him. I said that the credibility of ACAS could be impaired, and no purpose would be served if meetings took place under their auspices, because we had no material concessions to make. Although there was, in the event, no final resolution at the ACAS talks, this was no fault of Pat Lowry or of ACAS, for agreement was indeed reached – but politics outside management, workforce and unions, caused that deal to come unstuck. The ACAS conciliators played an important and highly professional role during the 36-hour crisis, skilfully assembling both parties and involving both the General Secretary and the deputy General Secretary of the TUC.

Pat Lowry is a specialist in this sophisticated atmosphere of nuance and counter-nuance, and we subjected ourselves to some very thorough professional probing by him and Dennis Boyd: both were in their elements in this role. It was then that we learned that this was no ordinary summit. Besides the national union officials there was the full shop stewards' negotiating team in the basement – about 40 in all – as Alex Kitson had asked ACAS for a room for them, rather than leave them at Transport House, a few hundred yards away. The national union officials would not necessarily have the final say.

We quickly established with ACAS that there were fringe areas in which we could make concessions, but these added up to about 0.1% of the payroll. There were no material concessions that could be made for we were struggling to compete with the unit costs of European cars; and the Japanese could eat us for breakfast! Pat Lowry and his colleagues took it all calmly and cooly.

At this stage the union delegation returned from the Secretary of State and we learned that Patrick Jenkin had quite properly declined to intervene beyond having that Saturday morning exchange of views. Both parties met just before lunch and made their positions clear – we seemed miles apart. Over lunch the BL team agreed that while we could not move on pay, we could be encouraging about the question of closer employee involvement and play our part in trying to move away from confrontation. So when both sides reconvened I emphasised our willingness to move forward with the unions on this issue. Give and take was needed. We would make strides in this direction, if the unions would resolve their hiatus on the structure of employee representation for here we were, in as big a crisis as we had faced, with no structured interface with whom to negotiate the pay deal, and no opposite numbers with whom to resolve the present crisis.

And so we sat around the ACAS table; half the main BL Board, the heads of our operating companies and all the General Secretaries of the unions directly involved in the shop floor pay offer. Quite simply, I said that we were not proud of our level of employee involvement, and we wanted to do something about it – provided we had someone to negotiate with. Len Murray quickly acknowledged the latter defect, and he agreed to take this up at TUC level and, indeed, this was resolved some months later. The unions gave their point of view, welcomed the management recognition of the need to involve employees in a more meaningful way, and made a telling observation that Alex Kitson was to repeat in public the next day: 'You have tried to do in three years what a normal company would have done over 20 years.' In short, we shouldn't be surprised if the workforce found it difficult to stomach our drastic action.

Both sides withdrew, and then we were treated to the spectacle of the ACAS 'shuttle' between the two parties. As I recall, neither side met the other in the many hours which followed. We were in one room, the national union leaders in another, and the stewards in the basement. Pat Lowry impassively and objectively moved backwards and forwards between us and the General Secretaries, endeavouring to build upon the fragile common ground which had appeared over employee involvement for the future. Eventually – perhaps after eleven hours – there appeared a glimmer of hope and the management group were asked: 'Could Len Murray, Alex Kitson and Sir John Boyd see you privately?' I readily agreed, and the four of us entered Pat Lowry's office where we sat down to define the gap between the two sides.

Sir John Boyd, with great skill, nudged us into quantifying what we had not quantified all day – the modest value of the fringe areas where we were prepared to concede some costs. Everyone present knew, after what now amounted to 12 hours, that this was it. If this wasn't acceptable, we would take a strike. And if the men did not return to work, we would dismiss them, and close the business. Throughout these talks our original letter of the 14th October remained on the table, despite requests that it be withdrawn. At the fourteenth hour agreement was reached, and Len Murray and Sir John Boyd showed visible relief; Alex Kitson was definite but apprehensive for he had some 40 stewards to 'sell' it to in the basement. But all the General Secretaries agreed to help him in that difficult task: for him it should have been merely a part of the day's work.

While the union leaders went down to meet the stewards – for the first time that day – and my colleagues debated the mechanics of getting everyone back to work, I reflected upon the negotiations, and why it was that virtually all the General Secretaries were in favour of a deal, when we had made no material concessions except the promise of deeper employee involvement. I believe there were two reasons. The obvious one was that they did not want to take direct responsibility for the closure of our Cars business, with the consequent loss of jobs. They were losing members anyway, and the prospect of wholesale job losses was not appealing – their union finances could not stand the loss of subscriptions. (In 1981, trades union membership in Britain dropped by several hundred thousands.) There was also a more cogent reason – had we applied constructive dismissal, so that the men would have in effect dismissed themselves because they would have been in breach of their employment contracts, the unions would have been liable for strike pay for a full 12 months! We estimated that this would have cost the AUEW up to £12 million and the TGWU some £24 million for the ensuing year. I believe this was an important consideration. A third reason, and I suspect the major consideration, was the fear that employees would in fact defy union instructions to strike and report for work. On this point the union assessment was probably no better founded than our own. Our instinct led us to believe that many would, indeed, walk through the pickets and in to work.

But we were in for a shock, for there was to be no deal. Len Murray and his colleagues were in the basement addressing the shop stewards, a militant group of people, who were by no means looking for a settlement. Some had other aims. I am told that each General Secretary had his say, and apart from the Communist, George Guy, and one other, all spoke in favour of the agreement that had been reached upstairs. Much was made, quite rightly, of our intention to improve employee involvement. Twice during this fairly laborious procedure and before he addressed the stewards, Alex Kitson went out of the room to telephone. And then came the bombshell. Having led the union team in the private talks with us (with Len Murray helpful but insisting that he was an observer), and having firmly settled the deal, Alex Kitson spoke up last and spoke *against* the deal, to the absolute astonishment of John Boyd and others. He literally said, 'I am not sure that this is a good deal; you, the lads must decide.' The stewards, who had been kept in isolation for over 12 hours and were clearly in no mood to be steam-rollered into acceptance, were given the lead to continue their opposition.

And so in the fifteenth hour we reconvened upstairs, not to confirm the deal, as we expected but, to hear some very embarrassed men, and a very lame and unconvincing Alex Kitson, tell us that the stewards would report back to mass meetings 'to let the lads decide'.

I kept my temper for virtually the whole of my five years at BL – when I was very angry inside I merely became 'ice cool'. On this occasion however, I let my opinion of this 'grand renege' be known, with heated clarity and without any reservation. Recently, Pat Lowry told me that had ACAS officials not buttonholed the union side as they came out of the meeting with the shop stewards, they would have left without giving us even the courtesy of an explanation. Pat Lowry, who normally remains calm under the most trying of circumstances also showed his anger – the first time since he joined ACAS – at the way in which the negotiations had ended. The BL team were all utterly contemptuous of what had been done, and we said so.

It was well past midnight and the press had been waiting since early morning. In ten minutes' time we were to face them – and during those minutes my management colleagues and I quickly discussed our strategy. We decided that we could only put a brave face on it, and reserve our position in public, at least overnight. And so in the early hours of Sunday we met the press with the unions; we heard Alex Kitson solemnly speak for his colleagues – despite having reneged on the deal, he was still their spokesman – and I said a few cautious words, and then we headed for home. The press were not fooled – they sensed that something fishy was going on.

But the battle was far from over, for we had a long Sunday ahead of us. I returned to Richmond at about 2.00 am on Sunday morning feeling utterly disillusioned and let down, but ready to start the telephone debate with colleagues and others later that day. Terry Duffy was due back that Sunday, having attended a union meeting in Kenya through the critical week. His deputy, Sir John Boyd, was too honest a man not to be very angry indeed, and as I fumed and racked my brain, as I consulted and debated that Sunday morning, so too did Sir John Boyd. I know because I exchanged views with him on the telephone. He was appalled at what had happened and he was prepared to say so – as did Terry Duffy on his return.

In mid-morning we learned that Alex Kitson was to appear on the Independent Television programme 'Weekend World' at midday. An urgent message was sent to Michael Foot explaining what had happened the previous evening, and we asked him to intervene and reason with Alex Kitson to get him at least to moderate his public stance, so that he would not inflame the workforce and make a strike decision inevitable. I believe Alex Kitson was so contacted and in a very rough interview with the programme presenter, Brian Walden, he came off second best. I learned that day that there is a sort of rude honesty among the media and when their instincts tell them that all is not as it should be – that there has been dirty work at the crossroads – they can be quite cautious in their reporting. Their hunch that all was not above board, was confirmed when Sir John Boyd went on the radio later in the day. He openly supported the ACAS deal and put Alex Kitson under pressure. That evening I telephoned Harold Evans, then Editor of *The Times* and said:

> I am fighting mad, and I don't want you to accept a word I say but let me tell you a story and then phone Len Murray, Pat Lowry and John Boyd – plus Alex Kitson and others if you wish – and then decide whether your sense of fair play requires a probing story into the background to yesterday's ACAS negotiations.

This was at 7.00 pm and by 9.00 pm he phoned back; told me that what I had said had been substantially confirmed, and that he was running a strong article on how we had been let down. It was published under the headline 'Union Leaders Split over Settling BL Strike' and went on:

> BL shop stewards meeting in Birmingham this morning hold the key to an early settlement of the company's first national official strike. They will be given a report of the new deal proposed by Sir Michael Edwardes, the company's Chairman, without a recommendation from national union leaders.
>
> Usually reliable sources in the Labour movement last night predicted that shop stewards would seek to continue the strike, though they will come under strong pressure from some national negotiators to recommend the rank and file to accept the package. Indeed, at the climax of Saturday's negotiations no national leader sought rejection of the offer . . .
>
> The strike was 'within a whisker of being called off', said one high level participant.
>
> It went ahead with Mr Alex Kitson (transport workers') playing a disputed and apparently shifting role as chairman of the final meeting of the 38-strong negotiating committee of the BL Cars union side, including Communists. They decided not to reverse the strike call and to

put the new offer to shop stewards today and to mass meetings of the work force tomorrow.

What hope this held out began to crumble last night amid bitter recriminations.

Mr Kitson, acting general secretary of the Transport and General Workers' Union, was accused by BL negotiators of reneging on an agreement he had given to them to recommend acceptance. And in the early hours of yesterday morning he angered union colleagues who had been in the negotiations with him when he told the press that they had agreed to call off the strike.

There were scenes of bitterness and anger when the union side came back and the BL team asked, 'So the strike is suspended?' Only to be told that it was still on.

BL negotiators insisted this was against the understanding given to them in the presence of Mr Pat Lowry, the Advisory Conciliation and Arbitration Service negotiator.

But the damage was done, and we were back on the brink.

And so the tempo built up, and the whole issue was to go back to mass meetings at plant level. Before the mass meetings – first thing in the morning of the 2nd November – Patrick Jenkin phoned me. He seemed very nervous about the outcome, and I was very uneasy when I put the telephone down after his call. It was therefore with immense relief, when only minutes later I heard that Longbridge, of all places, had voted to accept the offer; certainly we were back in with a chance of saving BL. And then plant after plant accepted the 3.8%. The crisis was over but at what a price in time, effort and image. In terms of government attitude, it was important that the Prime Minister was ready to stand firm and not intervene; she confirmed that this was so a week or so later. I was grateful for this, but I didn't know it at the time.

Of course, even if the reneging was not totally politically motivated, it was symbolic of a great problem: the avowed policy of the TGWU to lead from behind – to follow their militants. They refer to it as 'putting it to the lads', but it doesn't work that way. In their hierarchy 'the lads' are invariably the vocal militants who, even if they know what the lads really want (and that is often doubtful for they have such different objectives), ride roughshod over their wishes.

And so once again we had been involved in brinkmanship – out of need, not out of boldness. Was our approach, and our success, due to fear on the part of our employees? I think not. I firmly believe that managers, if they are to be leaders, must be firm and honest and do what they say. The BL Board has done just that for five years, and perhaps gained more credibility than friends. Our employees respected this, and they voted for the management offer against the advice of militant leaders.

The pay dispute of November 1981 pushed BL Cars closer to disaster than at any time in the previous four years. But there was another problem on the horizon. Within a week of the dust settling, this manifested itself in another dispute. The media dubbed it the 'tea break strike', and no doubt it reinforced the jaundiced view of Britain from overseas. In reality the dispute affected just the Longbridge factory and was caused by the need to implement a national Engineering Employers' Federation agreement to reduce the working week to 39 hours. This agreement had been reached two years previously between the unions and the Engineering Employers' Federation, for implementation on the 1st November, 1981. But it contained the fundamental proviso that the loss of one hour's work would not increase costs and the full implications of this were not realised by the unions until companies began to seek ways of achieving the cost containment. Although BL had since opted out of EEF negotiations, the company was bound by that particular deal.

While there may have been a temptation on the part of some employers just to absorb the extra costs, BL's financial position dictated otherwise. An hour's production was the equivalent of 2.5% of weekly output and this could not just be written off. Our proposal was to reduce relaxation allowances by about eleven minutes a day thus achieving the '40 hours' production in 39 hours. The unions, on the other hand, felt that the productivity increases already achieved, and which were providing good earnings, were sufficient and should be 'traded off' to cover the cost.

The timing of the dispute, so soon after the pay settlement, was unfortunate, but had we delayed implementation of the 39-hour week, the unions would have taken industrial action for failure to honour the introduction date, which would have wrong-footed management. Therefore we implemented the deal, but demanded a cost offsetting arrangement at the same time. We were mindful that in this case there was room for a degree of flexibility about how the reduction in the working week could be achieved, provided there was no cost penalty. In the event there were concessions on both sides; the rest breaks were reduced by five minutes with increases in the speed of the production line absorbing the balance. This agreement was arrived at by burning midnight oil, with the management team working through the night with employee representatives to finalise the deal. I well remember Harold Musgrove phoning me at 4.30 am in the morning to tell me that he had reached an informal agreement, which the senior stewards were prepared to recommend to employees.

Longbridge, in fact, had been on strike for four weeks, and this was far more serious in terms of lost production and sales than the pay row. The company lost production of 24,000 cars – most of them the best-selling Metro, with a showroom value of about £100 million. At our other factories the 39-hour week was introduced without major disruption as local management negotiated various permutations to meet the company's 'no extra cash' objective.

While the tea break dispute rumbled on during that November, Leyland Vehicles management had its own problems; the business had lost £47 million in the first half of the year. The problems were two-fold. Firstly, the British market for trucks had dropped alarmingly, from some 80,000 a year in 1979, to about 40,000 18 months later. Overseas sales, which traditionally accounted for half total sales, were stagnant, and losses were mounting due to the strength of the pound which enhanced the superior competitiveness of overseas manufacturers. The second factor was that the Commercial Vehicle operations had far too much capacity, and overmanning was still rife. New products were being introduced successfully, but it would take at least three more years to replace the existing range with new models.

A wide-ranging survival plan was announced in which management proposed a concentration of manufacture on fewer factories, less 'in house' manufacture of uneconomic components – like gearboxes – and collaboration arrangements with other companies to maintain a full commercial vehicle range. The plan also required about 4,000 job losses out of the 18,000 strong workforce.

The proposals were put to union officials and employee representatives on the 20th November and met solid opposition. As with similar situations in the Cars operations, the shop stewards saw the solution in terms of greater investment and expansion, regardless of the realities of the market place. The cutbacks may not have been quite as drastic as those suffered by the Cars business over the previous two years, but the announcement had a traumatic effect on the workforce at Leyland and Bathgate. The social and economic impact of the changes was disproportionate on a business of only 18,000 people located in relatively isolated areas, without much alternative employment. These factors, together with malicious rumours that management were intending even more drastic measures in the future, explained the opposition to the recovery programme, and they led to a strike of several weeks at Leyland and Bathgate, led by the Communist shop steward at Leyland, Michael Coyne, who had held his shop steward job for only two weeks.

The build-up to the strike started when Leyland management began to implement the Plan in a low key by the transfer of development work on a new vehicle from Bathgate to Leyland. A dispute arose, initially involving one man, then 180 men, and then escalated until some 14,000 employees at both plants went out on indefinite strike. It was the first time there had been a strike against a recovery programme and for the specific purpose of stopping a closure or redundancy programme, anywhere in BL. It was in fact the only incident of this nature during my time with BL. The BL Board was in no doubt that, unless the Commercial Vehicle Plan could be carried through, the whole Truck business would have to be closed. We decided that time was needed to allow realism to grow amongst the workers.

The strike lasted for four weeks, and if Michael Coyne had had his way it would have lasted longer. For at the Leyland mass meeting which followed a late-in-the-day, but comprehensive management communications programme – including newspaper advertisements – the mood was overwhelmingly in favour of a return to work and the vote at the mass meeting clearly reflected this. Yet Michael Coyne at first declared the vote was in favour of the strike continuing! I remember the graphic television news coverage of the meeting which captured the anger and frustration of the men, who were clearly not going to be manipulated; they made their feeling known for 30 rowdy minutes before Michael Coyne conceded that his verdict 'may have been a little exaggerated. . .' (The news of the staff union vote, which had gone in favour of ending the strike, may have assisted him to reverse his opinion.) The democratic vote to return to work was followed the next day by a similar vote at Bathgate. The issue at Bathgate was further complicated by resistance on the shop floor to the ending of tractor production, and the militants sought to combine the two issues and create uncertainty and confusion to influence the vote by employees.

Had the Bathgate vote gone the other way or had Michael Coyne been successful in keeping the Leyland men out, the BL Board would have announced large-scale closures and possible liquidation, as the business was losing £2 million each week, and there would have been no point in continuing without the support of the employees. Equally, if the execution of the Recovery Plan had been frustrated there would have been no point in continuing in business.

The stewards put an interpretation on the Plan that was not accurate, and this fuelled the fire. They must have known that Leyland Trucks had a chance of survival with our planned action, but had no hope without it, especially as the top management team had spent many hours explaining the logic of it to the stewards. The initial failure was in not getting it spelled out early enough and beyond the stewards to where it really mattered – on the shop floor. Once we had communicated forcefully, commonsense rather than Communism won the day. And so the men returned to work, and the Leyland Plan was accepted.

There have been times when I have felt fairly certain that politically motivated stewards were provoking closure, in the interests of wider political aims. Perhaps we will never know why the rank and file at Leyland and Bathgate decided to end the strike; my guess is that their instinct told them that they were being used for political ends.

I have described the major industrial relations crises, but reading them one after another may give an erroneous impression. There really was more to it than a running battle between manager and militant, for while we had these peaks of crisis they generally erupted quickly and were resolved within a short period of time. For the rest of the five years we made steady if less spectacular efforts to bring the business under control.

From the start everything we did in employee relations was tested against the broad strategy of regaining management control of the business, and many of the management initiated problems – the factory closures, the implementation of working practices, the discontinuation of models, the modest pay offers – were simply a reflection of agreed plans and policies. The thoroughness with which the employee relations people and the finance people prepared the plans, drew up the options, quantified the impact, determined how long the cash flow could stand the buffeting – and therefore how long we had before we must end each upheaval – was impressive. This stood us in good stead for the two years of highly damaging pay disputes in 1980 and 1981.

By contrast the 1983 pay negotiations in October 1982 were conducted in an atmosphere of hard yet responsible bargaining and out of them came a two-year pay agreement which will do much to give the Cars business a stable platform for the hectic and crucial period of new product announcements in 1983 and 1984. The deal was concluded within the new negotiating machinery between management and employee representatives without the need to bring in national union officials or to escalate the issue, and attract highly damaging publicity. It is, I believe, significant that the structure for greater employee involvement had been finally agreed in April. Before then, when things became tense there were differing reactions among our various 'interested parties'. Most of our suppliers were calm, and so were many dealers, but not all. The group who surprised me most and for whom my respect grew, were the top 300 managers in the company. Calmly and deliberately they put their jobs on the line, and particularly so when 150 of them agreed to put the future of the company to a vote by the whole of the workforce. They saw that unless we regained control the business would collapse, perhaps not in a spectacular way at the height of one of the crises, but through insidious erosion, until there would be no pretence of a business left. The fact that many national union leaders were nervous, whenever we went to the brink, was neither surprising nor any reflection on them. They live by membership, and for them to have membership, people need jobs. The prospect of a few hundred thousand jobs both within and outside BL disappearing was not one they could view with equanimity, and there was therefore a great deal of pressure on us to compromise in those crises. Honest well-meaning union officials, and some interested parties who were not actually union people, tried to prevail on us. 'You wouldn't really do it, if it came to the crunch? Would you?' We gave them no hope, for each time we faced a crisis situation, we all knew that it would only be resolved in one or two ways: a climb down by the militants who initiated the action, or the closure and break-up of large parts of the company. For 20 years we had seen management's authority challenged and eroded, and it had to stop, otherwise the business did not deserve the vast funds which taxpayers were pouring in through our major shareholder – the Government.

Paradoxically even quite sensitive political issues were seldom the subject of advance consultation with the Labour Government, because during their administration we had the structured form of employee participation, and the drill was to consult the 'machinery' first. As the more politically motivated of the stewards on the consulting body – the Joint Management Council – invariably leaked these matters to the press, the Government usually learned of our plans through the media. That was, if you like, the price they paid for this somewhat idealistic democratic experiment.

After the 1981 pay agreement when the TGWU conceded overall control of the negotiating body to the ten other shop floor unions, we moved into a new phase of employee involvement. Before this helpful development we had used thousands of man-hours explaining our strategies on particular issues to employees direct, through managers at all levels and throughout our factories, and our intention was to continue to do so, in parallel with the union machinery.

An excellent example of direct communication was when Harold Musgrove and his team put the product strategy across to some 18,000 employees – on day and night shifts – talking virtually continuously to groups of 1,000 people at a time, prior to the Recovery Plan Ballot in 1979. Jaguar have more recently involved their workforce in depth on the new lightweight engine project, and when I went over the engine plant at Radford in mid-1982, the seven stewards who accompanied the plant director, the head of Jaguar, John Egan, and me showed a deep knowledge of the financial, commercial, productivity and manning implications of this new investment. Rightly so, for it is vital that they should be well versed in facts and statistics that affect jobs. The correlation between disputes and market share shows how jobs are affected by mindless industrial action, and if deeper involvement reduces disputes, then, for this reason alone, it is worth it. At the employee relations level, this necessitates manager and employee working directly together – it doesn't benefit from third-party do-gooders or from government intervention.

With this process goes the need for balance, moderation, and dignity; it does not justify 'hob-nailed boots,' and whenever my senior colleagues have had evidence that someone has abused his new 'strength', changes have been made. These unhappy incidents have been the exceptions, but they have on occasions been publicised, which is fair enough. Abuse must be discouraged for if men give up some liberty and accept discipline in its place, those applying the discipline must earn the right to do so. The balance is a fine one; if management doesn't lead firmly, militant shop stewards will fill the vacuum, and it will be the moderately minded worker who will be the 'pawn in the game'. It is management who have responsibility for the business; if the power is to move to the shop stewards, let them have responsibility for the business, let them find the banks to lend the money, let them persuade governments of any colour to tide them over bad times, let them persuade competitors to collaborate; and let the unions persuade customers to buy the products they design, build and deliver. And above all, let them create the excellent working conditions – and much improved bonus earnings – that we are now proud to have in those of our factories that have come through the management and investment revolution of the past three years. For you cannot have responsibility and authority without accountability, and it is at this last fence that the militant falters and falls. Having learned to exploit, he has not yet learned to create and construct.

8

Metro Breeds Success

Before the new team went into BL, attempts had been made to save the company as a single entity on a highly centralised basis but BL is not a single integrated business; it is a group of several distinct businesses, each of which have their own problems, requiring individual tailor-made solutions. This was sometimes all too easy to forget when the sheer size of the volume car business (and its problems) tended to dominate the BL Board's deliberations, and to capture public attention. To bring about attitude changes meant breaking the inertia, the resistance to change, and we used organisational adjustments, to good effect, as one way of doing this. This, however, led us to make an early structural mistake; not in concept but in implementation.

'Separate out the specialist car operations – those of Jaguar, Rover and Triumph and Austin Morris's true position will become painfully clear,' was the recurring theme. This view was intuitive for the sums had not been done. When they were done, the weaknesses did become apparent, but not quite in the way we expected. Austin Morris certainly had problems, but if anything Jaguar Rover Triumph Limited was in worse shape – not an easy message to get across, even to JRT employees.

JRT lasted from early 1978 until mid-1980 when it was dissolved. It was really only a holding company with Rover and Triumph still separate identities in the minds of many managers and employees and with Jaguar, quite rightly, looking for greater independence. The workforce involved toiled manfully to make it work; decentralisation was right but its execution was not, thus fuelling the fire for the 'centralisers'. We recouped the position, but only just. The situation highlighted the vital need to make the right appointments and also the need to get a balance in which 'staff' men and 'line' men each make their separate contributions. Our difficulties were not helped when we made two wrong appointments and, at the same time, too many 'non-car' men were brought together in one group.

In the case of Jaguar we failed to solve its many problems at the first go; the product was not reliable, the paint finish was well below par, and productivity was abysmal. Losses were enormous, but the structure of the total cars business was such that it was impossible to pull out separate results for individual operations. We only knew the profit and loss across the vast and complex business of BL Cars as a whole. Even without the benefit of proper figures, it was obvious that Jaguar was losing a great deal of money – losses were running at millions of pounds a year. The attitude problem was enormous; the men on the shop floor, and indeed many of the managers still considered Jaguar to be elite, and their own contribution to be unique. Some managers, were more concerned with producing new models and reaching new standards of engineering excellence, than with managing the business. It proved difficult to get across to them the simple fact that Jaguar was not being managed – despite the fact that warranty costs were too high; that dissatisfied customers wrote or telephoned us from as far afield as the west coast of the United States; and that the failure of components, particularly electrical, was putting the reputation of the car at great risk.

After considering various permutations, in early 1980 I suggested to Ray Horrocks and Berry Wilson that John Egan, who had left the company some years before and whom we had failed to recruit the previous year, might be worth approaching again. Between them they very quickly had John Egan in the top job at Jaguar reporting to Ray, and within days of his arrival things started to happen. He rejoined the company in April during a strike at Jaguar over a grading issue and immediately became deeply involved in the negotiations. Bridges were built with the workforce from that the first day. Furthermore, John Egan believed what other Jaguar executives would not; that mounting losses made Jaguar's demise a certainty, unless the turn-around could be accomplished so quickly that the 1981 Plan would show a vast improvement and the company would project a break-even, or better still a profit for 1982. There was no other way in which major investment in the new light-weight engine could be justified, still less the even larger investment in the new prestige car for the mid-1980s and early

1990s. He won over the workforce, the suppliers, the dealers and with the appointment of two new managers, and very firm leadership, he transformed the top team. In the one year, 1981, Jaguar was truly reborn. Sales in the United States – Jaguar's major export market – responded as word got around that the cars were at last reliable and were very good value. Sales there went up by 55% in 1981 and doubled in 1982. Back in Coventry productivity in the first quarter of 1982 improved by 75% over the same period a year earlier.

The problem of quality and reliability was a thorny one, for even many of Jaguar's most enthusiastic owners in the United States would say, 'It's better to have two, if you want to be sure one stays on the road.' The new team tackled the reliability problems methodically by first ascertaining the failure rate of Jaguar components versus those of our major competitors and then by debating the facts with each supplier – usually by inviting the whole Board of the supplier company to visit Jaguar's Browns Lane factory for a full discussion. Although improvements were literally demanded of suppliers, the aim was usually to go to these meetings armed with positive suggestions and solutions. Seemingly intractable problems were solved by setting up joint task forces; to provide the right sense of urgency, the approach to warranty costs was modified when the full cost was charged to the supplier. Those suppliers who could not meet our requirements lost the business. Inside Jaguar itself some 50 'quality circles' were set up, and standards were lifted to achieve the levels of quality needed.

Success is about leadership and the test of leadership is success. Sometimes success will inevitably be limited, because of the nature and size of the task, but its presence is a necessary ingredient in the more difficult situations. There were few more difficult situations than in the volume cars business – now concentrated on the Longbridge and Cowley factories – where the immense task has required a robust leadership style. It was not possible to make fundamental change; to shake off generations of ingrained and obstructive attitudes and practices, both among management and on the shop floor, by skating around the problem. The Austin Rover team had an almost impossible brief, to win back the right of management to manage where militants once ruled, and indeed more often than not actually made the rules. The continuing turn-around of the Austin Rover business is a major British industrial success story with credit belonging both to management and the shop floor.

Critics speak of the pendulum swinging towards management, and suggest this might be only transitory; they argue that there will be a swing back followed by a backlash of militancy. There may be a few activists whose cause would be well served by such an outcome, but the experience at BL would indicate they are vastly outweighed by a majority of people with commonsense, working to bring about the recovery of the company in a constructive way. On issue after issue it was not the militants, the local or national union hierarchy or management who decided the outcome: it was the majority of moderate employees. On no occasion when the company came close to the brink, did the workforce take the irretrievable step over the edge, although at times there was intense pressure for them to do so from the politically motivated minority. Leadership at Austin Rover has kept the company on course for recovery – first directly under Ray Horrocks and then under the operational control of Harold Musgrove.

Land Rover and Unipart, both managed by executives in their 30s, are very different businesses, but both have been profitable, and neither has been in the depth of trouble that befell Austin Rover and Jaguar. These businesses, managed by Mike Hodgkinson and John Neill respectively, are good examples of the BL policy of putting specialist areas of the business on a relatively free-standing basis under the right management: people who thrive on having full accountability for the performance of their businesses.

A recent example of the transformation of a specialist unit is the Freight Rover business, which manufactures and sells Sherpa vans. In fact, until it was taken out of the volume cars business at the end of 1980, Freight Rover had no separate identity. Until then, its very distinct needs in the marketing, manufacturing and product development areas had been given little attention because of the Cars management team's absolute priority of saving the volume car business. Against intense competition from the Japanese as well as European manufacturers, the Sherpa van was losing market share and thus running up trading losses at an alarming rate. Closure looked to be on the cards in 1981, and decentralisation seemed to be its last chance. We therefore made it a first cousin to Land Rover, under the designation 'Freight Rover'. We gave Tony Gilroy, fresh from a superb job of work at Longbridge where he was part of the

Metro launch team, 18 months to swing the van business around. Because it lacked the inertia of some of our larger businesses and was of manageable size, he was able to make a very speedy impact. The results have been inspiring and with the launch of the new Sherpa range of vans in June 1982, the business moved out of its heavy losses. In mid-year they obtained an order worth about £10 million from British Telecom, which gave them a useful boost, not only in sheer sales volume but because it was a public demonstration of their new-found competitiveness in the market place.

The problems of Leyland Vehicles, the truck and bus business, were even more intractable, not only because the cost base of the business was far too high, as it faced the commercial vehicle market's deepest recession for 50 years, but because complacency was rife among the management team as well as the workforce. This despite all that was happening and was being seen to happen on the Cars side. As a result, although sterling work had been done to bring in new models, so that some 40% of the truck range would be totally renewed by the end of 1982 and much effort had gone into bus development, there was insufficient realisation of the extent of over-capacity in the industry as a whole – and in Leyland trucks in particular – as the slump in demand hit the truck industry. Fixed costs needed to be cut to the bone. No company that failed to grasp this nettle could possibly live through the recession. In addition, there were the more endemic problems of lack of competitiveness compared with European manufacturers in terms of productivity, quality and reliability.

There was a fundamental need for Leyland Trucks, as a relatively small truck business in world terms, to look for economies of scale through collaboration without, however, losing its identity in the market place. In retrospect, we at the centre were also slow to appreciate the extent of the problem. This was in part due to the attention we had to give to the Cars business, and in part because warning signals did not flash as brightly as they should have done.

What Leyland management did tell us constantly – and with a degree of justice – was how their business suffered in the market place, especially overseas, from its association with BL Cars. Apart from the unofficial and unconstitutional strike at Bathgate in 1978 our employee relations problems in Leyland Vehicles never reached the horrific proportions they reached on the Cars side. But the image generated by strikers in the Cars business rubbed off and damaged customer confidence, particularly as the foreign media were even less inclined than their British counterparts to draw distinctions between BL's various businesses. Leyland Trucks, with some 60% of the output exported and Land Rover with 80%, were especially vulnerable to this projection of a bad image overseas.

The full extent of the Leyland Trucks problem began to come through to us during 1980 as the British truck market fell away and the profits of early years turned into trading losses. David Abell, then Managing Director of BL Commercial Vehicles recognised that fundamental change was needed, but he was keen to branch out on his own. The timing could not have been better, for we were in the process of selling a business that he knew well. He, therefore, resigned and negotiated to buy our Prestcold refrigeration business, which as a non-mainstream business had been available for sale for some time.

It therefore fell to David Andrews, appointed Chairman of the reorganised Leyland and Land Rover Groups at the beginning of 1981, to take on the formidable task of reversing the decline of Leyland Trucks. To direct the Leyland Truck, Bus and Parts business as Managing Director under David Andrews, we brought Ron Hancock back from Leyland Australia where he had been Managing Director. The new top team took over with the recession at its deepest and the pound – affecting Leyland's competitiveness – at its strongest. There were many inside and outside BL who doubted whether Leyland Trucks position was recoverable. The recovery programme took nearly a year to develop, and it showed that far-reaching changes were required. These were finally accepted by employees, following the strike in 1981, and are now being acted upon with their cooperation and to good effect. Streamlining is well under way, and even if the truck market does not recover quickly, the financial haemorrhage will have been stemmed and the businesses will be organically stronger to cope with external vicissitudes. Most important of all, it has a management team which is realistic and determined to carry through the Plan.

There were other instances of key individual appointments transforming the prospects for businesses within BL. They all reinforce my view that business is about leadership; it requires understanding, courage, single-mindedness, drive and an ability to persuade and lead others. To manage change one often needs to change managers, which is not much fun; particularly managers who fail to involve their people and so secure their full commitment. British industry needs change: the scope for bright effective managers is unlimited for there are too many ineffective managers in key jobs. Yet why do our best young men and women shy away from the manufacturing industry – for where else is there such a challenge, where else are talents and resources so fully stretched? Where else do relatively young people have 'space' to grow and change. The concept of creating space to allow growth, of elbowing inertia, apathy, and resistance to change aside was well illustrated in a relatively small corner of the BL empire, but a part which was being suffocated for lack of breathing space.

Scattered around the company were pockets of highly skilled 'systems' specialists – the people who apply new technology, usually computer-based, to factory and office ways of working. They are the people who actually make the changes happen by devising micro-wave communications networks, computer-aided design and manufacturing programmes, and automated factory systems. Before 1977 the systems function within the company had on various occasions pointed out the benefits of bringing all this expertise together under one organisation to provide a service to the operating units. There was a pressing need to dissociate those few specialists from the wage bargaining morass of the rest of the Cars operation. Not least because of the severe constraints on salaries this imposed, in contrast to the quickly escalating pay for computer professionals throughout the world. As a consequence staff turnover was reaching hideous levels – more than 30% a year in some cases – and it was proving impossible to keep some vital systems running reliably, let alone plan and implement the far more sophisticated and technologically advanced systems of the near future.

The logic of establishing a separate systems function was accepted after the new Board was appointed and the decision to do so was taken by the BL Cars Board in early 1978 as part of the COG review. John Leighfield, was given the task of creating the systems company. He battled on and throughout 1978 tried to wade through the internal politics, the resistance to change, and specific opposition from the employee relations area, who were fearful of the effect this fragmentation of central bargaining would have on the rest of BL Cars. It was hardly a problem: the systems specialists numbered less than 1,000: the BL Cars wage bargaining unit represented close to 100,000 people! The inertia and opposition

I THINK IT STANDS FOR BREAD LINE

was immense and it was a year before action on the decision to centralise took place. When to my horror I discovered that virtually no progress had been made we immediately escalated the issue to the BL Board for a firm and final decision. The Board decided formally to establish BL Systems Limited as a separate company and it became a legal entity in June 1979. Even then the rearguard action of the status quo faction put up a spirited, final resistance in the form of protracted negotiations to 'separate' BL Systems from the wage negotiating unit and this took a further 18 months to achieve. This was the only major case of a continuation of the internal politics which we had taken steps to stamp out in the early months of 1978.

In November 1980, BL Systems finally became 'independent' – two years and nine months after we had decided that it should, and from that time onwards John Leighfield and his team established the company as a profitable European leader in manufacturing systems technology. The various applications spin-off from the high technology projects they and their colleagues in the operating companies devised – like monitoring systems for Land Rover and Metro production – have been bought by top European companies not connected with the motor industry, and have been small but prestigious 'invisible exports' for BL as a whole.

Metro was of course on the horizon and Metro was very much a child of information technology. It was to represent a major leap forward in how people coped with technological change and required a major change of attitude towards working methods. That our workforce at Longbridge rose to the challenge, is shown by the remarkable improvement in productivity that came in the wake of Metro, which went into production there in the second half of 1980. The fact that Metro was born at all, is a fascinating story.

From the start, back in 1977, we knew we had two major product problems to overcome. Until the launch of Metro due at the end of 1980, we had a serious gap at the small-car end of the market. In addition, Maestro – first of the new family of mid-range cars known as the LC10 range – was not due until more than two years after that. The product gap between 1977 and 1980 in the small-car market and between 1977 and 1983 for the medium-sized market was on our minds night and day for the five years. Knowing that we could not launch Maestro before early 1983, we held our market share together as best we could: we replaced the Austin Princess with the far more acceptable Ambassador; we updated and widened the Rover range, adding a 2-litre and a diesel, and made detailed improvements to the rest of the car range. In the commercial field we introduced a new Freight Rover-Sherpa and Land Rovers; new trucks and buses were brought out by Leyland, whose market share had also declined steadily over many years.

But whichever way we looked at it, the problem of the mid-car product gap was always the overriding issue. Even if our many other problems were overcome, this one would be there to haunt us until 1983, and in January of 1978 that looked a long way away. Competitors and motor industry 'experts' who analysed our situation clearly felt that we couldn't make it until then. It wasn't in our interests to show them the extent of our nervousness, but even if it didn't show, it was there!

The first gap we tackled was the sector one size up from Mini – first because we knew that we could fill it in 1980, well before the other and more serious sector gap. Work already done on the Mini replacement could be diverted to what we referred to publicly as a 'Mighty Mini', but no amount of adjustment to engineering priorities could bring Maestro forward to 1980 to substitute for its smaller brother. In other words, we were stuck with the predetermined order – first the small-car, then the medium-sized car.

173

We didn't have the engineering resources to alter the order, for work had been concentrated on the smaller model and it was well advanced compared to the Maestro. Switching the order would have meant that *neither* could have been launched in 1980. In fact, the engine strategy and development of the new 1.6-litre engine for Maestro did not mature until much later.

Having accepted this as a fact of life, we analysed the implications for the company, and we did not like what we found. The major sector of the market was the very one in which we had our biggest problems. Models like Allegro and Marina, which did not exactly set the world on fire when they were first announced, were now facing very strong competition. We decided to deal with this problem in two ways, bearing in mind that not all the funds in the kitty would enable us to launch Maestro or the next mid-range model, known as LM11, any earlier than early 1983. First, the small-car had to be a certain success; it had to have an aura which would make it a real winner, and would more than fill its particular market segment, to give us the momentum to get through the barren period from the end of 1980, when it was due, to early 1983. Second, we had to find a model – someone else's creation – to help bridge the gap, to make the barren period a lot less unpalatable.

We made the first decision very early on – on the 20th December, 1977, only weeks after the new team arrived on the scene. It was, in fact, the first major decision made by the newly appointed Advisory Board. We would scrap the Mini replacement, the so-called small-car project, and go for a rather larger and more ambitious car: a winner on all counts. A car that would beat all-comers on space and economy; a cheeky car that would capture the imagination – and one which would perform both in drive-ability and reliability. This meant an eleventh hour death sentence for ADO 88, the project to replace the Mini; it gave way to Metro . . .

ADO 88 had been the final, agreed design for a replacement for the revolutionary Mini which had so caught the public imagination after its launch in 1959. At regular intervals since this remarkable small car first appeared on the road new designs and concepts were developed, but came to nought. 'Small cars don't make money' has been the conventional wisdom of the motor industry worldwide, and stories abound of Ford executives tearing the first Minis to pieces and shaking their heads about its being over-engineered and under-priced. There was a measure of truth in this, but in a properly ordered business small cars help to cover the fixed expenses and are an essential part of a total car range. This is why the launch of Maestro and then LM11 and the XX car are all so crucial. Metro cannot stand alone, and was never meant to.

At the time of the formation of BLMC in 1968 what money was available was spent on designing larger cars like Marina and Allegro, the short-lived Triumph TR7, and the initially under-developed Princess and Rover saloons. By 1974 there was felt to be a need for a new small-car to take over the mantle of the Mini, and ADO 88 was seen as a direct replacement in a market sector created solely by the Mini's uniqueness. The very heavy capital cost of this project became a major plank in the company's platform and plea for state aid later that year, and the project featured prominently in the Ryder Report product plans. In the two years after the Government bail-out in 1975, development had continued, but by mid-1977 real doubts were beginning to surface inside British Leyland and the NEB about ADO 88's commercial prospects. The implications were quite staggering; a near £300 million investment which looked like turning out to be a national disaster. Momentum had built up over the previous two years to the point where fully engineered prototypes were on the road, and work was poised to start on a new £200 million factory at Longbridge to build the car. The doubts grew into serious misgivings when the results of UK and European 'clinics' of ADO 88 became known.

The clinic is an important part of every manufacturer's design and development programme. A representative cross section of potential customers owning either the company's or rival manufacturer products, are shown the new car, unbadged and anonymous, along with competing models; their reactions are carefully noted. They are asked a series of questions covering their reactions to all aspects of the car and their responses are analysed to build up a picture of how well it will sell – and at what price. The clinic tests of ADO 88 turned out to be discouraging in the extreme. The result of one clinic showed that out of 500 people just 3% made it their first choice, against 39% for the Ford Fiesta. In France, Germany and the Netherlands the results were correspondingly bad. The car would not command a price sufficient to make the project profitable.

While these facts were known to management before the new

BL Board was appointed, the crunch decision had hung fire, and so a major problem fell into our laps literally as we walked through the door. The company desperately needed a new small-car; the world expected ADO 88, but to carry on with a loser would almost certainly put the volume car operations out of business; and yet to cancel it would be a further blow to the company's image and credibility. It was a 'no-win' situation.

In product terms there was no greater priority than finding a way out. The options were stark if simple, and were debated by the Advisory Board at the 1977 pre-Christmas meeting. No one around the table was in any doubt that ADO 88 had to go, but how could we get out of the fix we were in? We could cut our losses, cancel the whole programme and hope Mini had the staying power to keep up with the competition in the small-car sector. But with the Ford Fiesta and VW Polo setting the standard in the next size up, that was too much to expect, even of the evergreen Mini.

Alternatively, we could make a fundamental change of strategy to produce a 'Mighty Mini' which did not try to replace the Mini directly, but would be its big brother with interior space no manufacturer could rival, yet in a car which would still be shorter than competing models. Such a radically different concept would once again establish the company as the best in the world at squeezing extra inches of space seemingly out of nowhere – and at the same time, command a better price than ADO 88. It would defy conventional wisdom by selling at a profit.

The new concept was called the LC8. Such were the changes from ADO 88 – virtually every exterior body panel was altered to give extra length and extra width, and much more glass area – that the public announcement of the new small-car would have to be delayed by a full year, to October 1980. Better a good car in 1980 than a disaster in 1979, we decided. Even on that time scale the pressures on everyone – senior management, designers, vehicle development engineers and manufacturing staffs would be unprecedented. There were two crumbs of consolation. First, even with all the changes and upheavals the £270 million estimated cost of LC8 and its new factory was calculated to be marginally lower than the ADO 88 programme. Second, the management team was solidly behind the change to LC8; without this commitment, we could never have taken on the enormous task involved.

The LC8 project was formally approved by the BL Board in July

1978 and handed over to Ray Horrocks and his team at Austin Morris. It was picked up with gusto. LC8 would be the first new car to appear from the new management and everything depended on its being right from day one. This time there would be no second chance. Mindful of this commitment to perfection, the project team expanded the already hectic development programme to include an extra 70 cars, not special hand-built prototypes, as is the usual case for development work, but made by normal production methods. These were to be used exclusively for testing and proving, well before the launch date. This meant that there were intense pressures on the manufacturing team to get the new highly automated factory commissioned even sooner, and with its revolutionary robots in full operation. The factory project would therefore have to go forward even before the car was fully developed.

In fact, the development of LC8 and the building and equipping of the 725,000 square foot-factory at West Works, Longbridge, proceeded neck and neck. As the foundations were being dug, the car itself was being subjected to major changes and modifications which, in turn, required alterations to the manufacturing programme. People worked around the clock for days at a time. Wives complained bitterly, and with every justification, that their husbands were being enticed away from them. 'Another woman – I could understand, but not to play constant second fiddle to a factory and four wheels,' was a common reaction in the Midlands throughout those three years. The excitement infected people outside the company too; contractors and site workers, suppliers to both the car and the new facility – all worked miracles as a matter of course to keep the project on time. Some of this excitement comes through in the recently published book on Metro by Graham Robson. Metro represented a superhuman collective effort, not least of all by the Longbridge workforce. The attitude in West Works, the new factory, was noticeably different, even in the days before Longbridge as a whole changed to the hard-driving factory it is today. Commitment was infectious. Britain and BL needed a winner and they were going to get one. Old ways were discarded as shop floor and management worked together to agree manning levels, flexible working, mobility of labour and a myriad of other issues which had to be settled if the new factory was to achieve its aim of being the most efficient of its kind in Europe.

There were employee relations problems to be solved. A few

managers took a while to realise that second best was no longer acceptable; for those who never did, there was a parting of the ways. Pressures were unrelenting and inevitably took their toll. But the sustaining factor was that, at last, real tangible progress was being made. LC8 was more than just a new car, it was the yardstick by which the whole company would be judged. At last employees were seeing the bricks, mortar and machinery of new investment which had been so lacking during the previous 30 years.

Just as important as commitment was another factor which was growing inside the company throughout 1978 and 1979 – confidence. While this was true of the LC8 project, it was having a dramatic influence on other parts of the business. People found that they could do things which years of wallowing had made impossible. On LC8, this new-found confidence was leading to the setting of tougher objectives for the car – targets which none of us had in our minds when the decision was made to change ADO 88. The knife-edge of the development programme showed when the BL Board met in Warwickshire to road test the latest version of the LC8 at the end of 1979, less than 12 months away from the launch.

We drove Fiestas, Fiats, VW Polos and other competing cars to give the product engineers our opinion on how much work remained to be done to put LC8 ahead of its class. The consensus was – a great deal. The concept, shape and the interior space were all basically sound, but overall the car lacked refinement in major areas. It was sluggish because the differential gear ratio was too high; we were still in the process of replacing much of the tooling to make the engine and gearbox with much greater precision, and the car reflected this. As 'non-motor' men the Board weren't able to tell the experts anything they didn't know, but confirmed the view that there was still a long way to go. It came as no surprise to learn that some 250 issues were felt to be unresolved, requiring engineering resources which were already stretched. But one thing we all agreed on – we had a winner in terms of 'miles per gallon'.

I am often asked whether my lack of knowledge of the motor industry was a handicap at BL. In fact I was less innocent on the subject of cars, trucks and engines in general than my colleagues in the company appreciated. I grew up in a motor family. My father was involved in the affairs of the South African Motor Trade Association, being the owner of a motor business for much of his life. I filled the petrol tank of his 1933 Buick Sedan when I was four

"BETTER STICK A GALLON IN . . .
. . . WE'RE GOING ON HOLIDAY."

years old – with water! He had complained about the cost of petrol in my hearing and so the emotion which the cost of motoring caused first came to my notice when I was four, although my efforts to solve the problem were singularly unsuccessful! Eleven years later, at 15, when my father was short of a driver to take an open-back DKW with a load of food and water to the holiday cottage – a journey of some 80 miles – I had my second experience of 'miles per gallon'. The car had only 60 miles worth of petrol for the 80-mile drive. Dad had driven on well ahead when I spluttered to a stop, alone and miserable. Having walked the four miles into Humansdorp, the nearest dorp (or village), and having returned carrying 20lbs of fuel I duly arrived at the river three hours later than planned. The need for fuel economy was well and truly brought home!

In early 1980, 35 years later, all this came back to me as the BL Board put the remarkably fuel-efficient LC8 through its paces for a second time.

This test took place appropriately at the newly opened BL Technology Proving Track at Gaydon, built specifically to make good the research and development deficiencies from which BL had suffered for so long. This time the 'Mighty Mini' was an entirely different car – a dream to drive. The rate of improvement had been phenomenal and everyone was excited about the whole character of the car. We knew from the performance figures we had a winner in terms of all-round performance combined with outstanding fuel consumption; but statistics alone couldn't convey the sense that everything had fallen into place and felt right. One after another we drove it and came back quite astonished at its improved behaviour – and above all the comfort and spaciousness within such a small interior. The designers and engineers had achieved a remarkable balance. The confidence of the project team had somehow been transferred to the car itself. It had character – just as the Mini before it. It also had a name; LC8 had become the Mini Metro.

The name was the choice of employees in the Austin and Morris factories. An original list of 8,500 possible names had been narrowed to three; Metro, Maestro and Match. About 20,000 employees returned ballot papers and Metro won by a bumper – only 267 votes ahead of Maestro. Involving employees in the name was important for morale, and the fact that the vote was evenly split between Metro and Maestro was significant, for the new mid-car would need to be named in due course!

By courtesy of the Daily Express

" A very nice lady saw your Mini Metro outside, and asked me if I'd like to do a straight swop."

The immense effort which had pushed the project along had now created its own momentum; we were really driving forward and could begin to think of success, whereas we had seen disaster staring us in the face only 20 months earlier. How was it achieved? By leadership. Ray Horrocks and his top Austin Morris executive team, particularly Harold Musgrove and Mark Snowdon, led from the front and involved everyone with a sense of urgency and a conviction that everything was possible. They kept a watchful eye on every step in the car's progress, and they short-circuited the bureaucracy, and broke rules to do it.

The response was unbelievable. Managers felt that here at last was purpose and determination. They may on occasions have been virtually driven to distraction but the end justified the means. For years there had been inertia and complacency. The 'not invented here' syndrome had had a widespread demotivating effect and had shown through in the products. Now the team had lifted its head and had its eyes on larger horizons. It showed in all aspects of the business; Metro was a catalyst for much bigger changes than just the production of the new motor car. New and tough criteria were set up by the top team at Austin Morris, supported by Tony Gilroy, Operations Director and his project manager Jim Donaghy whose job it was to get the factory built and running; Ray Bates, Product

Engineering Director and Fred Coultas, Chief Engineer for small-car engineering; Steve Schlemmer, the Product Planning Manager, and many others all made Metro a way of life for two full years. They in turn were not let down by the hundreds of other people whose contributions played a vital role in Metro's success.

During this period there were some formidable obstacles to be overcome. For example. . . . In the new West Works, when one of the massive automated machines was installed it was found they could not produce the complete assembly. After many days of trying to establish what was wrong, it was found that the machine had been damaged in transit – it had actually been damaged against a bridge in Europe. This was one of the times when the management of Austin Morris reached a state of despair because the second facility was running six months behind the installation of the first, and if the automated plant could not be brought on stream the launch would have slipped and we would have missed the Motor Show. However, the supplier, together with the Austin Morris manufacturing management, found that by working seven days a week and 24 hours a day they could bring the second machine on stream with a loss of only one month – and even that month's slippage was recovered in order to achieve the target of some 6,000 cars by the time of the launch.

The 55 robots building the body started work right on time and by June 1980 the first cars came down the assembly line, and were whisked away for the closest scrutiny and testing. Throughout the summer, production built up sharply to support the launch on the 8th October (which was timed just before the start of the Motor Show at the National Exhibition Centre in Birmingham), and the Longbridge factory began the climb in productivity which has taken it up to the top of the European league. There were virtually no major teething troubles, for the planning and execution had been superb. And due to equally disciplined financial planning and tight discipline, the target cost of the investment and the marginal cost of the car were both met – Bob Neville, the Financial Director of Austin Morris saw to that.

Weeks beforehand several hundred highly critical journalists from around the world had driven the car, and although their public judgment would not be known until announcement day, their off-the-cuff opinions as they came and went in the various models were very encouraging.

We also had our long-suffering dealers to win over. For years these loyal people had seen false dawns briefly brighten the gloom and then fade, and we were determined to infect them with the Metro fever which we had caught with a vengeance. We went a long way towards regaining their confidence by producing the target number of 6,000 Metros and getting them into their showrooms for launch day – something which, sadly, had never happened before in a British Leyland launch. A very few of them had some idea of what to expect for we had involved the members of the Dealer Council Executive Committee in the testing and development programme. This was also something else which had not happened before and their contribution and positive attitudes towards Metro not only helped us produce a better car but they were able to tell their colleagues in the dealer network what we were doing and so keep morale up at a very critical time, in the difficult months before the launch.

All our dealers were introduced to Metro on a short cruise between Liverpool and the Isle of Man aboard the *Vistafjord* – British built despite its name. Tony Ball, Trevor Taylor and their colleagues in sales and marketing made it one of the most exciting launches of all time, in an industry not noted for its backwardness in promoting new products. I well remember an evening newspaper criticising the cost. How shortsighted it would have been to play down that launch. To prepare the dealers, there were comprehensive business sessions covering the state of the industry, market opportunities, promotional plans, future product action programmes and other topics, all against a none-too-smooth background of rolling and pitching. The Irish Sea in September can be very rough. Then in the morning of the second day, the Metro emerged amidst billowing mist from the centre of a globe and was unveiled right in the midst of the audience, just as the presentation reached its climax. The dealers went wild. They clapped and stamped (a few cried) for they were convinced that here was a success story from BL and a car that was a world beater. The next day they test drove Metro on the Isle of Man and came back ecstatic. It was even better to drive than it looked. Dealer commitment and loyalty rose through the roof and their motivation showed through in the way they went out and sold Metro from the first day some held midnight launch parties, others invited customers to breakfast in their showrooms en route to work.

On the opening day of the Motor Show, Alan Jones, the racing driver, and I drove in a metallic blue Metro from the nearby Metropole Hotel to the Exhibition Centre, where we were met by a massive press gathering. The atmosphere was electric. Hundreds of journalists surged around the car anxious to exploit this golden opportunity of recording good news. 'Austin Mini Metro' rang around the world and I couldn't have had a better 50th birthday present than the remarkable reception accorded the car; a real tribute to the quite prodigious efforts put in by so many people in BL Cars and by the hundreds of component suppliers who worked so hard to meet near-impossible demands and deadlines. For Metro wasn't just a BL success – it was a British success.

The evening before, at the Motor Show dinner, the Prime Minister, conscious that she was in the heart of the Midlands, had some encouraging things to say about the motor industry, with helpful allusions to Metro, and as I recollect it, she emphasised the need for an entrepreneurial spirit. Her audience received her speech well, although officers of the Society of Motor Manufacturers and Traders were lukewarm about her Government's approach to the industry on a number of counts.

The next morning I looked out of the window, over the sheet of water immediately behind the Metropole Hotel, and I thought again of how great industries can be built up from small beginnings, given the man with an enterprising mind and the drive and faith to pursue his ideas. Sir William Lyons was a case in point; I had recently had tea with him at his home near Coventry, chatting about the future of Jaguar. It had gone through a bad patch, and we were determined to get it right. Sir William, who recently celebrated his 81st birthday, is an excellent example of the British entrepreneur – and without this breed of man, the future of industry in Britain will be grim indeed. Look what Alex Issigonis did for Austin with his revolutionary small-car concept which became the Mini – the tragedy was that for many years Austin Morris failed to update the Mini after its launch. And flying gracefully over the Exhibition Hall was a hot-air balloon, reminding me of how a long-standing friend, Colin Prescot, came to dinner one evening and said, 'I plan to give up my job and start a hot-air balloon company and everyone says I'm crazy to do it.' I opened my mouth to join in the chorus, and then thought – why not? Why shouldn't it be successful? He had the drive and the imagination. Now, six years later, 'The Hot-Air

Balloon Company' has gone from strength to strength and is the largest company of its peculiar kind in the world.

Metro, too, set new records. After its launch, it went on to win numerous awards and prizes. It is currently the best-selling small-car in Britain and it quickly established itself as our top-seller in Europe. This was not surprising for it was developed for Europe and in Harold Musgrove's words:

> We were so concerned to ensure that we reached European quality levels on fits and finishes that we sent a Metro to Europe at considerable cost to have the car brought up to their level of fits and finishes by external design consultants. When the car was returned to us with all the improvements that they believed were necessary, it was viewed and the cars being produced at Longbridge were *so much better* that we decided to put a sheet over the car and to hold it in case anyone at the time of launch should criticise its fits and finishes against European standards. That car has only recently been disposed of.

> When production first started, the cars were rerun down the assembly lines four and five times for improvements to be made. This in no way was a reflection on the assembly workers; it was because management realised that the standards had to be raised and then raised again. The cooperation from the workforce was magnificent and without the dedication of these people the car would never have been the success that it undoubtedly has been.

Metro's crucial job was to halt the sales decline which had gone on for many years while we pressed on with developing its big brother, the Maestro, and it has done that job in fine style. However, even more than that, I will remember the car as a symbol of the changing attitudes inside the company which helped to transform the gloom of December 1977 into the glow of immediate success in October 1980.

But when all this was said and done, we still had the gap in the mid-car sector; to bridge it until Maestro appeared meant collaboration, and this we did to great effect. The Triumph Acclaim was conceived out of this seemingly intractable problem. Joining forces will be the new way of doing things in the 1980s, and a new way of life for small, medium and large motor manufacturers.

9

Joining Forces

A great deal has been said about the need for BL to collaborate with other motor manufacturers, and there has been much speculation about the subject – much of it wide of the mark. At some stage I think BL has been reported as being on the verge of collaborating with every manufacturer in the world. The realities have been less widely drawn, but the possibilities which arose during the past five years have, on occasions, been stranger than fiction.

Collaboration quite simply is the art of synergy, of joining forces with others to save funds, or to optimise cash and engineering resources; or simply to achieve a larger scale of purchases or production, to cut the cost of components and of complete vehicles. Some companies collaborate for any one or more of these reasons: BL had another and even more pressing reason – shortage of time. Years of indecisiveness, of inadequate product strategy, of lack of profit and money, had eroded our product base. We had to catch up by every conceivable means, or go out of business. Had Metro been delayed beyond October 1980 I am convinced that the Government's marginal decision to provide £990 million for 1981 and 1982 would have gone against us, for the euphoric success of Metro made a big impression on the Cabinet when it met to decide BL's fate, just 90 days after Metro won the hearts of Britain.

Having made the first decision – to cancel the unviable Mini replacement and redesign the car as a Fiesta competitor – we wrestled with the problem of filling every product gap, whether car, truck or major component, by collaboration.

From the beginning, I was in complete agreement with Sir Leslie Murphy and the NEB on this subject: that substantial parts of BL would not survive without this type of in-depth collaboration. But this did not mean that collaboration could and would be brought about. There were two groups of people to be won over – the management inside BL, and potential collaborators outside.

Intellectually, the vast majority of senior managers could see the case for collaboration, but there was a considerable variety of more instinctive hang-ups to be overcome. Occasionally, the 'not invented here' syndrome would surface, or the sheer dislike of working closely with foreigners, or simply of having to surmount the language barriers. But there were other more understandable worries – the feeling that BL's recovery could not be secure unless it was totally self-sufficient, and the practical concern that a collaborative project would be difficult to manage with the necessary momentum and flexibility if the two partners' headquarters were a long distance apart. All these reservations took time to overcome – sometimes by a very firm steer from the top, sometimes by persistent argument. Fortunately experience of how well collaboration can work at all levels, when there is goodwill on both sides, has consolidated attitudes. The problem now is not so much persuading people in-house, but finding the right partner. It is not simply a matter of saying Tom or Dick would be the ideal partner in this or that venture. It requires a commercial coincidence, for the partners must find that they have similar but complementary needs and aspirations in a particular segment of their business. There must, in short, be something in it for both parties. Furthermore, the merit of a technical partnership can sometimes be offset by the commercial or marketing disadvantages associated with the deal. Above all it needs a meeting of minds between the companies involved.

There was very little meeting of minds in the proposed association with Renault which had begun to form before the new Board took office. Renault had some important attributes as a collaborative partner – it was a well-managed company, with good products, based on a strategic and well thought out product plan – but the relationship had evolved in an *ad hoc* sort of fashion and all the signs were that there were some less satisfactory, albeit latent characteristics which might emerge and dominate the situation. Indeed almost all the other factors were against Renault as a partner. They were state owned; they were very large, and would have dominated BL Cars; they were, and are, nationalistic in attitude. From every point of view, Renault's centre of gravity, including employment, was in France for that was where policy was determined. Looking back on our deliberations we would have expected it to lead to the Peugeot-Talbot type of situation, where all the design and engineering – and indeed most of the manufacturing

– now takes place in France, with the British operation becoming very much of a local satellite.

Renault offered us one of their models to assemble in Britain. All the major components were to be made in France, and while BL would have had the right to sell this model, its market would have been restricted to Britain – and some Renault top executives envisaged that their version of the car would also be sold in Britain. In short, while it would have helped to reduce the inevitable paucity of the British market share while we developed our new models, its strategic implications were somewhat threatening in that the BL franchise would have helped to establish Renault in Britain without reciprocal benefits for us in Europe. It was not a two-way collaboration. Nevertheless, it warranted thorough consideration, and we put in a great deal of time before we finally decided that to join forces with our French colleagues would not be to our ultimate advantage.

Before arriving at this conclusion David Andrews and I visited Paris in January 1978 at the invitation of Sir Nicholas Henderson, then British Ambassador. We dined with the Chairman of Renault, Bernard Vernier-Palliez, and his then number two, Bernard Hanon. This was two and a half months after I joined BL, but our French opposite numbers had already been warned that the new top team lacked enthusiasm for the deal – their contacts in BL were highly developed, and the flow of intelligence seemed to be heavily in their direction. The Ambassador laid on the dinner, and for the first time it became really clear to us how Renault saw the relationship. Following the hundreds of man-hours of collaborative discussions on engines and gearboxes that had taken place, it seemed to David Andrews and me that what they really wanted was a foothold in the British volume car factories through a car built from French components, and more important they wanted access to Range Rover and Land Rover products. At that time, the latter objective made sense to them but it made no sense to us for we needed to approve £200 million worth of investment to increase and modernise production before we could meet strong worldwide demand for these vehicles. To channel Land Rovers and Range Rovers to France for the French sphere of influence would therefore be an unrewarding exercise. David Andrews was, if anything, more sceptical than I, and after the excellent dinner – the Hendersons being marvellous hosts – we chatted around the subject, while looking in vain for a deal that offered mutual advantage. David Andrews felt that Renault saw BL as a very weak partner that needed shoring up to keep Ford at bay. In those days they were very apprehensive about Ford for they saw Ford's strength in Britain as a threat to the indigenous European industry.

In spite of our misgivings, we agreed to continue the talks, partly on the basis of the 'Leyland/Renault' protocol of July 1977, which talked of component collaboration and rather more vaguely of model and marketing collaboration and partly on the broader canvas that had been drawn at the Ambassador's dinner table. Our lack of enthusiasm was partly fuelled by the difference in nuance between the two Renault directors. Whereas Bernard Hanon was prepared to make a new car available on an exclusive basis, at least for Britain, his Chairman was reluctant to weaken the Renault franchise in Britain. We were not confident that a deal could be done, even if we wanted it. Furthermore, before I became involved in the talks, I knew that Bernard Hanon was on record as suggesting that Renault should market all BL cars throughout the original six EEC countries. Although he did not return to this theme in Paris, the implications of this original proposal could not be ignored. The talks drifted on at other levels over the following months, but came to an abrupt halt when we read in the *Financial Times* on April Fool's Day 1978 that Renault had done a deal with American Motors, which included a marketing deal for the Jeep four-wheel-drive vehicle, cutting right across the areas we had been exploring. We had no prior warning – even the *FT* reporter had no trouble reading our minds:

> The agreement to sell Jeep through Renault dealers over-seas appears to rule out the possibility that Renault might have distributed British Leyland's Land Rover.

I had come to like the two Bernards, and we have subsequently worked together on matters relating to the European motor industry, especially in connection with the Japanese, but on that 1st April I was very angry with Renault. Subsequently, on the 10th October I read in *The Times*:

> Sources quoted a senior Renault executive as saying, 'We were making real progress until the end of last year, but since Michael Edwardes took over the chairmanship of

BL, we seem to have run into one delay after another. But crucial decisions must be made soon. Delays only help the Americans.

This was an odd choice of words, for since the April 1978 announcement by Renault, they have poured hundreds of millions of dollars into the American AMC company to develop their Jeep and other interests in the United States of America!

Shortly after the Renault debacle, an extraordinary opportunity presented itself. It was the most exciting collaborative proposal put forward during my time at BL. I had come to know Bob Price, who at the time was Managing Director of General Motors' Vauxhall company in Britain. We were fairly close to one another then, and the reason we knew each other so well, was that I had tried to persuade him to give up the security of General Motors for a life on or near the brink with BL. The mere fact that he thought about it carefully and thoughtfully, over several weeks, before deciding to stay with his great company, indicates that we were on the same wavelength. I will never know how much power he had to negotiate with us, and certainly he did not claim any, but I suspect we overestimated his authority. The fault was ours. I believe it was late on a Friday evening – I know he kept long office hours too, in those days – when he telephoned me for an urgent meeting. 'Yes,' I said, 'why not have a beer with me at Richmond on Saturday?' What he proposed could have solved all of our problems, and some of Vauxhall's too. He summed up his view of the BL situation:

> Your main problem lies in Austin Morris. You believe that your truck business and Jaguar have potential. Now we think that your Austin Morris problem is bigger than you think it is, for we believe you need not one, but two new models in the mid-car sector. But you don't have the people resource or the cash resource to do it. And time is against you.
>
> We have just completed our ten-year plan for Europe and we find we will be short of production capacity. This will involve two new factories at a total cost of about $1,500 million. You are using, at best, 50% of your potential capacity. What about forming a joint sales company, drawing on your factories and ours, for worldwide sales? We could build on our mutual strengths – we think the

Mini can be developed, and your new LC8 would give us a ready-made car in that sector. We can solve your mid-car problem quicker than you can and we will have two-car families in that sector of the market. You will drop the Maxi, the Princess – the Allegro and Marina. By developing Jaguar and Rover, plus Land Rover, our combined range will be unbeatable in Europe. You are short of engineering resource – we can help you.

We code-named the project 'Gemini' and for some weeks we roamed over all the possibilities for Gemini Limited. It would have loaded our factories to the gunwales and lead on to the possibility of a merger of the Bedford and Leyland truck operations. I was very excited at this grandscale solution. It was agreed Bob Price would consult his European colleagues, and would involve a top staff executive in Detroit, who would fly over to Britain to join a study team, working with David Andrews and Mike Carver. Regrettably, it transpired that his American bosses were not smitten with this imaginative concept. The grand design was not on; we would have to solve our problems the hard way, step by step. Even the by-product of 'Gemini' failed – our attempt to sell our Belgian factory at Seneffe to General Motors.

This brought home the difficulty of saving BL by a major strategic coup, either with a European company or an international one – for it is difficult to be partners and competitors at the same time. Alas, it was not easy to get across to Cabinet Ministers, that there were no quick and easy solutions for Britain's motor industry! The Renault and General Motors episodes reinforced our view that any meaningful collaboration would only be fruitful if the preliminary work was carried through in painstaking detail on a strategic basis. *Ad hoc* ideas were not likely to bear fruit, and this type of international cooperation seldom results from a straight takeover. Take Chrysler UK, which became Talbot. What isn't generally known is how carefully we looked at the possibility of a merger between Chrysler Europe and BL; we were, thank goodness, pre-empted by Peugeot, as a result of which the British end of Chrysler lost its independence.

When we looked at Chrysler Europe (literally at the time Peugeot and Chrysler were talking behind the scenes) we realised just how painful it would be for all concerned, were a merger of BL and Chrysler to be consummated. We looked at it under the code name 'Dovetail' and it is to the credit of the union General Secretaries concerned that when we involved them in our thinking, 'Dovetail' never leaked out. In fact, I believe this is the first time that our interest in the matter has been made public. What led us to research a merger with Chrysler UK through July and August 1978 was our lack of engineering resources. We simply did not know how we could engineer all the new car models quickly enough. The same problem applied to trucks. Chrysler had an excellent engineering centre, near Coventry. There were a number of areas of synergy, but the painful part was what we would have had to do to Linwood in Scotland and probably to Ryton in Coventry; in short, close them.

As we were weighing it all up, the French connection was announced: Peugeot had done a deal with Chrysler in the United States – they would be the new owners of Chrysler Europe including the operations in Britain. This was a shock to the British Government too. I believe they were given no advance notice whatever. But the people who were most put out at the news were the unions, for they were very quick to see that this would decimate the Chrysler UK infrastructure – even if there were assurances given on this score, it was inevitable that the centre of operations would shift to France. When the unions pressed us to intervene we confided in them that with excess production capacity in Britain we would have no option but to close at least one and perhaps both major Chrysler factories. Understandably their enthusiasm for our becoming involved waned at this point.

Another non-runner was our attempt early on to link with Iveco on the truck side. Iveco was a joint venture between Fiat, Magirus Deutz of Germany, and UNIC of France. The dominant partner was Fiat, but for one reason or another the original idea did not work out, and there has since been fragmentation of the business. The theory was sound but seemed not to work too well in practice. The Iveco proposal was that BL's Leyland commercial vehicle subsidiary should form part of the Iveco alliance. In fact, when the new BL Board came in we found that Leyland executives were well down a merger road, without apparently having cleared the matter with the then British Leyland Board, still less with the Government. It seemed to me that the intention was for Iveco to swallow Leyland. There were fundamental differences of management philosophy and the evidence was that Iveco was not profitable and therefore lacked financial strength; the scheme faded away, and surfaced again in 1978. There were indeed many points of common interest but in the later talks our executives and theirs never really established a rapport; in the earlier talks there had been lots of rapport, but no clearly defined objectives. In many ways it would have been a good solution, but it seemed destined not to come off.

In 1979 we came closer to a sensible concept when Fiat appeared to have put forward the concept of a pan-European truck company. When it came to the point, in discussion with the Agnellis, I was never able to obtain any workable commitment on a joint project. It was always talks about talks – one or other party always lacked enthusiasm at the crucial moment!

Our experience in trucks has been that talks about specific collaborative projects have been more fruitful than generalised exploration of broader possibilities. The prime example was the agreement announced in September 1982 between Leyland Vehicles and Cummins to manufacture a new range of truck diesel engines. The agreement has straightforward commercial benefits for both partners. Components will be exchanged across the Atlantic to maximise economies of scale in their manufacture; Leyland save development costs by accepting a Cummins design; and Cummins will be able to meet the European demand for their engines from a European source, which will be up to date technologically and cost-competitive.

Another failed initiative occurred in July 1980 in New York. This time the initiative came from John DeLorean who heard that David Andrews and I were in town, and invited us to his Fifth Avenue address for lunch. We preferred not to risk being spotted – for fear of rumours – and so we invited him to join us for lunch in a private room at the Carlyle Hotel. His proposal was of interest conceptually – that he would adapt the Range Rover to meet United States regulations, and undertake distribution there – but we were uneasy about the relationship, and declined to pursue the matter.

We had already started to look at all the world motor manufacturers to see if there were any companies which seemed to have complementary objectives to our own. We knew there would be problems within Europe, because it is difficult to collaborate with a direct competitor in what is one big market. The Renault talks had highlighted this, and we had developed exciting possibilities with other European manufacturers, but always the problem of a common competitive market frustrated us. The dangers of a link with a multinational – even if they were interested – would be that BL would become no more than an offshore assembly operation – not even the right wing of the Conservative Party would have been sanguine about that outcome. We looked west and then we looked east in our study of possible partners. At this stage it was purely a desk exercise. Our target companies were all blissfully unaware of our interest.

The result of this comprehensive survey of world competitors was Honda; we did the exercise from a different perspective and we still came up with Honda. Their size, their engineering skill, their remarkable track record, and a number of other key factors, made Honda the most desirable partner. Perhaps they would provide the answer to our biggest single problem; how to fill the yawning gap until the long-awaited launch of Maestro in early 1983?

Although Honda was the one company whose objectives seemed complementary to BL, at first glance there were major differences; on further study the fit was remarkable. Compare the two companies in 1978: BL had a large, complex and unprofitable range – 16 model families, no less. Honda had just two model families. BL had more than 30 car factories, with no less than eight assembly plants. Honda had two assembly plants; it was altogether simpler and more workable. BL was and is state controlled; Honda was and is owned by individual shareholders.

These were some of the differences, but there were many similarities. Both were free of complex collaborative commitments. Both were leaders in front-wheel-drive technology. In the United States of America, Honda was deeply involved in small volume cars and therefore they were complementary to our great strength there – the luxury Jaguar. Where Honda's other half is motor cycles, BL's is trucks, buses and Land Rovers. Overall the companies are comparable in terms of output. Both were open-minded about the desirability to collaborate in at least some aspects of their business.

In August 1978 I phoned Sir Fred Warner, a colleague on the Chloride Board, who had been the British Ambassador to Tokyo, asking if he would act as an intermediary on behalf of BL. After some initial and delicate soundings had been taken Fred telexed the President of Honda, Kiyoshi Kawashima, as follows:

I am acting directly on behalf of Michael Edwardes, Chairman of BL Limited. In the light of recent developments in the industry and of certain highly complementary characteristics in your company and his, he would like to know your views on certain possible future developments. Before meeting with you personally, however, he would like me to explain his views and consider with you whether it would serve your mutual interests to meet and take the matter further.

If anyone understood the commercial dimension of the foreign office role, it was Fred Warner, for he had gained a deep insight into the business world in Tokyo. He met Kiyoshi Kawashima on the 13th September, 1978, and set out our broad thinking on the subject. His note of the meeting concluded:

Mr Kawashima said the matter was so important that he would like a clear week to think things over before deciding whether or not to meet Michael Edwardes.

Six days later Fred Warner received from Honda an affirmative response – they felt that the summit meeting (if any) should be preceded by a working session of senior executives. A few days earlier the *Daily Telegraph* had reported that BL was to merge with Volkswagen or Renault! Honda found these speculations a trifle disturbing, and wanted to probe our intentions a little further before a Kawashima/Edwardes face-to-face meeting. I understood their concern.

Fred Warner, David Andrews and I met to discuss how best to respond to Honda. Should we agree to this preliminary high level meeting? No doubt. Where? Neutral half-way territory. What about San Francisco? When? Fast.

Our team, which included David Andrews, Ray Horrocks and John Bacchus, stepped off the British Airways flight to San Francisco in late October 1978 with no real idea of what the outcome might be. It had to be right for BL – but would Honda see the benefit for themselves? Would they be nervous of the BL situation? They must be. Would they consider the employee relations scene beyond recall? Surely, yes, for back in October 1978, we had not begun to grasp the real nettles.

Nevertheless our team flew back from San Francisco with an

outline proposal that was to lead to the Triumph Acclaim programme. There was to be a great deal of analysis and thought on both sides, before the bare idea could be taken further. But in January 1979 a BL team, headed by Mike Carver, Mark Snowdon and John Bacchus, and accompanied by Sir Fred Warner, who was to introduce them and add his weight as evidence of the seriousness with which BL was engaging in the discussions, flew to Tokyo to see what was then a styling model. From what they saw and from what they would be told about the model, they were to decide whether or not a joint programme was really feasible. The team saw enough to convince them that the model would fit BL's product range and, most important of all, that the timing which Honda proposed would fill the yawning three-and-a-half-year gap between the introduction of Metro and Maestro. Mike Carver flew from Tokyo to Frankfurt (where I had been on other business with David Andrews) and made the firm recommendation that the project should be pursued. After discussion with Ray Horrocks, this was agreed, and a series of meetings with Honda took place over the next few months aimed at reaching a firm commercial agreement. The BL team met with their Honda opposite numbers about every three to four weeks during 1979; about half the meetings were in Tokyo and half in London. These talks went well and there were no leaks. On the 3rd April, 1979 we told our employees and the press that talks with Honda were in train. The media reactions were interesting:

"I don't mind that—it's non-stop Madame bloody Butterfly that gets me"

By courtesy of the *Daily Express*

196

Honda and BL: lifebelt or Trojan horse? – *Financial Times*

Sir Michael's gamble. – *Daily Telegraph*

The *Scotsman* published a leader which reflected the views of many people. It read:

> The time to pronounce on the desirability or undesirability of a link between Honda and British Leyland will be when their negotiations have gone further and the proposals are clear. Since the National Enterprise Board are the major shareholders in BL, their approval, and that of the new Government, will be necessary. Meantime, it is surely premature to condemn the very idea of a link with Honda, as some of the MPs sponsored by the Transport and General Workers' Union have seemed to do. Perhaps the negotiations will not succeed, just as the possibility of a link between BL and Renault has faded. But if there are positive advantages for BL, as well as for Honda, then the scheme may have more to be said for it than the ritual resort to calls for formal import controls to prop up the British motor industry.

In short, 'we must wait and see.' Very fair, and they did not have too long to wait. In May we wrote to our employees:

> Exploratory discussions with the Honda Motor Company of Japan have reached a stage where there is agreement on the joint project. This will involve a licensing agreement to manufacture a new car being developed by Honda.

> Employee representatives through participation have been given full details of the joint proposal and a representative of the shop floor accompanied the BL team which visited Honda in April.

> Although the details of the joint venture have yet to be worked through and will be the subject of further discussion with employee representatives, the current thinking is that BL will manufacture a new passenger car designed by Honda which will have a high technical specification and will be a Triumph. BL will have exclusive rights to sell it in the EEC and in Britain.

Note the visit of an employee representative to Tokyo. The plan at that stage was to build the car in the Midlands, but it ended up at Cowley. The steward came from Canley, which in the event was closed as part of the streamlining programme.

The French reaction to the 'Honda' announcement was interesting, to say the least! The *Sunday Telegraph* described it graphically:

RENAULT SEETHES AT L'AFFAIRE HONDA

Whatever distaste the BL workforce may have felt on hearing that their chairman, Michael Edwardes, had been talking to Honda, was evidently nothing as compared to the anger with which Renault received the news.

Renault, after all, had been talking about a liaison with BL long before Honda arrived on the scene and it seems was under the impression that it was still talking – until it heard last week's news and assumed the line from BL had gone dead.

The line from BL may be dead. It is still, so it is said, 'absolutely furious' at having thus been jilted.

The Renault reaction certainly caused some people in influential quarters to wonder whether the Honda deal was right for BL. I felt that the French reaction highlighted the problems associated with dealing with a French state enterprise. They saw themselves as the spearhead for social change – as indeed Renault had been in France for 20 years – working very closely with the French Government of the day. The Renault reaction typified the French position vis-à-vis Japan at that time, and I can't say that it either surprised us or dismayed us. And, whereas Honda were not involved with other manufacturers, Renault itself was being pulled into AMC's problems of funding and model development, following their collaborative agreement.

The debate raged in the press, but at BL and Honda all was sweet and light, and progress was impressive. There was never a hiccough in relationships at any level.

And so we moved nearer and nearer the date for signing. From the start, the Department of Industry had been kept informed of the Honda discussions and BL's legal staff were in contact with the EEC Commission on possible problems over competitive laws and the vehicle's status as a model of EEC origin. By the 15th May, 1979, progress was sufficient for the two companies to sign a memorandum of understanding concerning the project – Mike Carver for BL and Noboru Okamura, then a senior Managing Director, now a Vice-President, for Honda – with BL committed by its partner to 'sign and settle' by the end of December, or forego the project by mutual consent.

From that point activity between the two companies accelerated, with product and manufacturing engineers from both companies meeting to develop detailed plans. The aim was to bring the joint venture car into production in Britain by mid-1981 for launch in the autumn. It was a mark of the growing confidence and developing relationship between the two companies that Honda was willing to provide much detailed information on the model and to set in hand costly provision of duplicate tools and other facilities well in advance of a formal agreement. Similarly, BL provided Honda with a great deal of detail about its plans and prospects which would normally be regarded as highly confidential. We had great confidence in Kiyoshi Kawashima and his executive team – and subsequent events showed that we had good reason to do so, for whatever Honda agreed to do was always done to the letter. The BL Board also agreed to the allocation of some 'long lead' funds for the project in advance of their approving the programme. Board approval was given in October 1979 by which time the draft agreement between the two companies had been finalised. The agreement could not be signed, however, until the 1980 Corporate Plan had been approved by the Government.

The Plan was sent to the NEB in November 1979, who forwarded it to the Government with a recommendation for its acceptance. This gave little time for the Government to form a view on the Plan and to give its approval in time for the Honda deadline of the year end. I will always remember the tense days leading up to the signing of that agreement! Sir Keith Joseph and the Cabinet pulled out all the stops to enable us to meet Honda's challenge, and to sign the agreement before the end of December.

The Honda collaboration was a far-reaching international venture, and the British Government as the major shareholder and as stewards of Britain's national interest, were right to take it seriously – and they did so with the minimum of officiousness. Clearly, it had many and various implications, not least of which was the EEC aspect. In order to save the deal from going by default, Sir Keith Joseph suggested that I should fly to Tokyo and wait to hear from him that Cabinet approval had been given. I was unhappy to leave it on such a last-minute basis and told him that the only satisfactory way to handle it would be to go to Tokyo with full Board and Government backing. I explained that the last possible day for signature was the 26th December – Japanese holidays start on the 27th – and that we would set up the meeting for that day, in the hope that he would secure his colleagues' agreement by Christmas Eve: 'I want to fly out with everything intact at this end – not before.'

This meant flying to Tokyo on Christmas Day, so that at least two families were likely to be disappointed at the news. I cleared the matter with mine, who took it in their stride, and then told John McKay – it was fine by him, but 'would you sell the proposition to my wife?' Mike Carver, the other BL party to the signing, was already in Tokyo. But as late as the 23rd December, I was still waiting to hear from Sir Keith Joseph. It was then that I had a telephone call from South Africa.

My father, who had had four strokes in the space of a few years, and had recovered remarkably well, had had a fifth; he had been taken to hospital and within a few hours he had died. It is customary for burial or cremation in South Africa to be held immediately and it was impossible for us to fly out in time. Close relatives and friends were arranging a memorial service for some weeks later, so we agreed upon a date, and set about cancelling our January holiday. Instead of flying off to the West Indian sun after my return from Japan, we would be flying to the South African sun, on less happy business.

On the 24th December the long-awaited message came through from Sir Keith Joseph. The green light having been given, John McKay and I flew from London at lunch time on Christmas Day. Interest in Tokyo was very marked and history was made when Kiyoshi Kawashima spelled out to the press the terms of the deal which was to create the Triumph Acclaim – to be launched just 18 months after signature of the agreement. The international press, there in force, received the details of the agreement very favourably indeed. The event was probably unique in the motor industry, with the heads of a British and a Japanese motor company participating in a joint public presentation.

And so the Honda deal was off the ground. The occasion

enabled me to make some pertinent points in Tokyo about our confidence in BL's ability to sustain a product-led revival with the help of this project. I also touched upon the need for continued restraint by the Japanese motor industry in keeping their exports to a reasonable level, and not exporting unemployment as well as cars to Britain, and said that whilst BL believed that continued restraint on imports from Japan was necessary while the British motor industry continued to recover, we did not agree that Europe should insulate itself in terms of collaboration. It is one thing to flood a market from behind a protective wall – like the Japanese had done for 20 years – quite another, to cooperate through a joint venture like the Triumph Acclaim to maintain jobs in Britain by building the car in Britain. At that time for every one vehicle the British industry sent to Japan, Japanese manufacturers sent 60 to Britain.

While in Tokyo I declined an invitation to see Nissan, who pressed to meet me. It would have been quite inappropriate, and would have been taken as an insult by our Honda partners had I seen their great competitors on this inaugural visit. And I still felt the scars from an earlier contact with Nissan. Following a very limited conversation over lunch with the Nissan Chairman, the affable Katsuji Kawamata, I was surprised to read of our discussion in the press, and was left to infer from the leaks that more besides – much more – had been discussed. This brief encounter with Nissan was to return in a quite dramatic form when the main ITN news bulletin one night announced, out of the blue, that BL and Nissan were to collaborate. It was totally untrue and without foundation and I called ITN as the programme was still running so that they could end it with our repudiation – which they did!

In fact, collaboration between Nissan and BL is an historical, not a current event. In the early 1930s the Austin Motor Company gave Datsun a licence to produce a car in Japan. The Austin–Datsun was the result and one of the few remaining examples is in the BL Heritage collection of historic cars. In the early 1950s Datsun obtained another licence to build, from parts supplied by Austin, the A40 Somerset. This deal helped to get the Japanese motor industry off the ground. Since then they have had exhaustive discussions about setting up in Britain to manufacture cars. The view in Japan has always been that the project will not go ahead. We shall see.

Looking back at the history of Austin it is intriguing to see that the little Austin 7 acted as a catalyst in the development of more than one motor manufacturer in the late 1920s and 1930s. It was built under licence in Germany by the Dixi Company which became part of the motorcycle organisation, Bayerische Motoren Werke AG – and the Austin 7 thus became the first BMW car. It was assembled in a part of the Peugeot factory in France as the 'Rosengart' and appeared in the United States as the 'Bantam', also assembled locally. Indeed collaboration is not a new concept and the present difficulties of manufacturers worldwide is turning the circle once again.

On Boxing Day we flew back to London and almost immediately my wife and I flew to South Africa for my father's memorial service in Port Elizabeth. His ashes were scattered on the river he loved so much at Tiger Bay, two miles from the mouth of the river Kromme. Mary and I agreed it was not such a sad moment for he had been a man of great energy; he had worked hard, played hard and Tiger Bay was where he would most want to be.

When I returned to London the BL–Honda agreement was still very much in the news and evoking strong reaction, for and against, but the overwhelming feeling was that BL had done a good deal.

On a company-to-company basis the relationship has been quite extraordinarily good, and both BL and Honda have benefited from it. This is not to say that negotiations were not tough – they were certainly that. But not only did the first negotiating teams find themselves at ease with one another, even across the wide cultural gap and language barrier, but so also did the engineers develop easy working relationships, with mutual respect, and this extended to all levels as more and more people in the two companies met. This shows what can be achieved when two companies adopt a positive and helpful approach towards working together.

In fact the only hiccough was when the press in Japan did some wild speculating about a secret meeting we had had in Anchorage in mid-February 1981. This indicated a need for both companies to tighten security, which we did immediately. That meeting gave birth to the new XX project, announced in November 1981, and once again our favourable instincts about the Honda relationship were borne out. The XX project is most imaginative, and could be the way things will be done in the motor industry in the 1980s and 1990s. International collaboration is quite different to 'takeover'; one doesn't lose sovereignty.

The XX project goes further than normal collaboration. Whereas the Acclaim is a licensing venture, with BL building in Britain a Japanese designed car, with some variations in specification, XX is a partnership of equals, with both companies deeply involved in the concept, its style and its design, and with both companies combining to engineer, manufacture and sell the vehicle virtually worldwide. It will be one of the most integrated collaborative projects ever undertaken in the industry, thus saving both companies millions of pounds, and much expert resource. Scale will be fully exploited by two-way sourcing of components: it will in truth be a world car, made in both Britain and Japan.

To find mutual synergy on a broader front is not easy at all, and so talks often come to nothing. You win some – but in the collaboration stakes, you lose some too.

10

Early Masters

In an ideal world, the chairman of a major company can devote his time to the key issues of strategy and man management which will determine his company's commercial future. But if he is reporting to an uneasy shareholder who owns more than 99% of the company, complications set in, and when that shareholder is the Government, the chairman has to accept that he may well spend as much of his time operating in the political and quasi-political arena as he does in the commercial arena.

In this sense, dealing with BL's different masters during the five years – the Labour Government up to May 1979, the Conservative Government thereafter, and overlapping these the NEB who acted as an agency of both – was a frustrating exercise. Yet it was also fascinating, as I experienced so many facets of government – not only Labour and Conservative, but dogmatic and bureaucratic, interventionist and *laissez-faire*, petty and statesman-like, vacillating and decisive.

BL faced a wide spectrum of political views and emotions. At the extreme left, there were MPs prepared to appear on almost any militant platform associated with a strike – in support of dismissed shop stewards or simply in relation to our annual pay negotiations. Nearer the centre of the Labour Party, there was a greater conflict of emotions about BL. To the extent that our brushes with the militants seemed to be weakening the trades union movement, which in my view was the very opposite of what they did, there was concern about our management style. On the other hand, there was a strong desire to see BL succeed, both for economic and social reasons, and to justify their original decision to rescue the company – to take it into public ownership in 1975 – and it was of course a Labour Administration that appointed me to take on the rescue 'part two' in 1977.

The Conservative Party presented an even greater spread of

emotions. Conservative MPs with constituencies around BL's main manufacturing locations such as Birmingham, Coventry and Oxford, were strong supporters of the company's battle for survival – even to the extent of being genuinely concerned, and perhaps alarmed, by our alleged brinkmanship in industrial disputes. A closely related school of thought among the Conservatives, which shared with the first group a refreshing lack of attachment to political dogma, saw BL as an engine of industrial recovery for the rest of Britain. They hoped that our plant closures, removal of restrictive practices, low pay settlements and the firm line we took with the militants would set an example elsewhere in industry and thus help to restore Britain's industrial competitiveness. Moving a little further to the right, another group of Conservatives conceded that there were benefits from our progress on the employee relations front, but would not have been too unhappy if BL had gone over the brink provided it was as a result of the militants' intransigence. They were part of the 'Militants rule, okay' perception of our motor industry – a somewhat out-of-date assessment. A catastrophic closure of the company would, in their view, have had short-term political advantages and perhaps long-term economic and social benefits if it were demonstrably the fault of militant shop stewards, combined with poor trades union leadership. The future of BL itself was less important to them than the shock-wave effects throughout the economy, which they felt would be invaluable.

There was an even more extreme version of this way of thinking which was put across to us very eloquently by Professor Alan Walters after he became adviser to Margaret Thatcher at the beginning of 1981. Shortly after his appointment a few senior executive colleagues and I entertained him to lunch because his arrival in such a key post was of no little consequence to BL. Not in any way abashed by being the only non-BL member of a gathering of six or seven, he quickly launched into the theory that the closure of BL, whether as a result of a strike or in cold blood, could have a positive effect on the British economy within six months. The short-term impact on regions such as the West Midlands and on the balance of payments might soon be offset, according to Alan Walters, by the beneficial effect of the shock of closure on trades union and employee attitudes across the country. Restrictive practices would be swept away, pay increases would be held down and a more rapid improvement in Britain's competitiveness would thus be achieved through the closure of BL than by any other means available to the Government! We had to admire the audacity and intellectual integrity of Professor Walters in advancing this argument right in the BL camp. We strongly disagreed with him but as the Government had just committed itself to meet our request for £990 million, we were not as alarmed as we might have been had we met him a few months earlier. Our position was understandably rather different from the one he had put forward. While we were prepared to close the business if it no longer had any reasonable prospect of viability (whether because of a strike or for any other reason) we felt that a more realistic view of the social and economic consequences of closure was that certain regions would take years to recover. Moreover, a closure instigated by the Government in cold blood was likely to backfire politically, and could well harden trades union attitudes. Some may say this was none of our business, but when you have responsibility directly and indirectly for the jobs of hundreds of thousands of people, and an annual £3 billion worth of business and £2 billion worth of purchase in Britain, you can't afford to take a myopic view of your environment!

There was also a school of thought within the Conservative Party, perhaps the most numerous and influential, which was focused not on employee relations but on the return of BL to the private sector. All Conservatives wanted to see BL back into private ownership as quickly as possible. But here again there were many differences in emphasis. Some felt that BL needed to be given time to recover to profitability, so that it could then be floated on the Stock Market. Others believed that it was politically necessary to show quicker progress towards privatisation – that is before the 1983/84 General Election; and that some major disposals ought to be possible without damaging the rest of the company. A minority of this group weren't too fussy about whether or not the rest of the company was damaged. Finally, a further group considered that BL would never recover, but paradoxically and unrealistically believed that if BL were effectively put into liquidation, buyers would emerge for most of the constituent parts!

I often reflect with some astonishment on how BL has managed to pick its way through this morass without opening up a fundamental political divide. During my time the recovery effort enjoyed bi-partisan support, despite the early and only division (in Ryder's time) when the Conservative Opposition voted against the

Ryder Plan in 1975. With Labour subsequently in Opposition our greatest worry was that our industrial disputes would become political battlegrounds. Would the Labour Party find itself under irresistible pressure from the trades unions and the 'left' to give them moral support? Worse still, would the Conservative Government succumb to the temptation to intervene publicly on the side of management, rather than adopt a neutral and unprovocative policy of non-intervention, which was what we always recommended?

This meant that not only the Government but the Opposition Front Bench had to be handled with great care. We consistently made it clear to the Government of the day that we felt it necessary to give periodic briefings to the Opposition, and Sir Keith Joseph as Secretary of State for Industry welcomed these contacts, saying how much he had appreciated this facility when in Opposition himself. Subsequently, we had many meetings with Stan Orme as Labour's shadow spokesman on Industry, with the occasional involvement of Michael Foot, and we valued the consistently responsible attitude of the Labour Front Bench during our employee relations crises.

Throughout, BL had to remain a-political, and on a more personal level I found myself having to stress time after time to different political audiences that I was neither an arch-opponent of private ownership nor (as popularly supposed on the left) an enthusiastic union basher. Neither the Labour nor the Conservative Prime Ministers, with whom we dealt, flinched when the going became tough – but some ministers were less resolute than others. I don't recollect Sir Keith Joseph or before him Eric Varley batting an eyelid when we stood up to unofficial wildcat action – and neither did the Chancellor of the Exchequer, Denis Healey under Labour, nor Sir Geoffrey Howe under the Conservatives do anything to weaken our resolve.

But what of our other masters – the NEB? Immediately after my appointment and indeed until the change of government 18 months later, the NEB was a source of encouragement – and there was no little experience around the Board table, with trade union representatives like Lord Scanlon and Harry Urwin, plus experienced top industrialists such as Bill Duncan of ICI and Alistair Frame of RTZ. But why did Labour Ministers vest the BL shareholding in the NEB in the first place? I believe they had two main reasons. First, they (but not perhaps their civil servants) felt ill-equipped to cope with BL and hoped that the business experience within the NEB would provide more effective scrutiny, as well as keeping BL's affairs at one remove from the political arena. Second, they obviously saw advantage in giving the author of the Ryder Report the remit to supervise its implementation in his new (and separate) role as NEB Chairman. As I described earlier, this can hardly be said to have been a successful arrangement while Lord Ryder was Chairman of the NEB. After his departure Sir Leslie Murphy stepped up from Deputy Chairman, and it was he who persuaded me to take on the BL job. Sir Leslie Murphy isn't everyone's cup of tea, but I found him competent and decisive. He had some unenviable problems to cope with, and he set about them with energy and determination. I cannot say the BL Board always welcomed his occasional intervention in our affairs, but then his job was to monitor and oversee, and these things cannot easily be done without ruffling the feathers of the target company! As time went on, and we found our feet at BL, the NEB's involvement became rather irksome, whereas at the beginning it had been more obviously helpful. There is no doubt that Sir Leslie Murphy's banking experience was helpful to him, and it gave him the standing he needed, for he was surrounded by industrial experts: both union and management. He used his expertise effectively, for he is both numerate and very articulate. It was no easy task to achieve a consensus within the NEB – the ideological spectrum of the NEB Board made it very difficult to arrive at decisions that could be made to stick, and it was a credit to his patience and persistence, and to the goodwill of the union and management representatives on the Board, that it was able to function reasonably smoothly. Nevertheless, it had its moments! There were times when informal committees of the NEB spent hours drafting public statements, and even internal decisions, in a form that could be 'lived with' by the individual members of the NEB with their disparate views, and their different constituents.

In my early days as Chairman of BL, I was effectively reporting to two people – Sir Leslie Murphy, who acted for our majority shareholder, and Eric Varley, who could not stand back as much as he would have liked as Secretary of State for Industry; he was continually pursued by a Parliament which was understandably uneasy about the amount of money being spent! Labour Governments may be obliged to spend money in support of their policies, but they don't enjoy doing it.

The situation was made palatable by Sir Leslie Murphy's

goodwill, and by two other factors. First, as a newly appointed Chairman having been subjected to the full glare of publicity, my bargaining position in the early months (but only in the early months) was strong. Neither the NEB nor the Government would have risked provoking my early resignation, or that of my colleagues, by obstructing me or the BL Board on fundamental issues. The decision to close the Speke assembly plant and our request for £450 million of equity funding in the early months of 1978 were two such issues, and BL therefore had a relatively easy ride with its masters on both. Anyway, to be fair, I believe they accepted the logic of both actions.

The other factor which made this three-cornered relationship workable was the personality of Eric Varley. He was in my view an excellent Secretary of State: he never lacked courage; he had strong civil servants, he used the resource well; and he was pleasant, firm and decisive. I believe that he was more effective than he was perceived by many to be.

The unfortunate rescue of Chrysler UK, when Eric Varley was overruled by the then Prime Minister, Harold Wilson, did nothing to help his standing and his image. And yet he had done what any honest man would do: he argued his case, because he believed he was right. At the end of the day he lost, and not many would now gainsay that the wrong decision carried the day. As time went on, it became more and more generally accepted that the decision was wrong – production capacity was preserved at a time when culling of the industry in Britain would have given the remaining three companies a far better chance of becoming stronger. Chrysler UK should have been allowed to go to the wall. Eric Varley was right.

Another, and equally serious consequence of the decision imposed on Eric Varley was the impact on the attitudes of motor industry employees throughout the country. The myth that motor businesses – or even factories within these businesses – were impervious to market forces, was given a shot in the arm, and those managers who had tried to put across the facts of life, were undermined. If the British Government was prepared to save a foreign company then who would dream of letting British Leyland go into insolvency? The disputes and wildcat strikes multiplied, until in 1977 British Leyland and Ford were clocking up 300 disputes apiece every six months. The message spread, 'They'll never allow motor companies to go to the wall.'

During this period my respect for Eric Varley grew. He made decisions fast, and if he was obliged to consult the Prime Minister on our affairs from time to time, it was not apparent – and if he did so, he must have done so speedily, for the BL Board was never held up during this period.

Speke was different: the first major car factory closure in Britain for many years in an area of high unemployment. It was highly sensitive. We did not seek or expect the Government to be openly associated with the closure decision, since in the BL Board's view this was just the sort of commercial matter which it had been appointed to handle. But we had to test the water with the Government, if only because any hostility from ministers on such an issue would have indicated to us that the task of recovery was impossible. Eric Varley's approach was impeccable. First, he took delivery of the views of the NEB – 'regrettable to have to close Speke, but commercially necessary . . .' was their reaction. Then he asked Sir Leslie Murphy and me to accompany him to Number 10 to explain the situation to the Prime Minister, James Callaghan. I have described this meeting in detail elsewhere, and will not labour the point. After a thorough, logical debate, the Prime Minister and the Secretary of State for Industry did not attempt to veto the Board's decision, and we proceeded with the closure.

I was impressed by the perceptiveness and firmness of the Prime Minister in facing up to an issue which was bound to give his Government a hard time, both with backbench Labour MPs and trades union leaders. I can think of few people easier to work with than the last Labour Prime Minister. James Callaghan is a relaxed but formidable man. In his quiet way he was persuasive and effective. He was a great delegator, even if some thought he delegated too much. I don't find this criticism compelling, for a Prime Minister paints on a very broad canvas, and how can ministers operate effectively unless they are given authority to do their jobs supported by broad direction from the Prime Minister and with his ultimate backing? And how can a Prime Minister provide broad direction, if embroiled in detail? His was a difficult, indeed an impossible task, for the opposing forces left within the Labour Party were being painfully exposed, and his government was nearing the end of the road. I found him firm and decisive, and he never involved himself in minutiae.

While I was not in agreement with the philosophy of the

Callaghan Government, I appreciated its very real management qualities. Having worked closely with both Labour and Conservative Governments, I found that we had a more workable relationship with the former. Not because they were easier to persuade – indeed they were at least as tough about providing funds – but rather because we knew where we stood with them. Whereas the present administration is heavily centred on Downing Street, the Callaghan Government was surprisingly decentralised: ministers seemed to have more delegated authority. It was indicative of the Labour Government's whole approach to BL. Once a Corporate Plan was approved, they resisted the temptation to pull the plant up by the roots to see whether it was still growing. They looked at the business strategically – there was minimal intervention, and when the Prime Minister did get involved he did so in a firm, friendly, but purposeful way.

Up to the General Election of May 1979, we had only three disagreements of substance with the NEB or the Government. The first related to the ill-fated 5% pay policy of 1978–79. BL was not of course the only sufferer from that policy, but our position was made more difficult both by the commitment we had inherited from the 1977 pay round (to bring about parity of pay rates between all BL Cars plants as part of the establishment of centralised bargaining) and by our desire to launch an incentive scheme to tackle low productivity. Consequently, although we could not afford generous increases on the basic rate, we had to fight to extract the last ounce of flexibility from a pay policy which was hopelessly ill-equipped to deal with the complex and varied needs of industry. This only served to confirm my distaste for the whole concept of pay and price controls. In seeking to limit the general rate of *increase*, the *structure* of pay and pricing tended to become frozen in a way which took no account of changing needs – moreover, norms were set which were often higher than would have been attainable in a free market. BL welcomed the refreshing approach of the Thatcher Government in this area.

The second disagreement was about BL's funding for 1979, and in this case the NEB rather than the Government were BL's antagonists. The Ryder Report had recommended in 1975 that £1,000 million of government funding would be needed over the following six years to support BL's recovery. In the two years before I joined BL, only £150 million of these funds had been drawn, mainly because of investment freezes during major strikes, and because of the generally slow progress in modernising and rationalising the business. Moreover, these funds were in loan rather than equity form, thus adding to BL's interest cost burden and giving the company a very weak balance sheet by commercial standards. In 1978 we paid up to 17% in interest charges on government loans. In early 1978, the newly constituted Board proposed a very different approach to the funding issue. We felt that the drip-feeding of funds in small tranches by the Government and the NEB should cease, so that BL could accelerate its modernisation programme with the assurance that the 'Ryder £1,000 million' would be available. I wrote to Sir Leslie Murphy on the 13th January, 1978:

> The British Leyland Board, however, feel strongly that a new approach to the provision of funds is required. The financial state of the company is such that, even though the Plan is expected to show the prospect of reasonable levels of profitability in the 1980s, the Board cannot recommend making the investments necessary for the 1980s without firm assurances of government financial support. The Board believes that the linking of financial support to day-to-day industrial relations performance is unhelpful in the running of the business. Furthermore, going from cash crisis to cash crisis will severely inhibit our ability to attract high calibre managers or to hold our best people. What is needed now is a government assurance that there will be adequate equity funding in the future, in addition to the funds that need to be provided at the latest by end March.

We felt that government funding should be provided in equity rather than loan form, so that BL could return gradually to the normal commercial disciplines of debt:equity ratios, to prepare itself for ultimate independence of government support. Albert Frost, who chaired the BL Funding Committee, was the main protagonist of this approach, and he was forceful and persuasive in putting it across. We pressed for no less than £450 million of government equity for 1978, with a further £300 million required in 1979 – still within the Ryder total of £1,000 million. The £450 million was approved, after due scrutiny of our Plan by the NEB and the Government. We felt that progress was being made towards a sensible approach to funding – though still not ideal, as we had judged it premature to press for more than a year's funding commitment in advance. At some stage however, we were determined to move to a two-year cycle of funding.

A year later, when our 1979 Corporate Plan was sent to the NEB for discussion, we carried forward the funding request of £300 million envisaged in our 1978 Plan. BL's immediate cash position had in fact turned out considerably better than forecast in the 1978 Plan, but we felt that the days of drip-feeding were over and that the NEB and the Government would certainly commit themselves to the full amount requested, while trusting the BL Board not to draw funds ahead of what it really needed. Our faith in human nature was not rewarded. The NEB felt that its duty to the Government required it to cut down the funding commitment to the minimum – which in their view was £150 million for 1979. A sharp debate ensued, which became three-cornered when the Government was brought in. Ultimately a compromise was reached, under which the NEB and the Government privately committed themselves to provide an extra £50 million on top of the NEB's £150 million if and when it was needed. In the event the £50 million was not required! The Board's irritation at the NEB's attitude was heightened by the rather patronising attitude of the NEB to our Plan. We had to fight hard to stop them describing it publicly as 'optimistic'. We could not object to the exercise of political judgment on the broad question of state support for BL – this was the Government's absolute right as ultimate owner of the business. But the 'second-guessing' of the BL Board's commercial judgment was another matter. The whole purpose of reconstituting the Board of BL to create a built-in majority of able and experienced non-executive directors, was in danger of being negated by too-detailed supervision of commercial matters by the NEB. Although the degree of NEB monitoring and intervention had been sharply reduced after I took over at BL, the message that there was not sufficient room for *two* non-executive Boards to oversee BL had not yet got through.

The third disagreement was rather more serious, as it arose from an attempt to involve BL in the political arena during the run-up to the 1979 General Election.

Prestcold – our refrigeration equipment subsidiary – was a peripheral part of BL's business and not therefore one in which we were prepared to sustain losses for an extended period for the sake of ultimate recovery. Like other non-mainstream businesses which we subsequently sold – Alvis and Coventry Climax are examples – we could not give Prestcold any significant degree of top management attention. If it had intractable problems, then it was clear to us that it must be sold or closed. 1978 was a bad year for Prestcold. Unfortunately, its problems were concentrated on its two Scottish plants at Hillington, Glasgow, which employed some 900 people and made hermetic compressors for domestic refrigerators. Excess world capacity for hermetic compressors was resulting in heavy undercutting of Prestcold's prices, and the unviability of Prestcold's Scottish operations had become clear as early as July 1978. Various options were explored, including the development of a new hermetic compressor and the possibility of selling the company to a competitor. However, none of these proved viable, and discussions about closure were then held with the Scottish Office, who were naturally reluctant to let the closure go ahead until they had satisfied themselves that all the alternatives had been exhausted. As a result, the Scottish Office offered to meet the losses incurred by the two Hillington plants for a further month between March and April 1979 while their own consultants examined the possibilities. We accepted the offer, but were not surprised to learn in early April that the consultants had endorsed our conclusion that there was no hope of viability.

However, we were now just a month away from the General Election, and alarm bells were clearly ringing in Labour Party headquarters. The Secretary of State for Scotland, Bruce Millan, pitched in with an offer of a further two-months' subsidy to meet the losses of the Hillington plants. Sir Leslie Murphy advised us to go along with this, even though it made no commercial sense. The possibilities for keeping the plants open in the longer term had been exhausted, and the local management had already started to leave because they could see the writing on the wall. Employees at the plants were aware of the extreme doubt about their future, and we owed it to them to make the position clear. As a straight business decision, the case for immediate closure was clear, and we felt that Bruce Millan's offer was no more than a delaying tactic. Accordingly, the BL Board decided on the 11th April to proceed with the closure of the Hillington plants and to issue the statutory 90-day notices of redundancy to the employees the next day.

Predictably, I was summoned to a meeting with Eric Varley and

Sir Leslie Murphy the next morning. Clearly no stone was to be left unturned in order to put off the evil hour. Couldn't BL put off the closure until a strategy for all our non-mainstream businesses had been worked out with the NEB? I pointed out that there was already such a strategy in our Corporate Plan. Couldn't the NEB instruct us to put off the closure until ministers had reviewed the wider issues? To his credit, Sir Leslie Murphy said that he could not see how this could fall within the NEB's terms of reference, since it was not charged with the day-to-day management supervision of BL. Couldn't the NEB take over the whole of Prestcold? Sir Leslie Murphy thought he would be unable to justify the price which he knew the BL Board would expect to receive. Finally, the Secretary of State asked for a few more hours to take legal advice on his powers to issue a directive to the NEB, and we agreed to this.

The BL Board was kept in touch with the drama as it was played out – blow by blow. Later that day, Sir Leslie Murphy told me that Eric Varley had decided to issue a directive to the NEB to acquire the whole of Prestcold from BL at a fair price. During the negotiations, Hillington's losses would be borne by the Government. This was the only option short of closure that satisfied the commercial requirements of the BL Board, and we therefore stopped the issue of redundancy notices. We had been in real danger of becoming a party to a blatant political manoeuvre, and we were very uneasy about the whole thing. The press reaction was predictable. 'Varley decision delights Prestcold unions' was the *Scotsman*'s headline – while the *Daily Telegraph* reported:

> Mr Varley's intervention had produced accusations from Conservatives that the decision was motivated by fears about the electoral consequences of the closure of Prestcold's two Scottish plants. . . .

Whether in practice, the Prestcold saga made a small contribution to Labour's better-than-average performance in the Scottish constituencies, I would doubt. Soon after the General Election, the new Conservative Government made it clear that they did not want the NEB to buy Prestcold, nor were they prepared to continue to meet the cost of subsidising the Scottish factories. BL was left to pick up the pieces. We therefore announced the closure of Hillington on the 7th June, and the incident lives on in the memories of the Board and top management, reminding us that approaching General Elections are to be treated with utmost circumspection!

So we said goodbye to the Labour Government on a somewhat controversial note – which was a pity, because our working relationship with Eric Varley and his colleagues had otherwise been excellent.

The Conservatives won a handsome victory which would not make it easy to fight BL's cause. We knew that Margaret Thatcher's Government, with its commitment to the contraction of both public spending and public ownership, would be a most reluctant owner. The various strands of thought, not to mention prejudice, about BL in the Conservative Party, all appeared to be represented in the new Cabinet.

The new Government launched an immediate review of the NEB, the whole concept of which was anathema to them. Predictably within two months of entering office, they announced a drastic cutback of the NEB's powers and responsibilities. In theory, the NEB's role as the dominant shareholder of Rolls-Royce and BL was to remain unchanged. In practice, the NEB's loss of credibility made the Rolls-Royce and BL Boards less willing to accept NEB supervision. In any case the long-standing tensions between Rolls-Royce and the NEB (much greater than those affecting BL's relationship) were being publicly aired at the time. The question was, should BL move directly to the Government if Rolls-Royce became detached from the NEB? There seemed little logic in having one report to the Government and the other to the NEB.

In discussion with senior civil servants, in which Sir Austin Bide accompanied me, it was clear to us that becoming detached from the NEB had its pros and cons. On the one hand it would eliminate the bureaucratic layer of NEB 'supervision' – on the other hand 'better the devil you know', and it was certainly possible that the Department of Industry would want to 'second-guess' the Board every bit as much. I know that this was the concern of Sir Keith Joseph who had been appointed Secretary of State for Industry, in the new Conservative Government. The BL non-executive directors at first strongly favoured moving to the Department of Industry, because they were becoming increasingly restive about the NEB. I wasn't quite so sure, but I had to admit that with a Conservative Government in power the NEB's currency would become eroded – it might be advisable to have direct access, in order to retain crispness in the decision-making process.

Over the months following the Conservative's election victory we vacillated on the issues, and towards the end of 1979 the choice was made for us. The problems between the NEB and Rolls-Royce came to a head: the Government sided with the latter, and the entire NEB Board resigned. Sir Arthur Knight took over from Sir Leslie Murphy as Chairman of the NEB and made it clear at the outset that because he had no effective control over them, he did not want to accept any responsibility for the affairs of Rolls-Royce and BL. The statement was thankfully accepted on all sides and the NEB withdrew *de facto* from supervision of the two companies, even though the necessary legislation to transfer the shareholdings to the Secretary of State for Industry did not formally take effect until the 31st March 1981. The press were often puzzled at how relaxed we were about the relationship – the fact is that for practical purposes there was by then no relationship.

Nevertheless, I was saddened at the way Sir Leslie Murphy and his team were treated; they were right to resign. It would be an incomplete account if I did not emphasise what great support the NEB gave to me personally. Nothing was too much trouble – all the key people (including the union members) were accessible 24 hours a day and over weekends – and I had some very helpful advice, not least from the trade union representatives, whose counsel was usually in the direction of cooling situations which could otherwise have led to difficulties for BL and for its employees. The NEB's problem was that it was charged with doing an almost impossible task, but the Board's members did it to the best of their considerable ability, and invariably they arrived at a consensus. At no time did the disparate make-up of the Board impact unhelpfully on BL. Always they had BL's interests at heart, and if BL eventually earns its spurs, Sir Leslie Murphy and his Board must take much of the credit for their faith and dogged determination – particularly during the dark days of 1977 and 1978, when anyone would have been forgiven for deciding to call it a day. I believe their faith and tenacity was good for Britain, for an overnight loss of its indigenous motor industry would not have been the best way to move out of motor manufacturing.

Knowing that the handling of the direct relationship with Government, particularly a Conservative Government, would be both tricky and time-consuming, and knowing too that BL's own managerial resources were already too stretched to do justice to this task, I suggested to Sir Peter Carey, Permanent Secretary at the Department of Industry, that he should second one of his promising young civil servants to work in my office as an assistant with special responsibility for liaising with the Government. The idea seemed obvious enough, but apparently it was revolutionary in the troubled history of the relations between government and public sector industries. Sir Peter Carey jumped at the offer, and the arrangement lasted from August 1979, until the end of my time with BL, when the change to a non-executive Chairman no longer provided scope for an assistant along these lines.

The arrangement worked extremely well. For the two civil servants concerned, it provided a stimulating challenge as well as the invaluable industrial experience which I believe is so lacking in Whitehall. If the Government is to involve itself as much as it does in industrial matters (irrespective of its political colour) then it needs the degree of interchange between civil service and industry which makes the French civil service so much more effective in this area. For BL the secondment provided an internal source of advice on how any particular proposal might look to the Government; plus being an informal supplement to the normal channels through which we dealt with the Government. This was of particular help in our relations with the Department of Industry civil servants. Information could thus be exchanged or draft letters cleared informally, without establishing precedents or commitments. It also contributed to establishing relationships directly with the other departments that had a voice in decision-making on BL – such as the Treasury, the Central Policy Review Staff, and Number 10 itself, since it became increasingly clear during Margaret Thatcher's tenure of office that the Department of Industry was but one, and often not the decisive, influence in such decisions. A public sector organisation which cannot play the Whitehall game – that is guessing down which corridor the real power lies and gaining access to that corridor – starts off with a crippling disadvantage in arguing its case with Government.

In assessing the pros and cons of vesting the responsibility for state-owned industries in an agency such as the NEB (rather than directly in the relevant minister) it is necessary to understand the impact which Parliament has on the relationship with Government.

There is constant pressure on ministers and senior civil servants exerted not only by Select Committees, but by the normal course of parliamentary business such as 'Question Time'. They are expected to be fully informed about the affairs of industries in the public sector. This pressure would be fine if it were confined to the strategic issues with which the Government needs to concern itself as owner and financier of these businesses. The snag is that it often extends to whatever trivia happens to have emerged in the media or interests a particular MP. More dangerously, it draws the Government into areas where commercial rather than political judgment must and should be paramount. It is fine when a minister finds it easy to say to an enquirer, 'I don't know anything about this, nor should I. It's the company's business – you had better ask them.' But this admission of division of political and commercial responsibility does not always come easily to politicians. So it is a constant battle for BL, and no doubt for other companies in the public sector, to keep the Government's hands off commercial issues which happen to catch the public eye.

Thanks to the understanding of civil servants at the Department of Industry, we largely succeeded in this task during my term at BL and more so in the first four years than in the fifth. Parliamentary pressure on ministers made the task more difficult, requiring them to be informed on quite superficial aspects of BL's affairs. Because of France's very different constitution, the French Government is not under similar pressure from Parliament and does not therefore concern itself in any way with the day-to-day affairs of the national-ised Renault – even when Renault is marginally profitable, or substantial parts of it are losing money. Government contributes to Renault's strategic thinking through representation on their Board.

I do not for a moment question Parliament's right to seek all kinds of information about activities in the public sector or to expect the closest possible government scrutiny of these matters. But if these tendencies are carried too far, then Parliament needs to understand the costs. First, state-owned companies will face sub-stantial penalties compared with their private competitors, because of diversion of top management attention from running the busi-ness, and because of the greater transparency of their affairs. Second, top flight management will not be attracted into these companies if they know that they will be constantly subject to 'second-guessing' and exposed to criticism; especially from quarters which have no basic expertise in the business field.

While it may be fashionable to belittle the role of Parliament, I do not share this view. Parliament can easily do a great deal of damage and it needs to recognise this potential so that it is not disastrously fulfilled. This applies also to the European Parliament, some of whose Members courted publicity in 1982 by encouraging the trade in parallel imports from the Continent, without the slightest regard to their impact on the longer term interests of the British motor industry or indeed the consumer, and with an astonishing lack of understanding of the principal reason for car price differentials – that is, the impact of currency ratios at any given time.

11

The Iron Lady

We may have thought we were picking our way through a political minefield under a Labour Government, but that was child's play in comparison to what was to come.

The first time I encountered Margaret Thatcher in full cry was at a luncheon to brief the Opposition in early January, 1979. She and the Shadow Chancellor, together with Sir Keith Joseph and James Prior, lunched with the BL Board at the Stafford Hotel – coincidentally, in the private room which was the venue for the hair-raising meetings with Terry Duffy and other union leaders in 1980 and 1981. In my innocence I thought that we would need to entice Margaret Thatcher to enter into a robust debate about the future of BL, so I placed her not on my right, but immediately opposite me – a technique that often gets a debate going. I need hardly have bothered. She had scarcely taken her seat before she fired the first salvo, 'Well Michael Edwardes, and why should we pour further funds into British Leyland?' She glared stonily around the table at each of us in turn. My Board colleagues, not normally lost for words, were halted in their tracks for a good ten seconds as we adjusted to the direct style of a very formidable lady. Thereafter it was difficult for anyone to get a word in. I cannot say that I felt she left the luncheon meeting any more convinced about our case than when she walked into the room. If she was, she hid it well. But I was wrong.

Two days later, a letter arrived to thank me for the lunch, 'I wish you well in the future in your very considerable efforts to restore BL to prosperity. If I may say so you have a thoroughly realistic approach.' She added in ink, 'I really enjoyed it, found it most valuable, and was most impressed by your open realistic approach.' Certainly, the letter softened our assessment of how the lunch debate had gone down with the then Shadow Cabinet – and perhaps in retrospect that lunch helped to give us at least a breathing space after the Conservatives regained power a few months later. This was the start of a relationship which tended to be conducted at a distance – she and I rarely met except at formal dinners – but despite that it did not lack in intensity at times. I was told by those who knew her better that she admired what she perceived as my persistence and courage in tackling BL's problems but was not at all pleased when these qualities were applied to the task of extracting money from her Government! Equally, I had the greatest respect for her courage, determination and hard work, even though I felt she sometimes discharged responsibilities which she could easily have delegated to her senior ministers – or indeed to the Chairman and Boards of major public companies who were actually appointed to exercise them!

With the Conservative victory in the May 1979 General Election, I found myself to all intents and purposes dealing directly with the new Secretary of State for Industry, Sir Keith Joseph. Many people have an impression of Sir Keith Joseph that is way off the mark. There is, of course, Sir Keith, the politician, and there is Keith Joseph, the man, but both personalities have one thing in common: great integrity. He may change his mind (and I can bear witness to the fact that he can and that this can be very disconcerting!) but I'm prepared to argue that he will only do so if he is persuaded by the intellectual case put to him. He changed his mind about BL affairs, as I shall explain – it was a mammoth reversal, and yet I have to say that he was easy to work with when he was at the Department of Industry; he is one of those people who is always 'a pleasure to do business with.' In a nutshell, I trust him.

I enjoyed our frequent debates, and despite his philosophical objection to public sector industry – which in many ways I share – I found him to be encouraging and supportive in our day-to-day working relationship. Sir Keith Joseph's intellectual integrity was helpful to BL because it made him a non-interventionist on commercial issues. He has no real interest in motor cars and did not see why he should struggle to understand them. He paid BL the courtesy of a few visits, but I well remember that when he visited our testing ground at Gaydon in July 1979, to see our new models, we had a real struggle to engage his interest in anything that was not fundamentally important. This did not worry us, because it encouraged him to stick to the strategic issues which the Government needed to tackle as owner of the business. He knew the BL Board was in a much better position than his Department to exercise commercial judgment, and until his departure to the Department of Education in September 1981, we enjoyed a period of minimal intervention by the Government on other than the broadest issues. We were therefore able to make great progress by concentrating on our proper business.

Our first task with the new Conservative Government was to convince ministers that they had no alternative but to honour the Labour Government's pledge to give BL the funds to see it through 1979. At that stage, any public hint of doubt about the availability of funds in the short term would have caused a catastrophic crisis of confidence in BL. Even if the Government wanted closure, it would have had no control over the speed and cost of it, if a crisis were allowed to develop. With the help of the NEB, we succeeded in convincing ministers that there were no quick and easy ways out.

The second phase in our dealings with the Thatcher Government came in the autumn of 1979, when we put forward our 1980 Corporate Plan together with a request for the government funding we needed for 1980. We knew that the odds were against our getting the funds. As the pound grew stronger and the two day a week engineering strike bit into our production, BL's losses were mounting. We were still a year away from our first major new model, the Metro. Although £225 million of the Ryder £1,000 million remained to be spent, we could foresee an early need for an additional £205 million, to finance our major programme of redundancies and closures. Moreover, if the economic outlook for manufacturing industry continued to deteriorate, we could not be optimistic about becoming free of government funds thereafter. The Iron Lady's axe was poised, perhaps rightly so.

Nevertheless, the BL Board felt that we were making progress in tackling our internal problems and that a real prospect of recovery remained. Knowing that this alone would not be enough to convince a very sceptical group of ministers, I reflected on the cards we had left in our hand. The depth of BL's plight was in one sense a point against closure, since there was no prospect of a buyer who would come along and take it off the Government's hands, or pick up the pieces. If buyers could be found for individual parts of the company (and there were few easily separable operations within BL in 1979), the overwhelming proportion of the company would still have to be closed. This would cost the Government far more in the short term than keeping BL going, for under the public government assurance, first given by Eric Varley in 1977, it would have had to meet all BL's obligations. In addition the cost to the Exchequer of the huge redundancies would run to over £4,000 a man in the first year. We then employed a total workforce of 160,000. Taking account of the likely impact on the component industry and on the regional infrastructure in such areas as the West Midlands, the Government would have had to find £1,000 million within a year in order to pay for the closure – more than enough to disrupt its plans for cutting public expenditure.

There were some positive points which had special appeal for a Conservative Government. We were making great strides in employee relations during the last quarter of 1979. We had won a 7 to 1 majority in a secret ballot of the workforce on our restructuring programme – thus nudging the country towards the 'realism' which ministers were preaching so fervently. We had sacked Derek Robinson and were awaiting the report of the AUEW's Inquiry into the episode. We had put forward a tough 5% pay deal for BL Cars with a 92-page list of proposed reforms in working practices; both were still under negotiation with the trades unions. At that time improvement in productivity and employee relations ranked number one as the Government's industrial objectives, later to be displaced by privatisation. Were they going to throw away this opportunity of a productivity and attitude breakthrough, and kick a realistic workforce in the teeth by going ahead with closure? A similar argument applied to the collaborative deal which we now had ready for signature with Honda. Would the Government be prepared to throw away this pioneering agreement between a British and a Japanese motor company, which might encourage wider moves to transplant the benefits of Japanese technology and efficiency in Britain?

We therefore made the tactical decision that we should ask for only one year's funding – amounting to £300 million for 1980. This went against all our wishes for a longer period of stability. But it made the decision to support BL more palatable for a Conservative Government. Could they refuse BL 'a last chance'? I knew that in a year's time we would have launched the Metro and it would then be even more difficult to close the company. The Prime Minister must have known that if she were to grasp the nettle of closing BL in cold blood (rather than as a result of a strike), she had to do it during her first few months in office. This could mean rejecting our 1980 Corporate Plan.

There was the usual detailed examination of the Plan at the official level, and the Board invited Sir Keith Joseph to dinner in November to explain its thinking. Later, John Nott, as Secretary of State for Trade, was asked to cast his 'City' eye over our figures, and this led to a tense meeting with a group of ministers at the House of Commons, where it was clear that the ministers did not give us as much as an even chance of succeeding with our recovery programme.

Thereafter we could do no more than wait, until one morning I was called off the squash court at the Lansdowne Club by Richard Bullock to sign a letter which Sir Keith Joseph wanted to lay before Parliament that afternoon, reflecting what I had already told him on behalf of the Board – that we would have no hesitation in abandoning the Corporate Plan (thus triggering total closure) if we were thrown off course by a strike, or indeed by any other factors. Subject to that, the Secretary of State would announce the funding decision at the same time. Richard Bullock, now retired from the Civil Service, has a dry sense of humour. There was I, squash racquet in one hand, towel in the other – he met me with outstretched hand, 'Sir Francis I presume?' I signed the letter, glad that this particular

By courtesy of *Private Eye*

battle was over; Sir Keith Joseph delivered his side of the bargain later in the day.

We got our £300 million – in the event the tactical points in BL's favour proved more weighty than the Government's free market philosophy. There had of course been much agonising inside the Cabinet. As the *Economist* put it after the Government's announcement, just as Parliament broke for the Christmas recess:

> On Thursday BL got early delivery of the most begrudged
> Christmas present ever shoved into a laddered stocking.

The Government were able to describe this decision publicly as a 'last chance lifeline' (as the *Daily Express* put it) rather than as a fundamental U-turn. This was hardly an expression of confidence in BL's future, but at least we had our funds, and the decision had come relatively quickly thanks to the pressure of the Honda negotiations. In retrospect ministers, and not least the Prime Minister, may have regretted this decision on many occasions over the next two years, as BL came forward with further large financial requirements; by then the combination of tangible progress towards the company's recovery and rising unemployment across the country made it difficult to close BL. Perhaps only now, with even longer hindsight, are some ministers accepting that they may well have taken the *right* decision after all, for BL shows signs of being capable of returning to the private sector (in due course) on a viable basis. But the growing ministerial mood of regret and frustration, and perhaps at times resentment, was to cause problems in our relationship with the Government for some time.

This, therefore, was the political scene at almost the exact mid-point of my five years with BL, and also perhaps the low point. It was ironic that, having successfully overcome the employee relations upheavals in the preceding months, the business was facing its most serious crisis yet – largely for reasons outside our control. With the recession biting into both the car and truck markets, and the devastating combination of high inflation and a strengthening pound destroying the competitive position of British manufacturing industry, BL's losses were projected to mount to record levels. What is more, we had not yet worked out a plan to deal with the situation, for it was literally building up overnight as the pound took off. We had progressed no further than the painful realisation that the drastic restructuring programme, which our workforce had so overwhelmingly supported seven months earlier, was now no longer adequate. Hundreds of millions of pounds of cash shortfall stared us in the face.

A few months earlier, as the pound gathered momentum, we had undertaken a major review to see whether or not we could survive 1980 without further funds. We were able to confirm to the Secretary of State that we could just about see our way through to the 1981 Plan, provided the employee relations scene calmed down in the wake of the dismissal of the Longbridge convenor, and the implementation of the wage deal. Throughout 1980 the pound continued its sharp climb upwards and peaked at the horrific level of 105 trade weighted average in January 1981, eroding in currency terms the increased competitiveness we were achieving through cutting our costs and increasing productivity.

Against this background, I faced the unenviable prospect of going to a working dinner at Number 10 on the 22nd May, 1980, with a Conservative Prime Minister to tell her the unpleasant news that she and her colleagues would be forced to choose between pumping more vast sums into BL to keep it going, or an even greater sum if they preferred to let the company go to the wall. Such a prospect would have caused difficulties with any government, but with a fiercely determined Prime Minister committed to reducing public ownership of industry, this looked like a suicide mission!

As I drove down the Haymarket, around Nelson's Column in Trafalgar Square, and into Downing Street – accompanied by Sir Austin Bide and David Andrews – we reflected that it would be difficult to put across the truth, which was that our latest predicament was largely due to her own high standing and its impact on our currency! With this weighing heavily on our minds we stepped into the lion's den. It didn't take her long to get down to brass tacks – one quality I understand, for I also have an inability to make small talk for more than a few seconds! A quick drink, and we were immediately ushered into a working environment, along with the soup.

The Prime Minister was very much in the chair. Her team included the Chancellor of the Exchequer, Sir Geoffrey Howe, and Sir Keith Joseph. She was in an enquiring mood, somewhat reminiscent of the Spanish Inquisition. 'Now what's this all about? You're not going to ask us for more money?' was her opening salvo. When I replied that we would certainly need some hundreds of millions of additional funds, this immediately established a frosty atmosphere for the early part of the evening.

We explained that BL's problems were complex; that the critical area was still product – great progress having been made in other areas – and that we would not have a fully competitive range of cars and trucks much before 1983. In fact, as each acceptable new product was introduced, it was burdened with economic factors that were rapidly moving against us. Although we expected productivity to improve dramatically in 1981 and 1982, and we would not concede extravagant wage claims, the new and unexpected rate of appreciation of sterling would severely erode our progress. It could be quantified, and it would be quantified, but as it was months before we were due to submit the 1981 Plan, we merely wanted her to be aware of the general problem. We said that it was not our place to make a political judgment about the impact of a possible closure of BL, but what was certain was that if the Government's economic policy was not successful, then BL could not hope to recover. In other words high inflation and a high pound (whether due to North Sea oil or any other distortion) was a combination we couldn't overcome unaided, especially if it was set against the background of a recession. One immediate effect of the currency shifts was that we were being forced to look abroad for some components which were substantially cheaper than ones bought in Britain.

Just in case there were any misapprehensions in the minds of the ministers, we explained that BL's problems at that time were not restricted to Austin Morris – the popular misconception was that Jaguar, Rover, Triumph and the Leyland truck business were all profitable, and this was far from the truth. At that time only Land Rover and Unipart made respectable profits. (Jaguar, which became profitable in 1982, had lost money for many years.) Product actions and modernisation were urgently needed in all parts of BL, and this meant continued heavy funding by the Government, particularly in the prevailing economic circumstances; it also required collaborative ventures to speed up the actions. We emphasised that apart from one or two parts of the company – perhaps 20% in sales turnover – the business was not saleable. Privatisation of sections of it might seem tempting, but it wasn't a practical option. On the other hand, as the recovery programme progressed, and as collaborative deals were consummated, we would hope eventually to bring in equity partners, which would strengthen BL and serve the

Government's purpose of introducing private sector cash.

Nevertheless, we had to be open with ministers – on present economic assumptions there was a real case for closure. This was becoming a political rather than a commercial issue. The Prime Minister asked what could be done about it, and I replied that the Government could fund the company over and above the present Plan – when the 1981 Plan was quantified, the Government could accept the need for finding hundreds of millions in extra funds – or it could close the business now, at a cost of arguably £1,200 million. Neither route would be palatable.

We were well past the fish course at this stage, and the Prime Minister was not enjoying the discussion one little bit. It didn't help when an aide popped his head through the door to give the end of the day's currency figures – the pound was still moving inexorably upwards. She had my full sympathy at this point; with public expenditure cuts proving difficult to push through, and the recession and the strong pound starting to accelerate the growth in unemployment, her sense of frustration with BL, as a microcosm of her wider problems, was understandable.

After our somewhat frugal meal, we moved into the drawing room to continue the cross-examination! 'What could *BL* do about it? – that was more to the point,' she said. Well, we were drastically cutting costs and would have to rethink our model programme; be much less ambitious. But even then the need for funds would far exceed that envisaged when the 1980 Plan was submitted in November 1979, only six months earlier. This was a political issue – yes, she agreed it was. Throughout the evening it was impossible to tell from her expression whether or not we were making headway in building our case for the future.

The biggest surprise was her next contribution to the debate. She asked the Chancellor how much he had in the contingency reserve fund! My immediate reaction was: we are in with a chance. My colleagues later concurred with this view. The Chancellor looked distinctly uneasy, and understandably was not too explicit in his reply!

The ministers looked tired – it was after 10.30 pm and we had been at it since 7.30 pm – 'is that about it?' Sir Keith Joseph asked. The Prime Minister said no – there were other aspects to explore. We ended by discussing the large wage settlements in the public sector; she doubted that interest levels would drop, or that the pound would ease in value in the short term. In this she proved to be only too right.

By the end of the evening we all agreed that no proposals were left on the table, because the BL Board were not yet ready to put forward positive recommendations – therefore no decisions were sought. We had had a useful exchange of views, and the climate which at the beginning of the evening had been frosty to cool, warmed up just a little. We trooped out into Downing Street at ten minutes past eleven.

I pause here to reflect on whether we were right to have initiated this type of debate. In mid-year, between Plans, one can only talk in very broad terms. We were postulating concepts – concepts which could not be quantified in any precise way for some months – and foreshadowing problems for 1981 which would only become crystallised when we submitted the 1981 Plan towards the end of 1980. We had reason to believe from subsequent feedback that the Prime Minister found this unsatisfactory. Our lack of precision, our lack of quantification of likely sums involved, was seen by her as a weakness – whereas we saw the working dinner as an opportunity to flag up problems on the horizon. As a Board we were used to dealing with concepts at the profile stage, and specifics at the plan or budget stage. We thought we were being helpful in doing this, but she expected a debate of the latter type, and our 'broad' approach was read as a lack of professionalism. To this extent we did not do justice to our cause. On the other hand, the message we were conveying was relevant not only to BL, but to hundreds of industries then being severely damaged by the over-valued pound. To be able to offer the Prime Minister and her ministers a meaningful example of the impact of her currency policy, seemed to us to be a very necessary exercise – perhaps even our duty, and subsequent events, in 1981 and 1982, showed that our concern was not without cause.

Sir Austin Bide, David Andrews and I chatted about the dinner; the only thing that was certain was that to continue with the Recovery Plan would cost a great deal more money, and we calculated that a large cheque – perhaps a billion pounds – would be needed to fund the Plan for 1981 onwards, when it was presented to Sir Keith Joseph in the autumn of 1980. (This turned out to be close to the mark.) Would they wear it? We simply didn't know – and we were wise to take nothing for granted, for the further funding requirement at £1,140 million was just about the estimated cost of closing the business. Too close for comfort.

It seemed that the 'BL dinner' became deeply engraved in the Prime Minister's memory and that it acted as the focus of her resentment about the 'BL problem'. She had no desire to repeat the exercise; it was the first and last working dinner! But this did not mean that she delegated the problem to her Secretary of State for Industry. In this respect she was the exact opposite of James Callaghan. Everything of any conceivable political consequence was referred to Number 10 – not only the strategic decisions on funding, but even matters such as the Chairman's remuneration. Moreover, this was no rubber-stamping process. Recommendations on other matters were frequently overturned. Quite apart from the Prime Minister's direct role in this, her general attitude to the sponsoring and spending Departments encouraged the central parts of the Whitehall machine – such as the Treasury and the Central Policy Review Staff (the Think Tank) – to indulge their penchant for 'second-guessing' the judgments of other departments. I cannot judge whether she was right to delegate authority sparingly to her ministers – but it certainly tended to undermine their credibility, and turn the already complex process of securing the right decisions from the Government into a fine art. Particularly in 1980 and 1981, under Sir Robin Ibbs, the Think Tank seemed to have an influence on policy which we felt went beyond its expertise. There are of course occasions when the staff experts are right, and can show that their point of view would have secured a better result. This is not always a good leadership approach, for if you 'second-guess' those responsible, you demotivate and sharply reduce effort and commitment. It doesn't pay to 'second-guess' 100% in order to lift correct decisions from 99 to 100, for the subsequent effort of those who are 'second-guessed' can be heavily diluted!

Whenever we met socially, the Prime Minister was extremely friendly. Just as I admired her ability and determination in pursuing policies with which I did not always agree, she seemed to recognise and applaud the progress we were making at BL, and in this she was generous, particularly as she disliked the whole concept of BL as a state-owned and cash-consuming operation. She could also take conversational ripostes as well as administering them. As I was leaving a dinner at Number 10 on the 10th September, 1981, in honour of President Mitterand of France, I was about to thank the Prime Minister for the pleasant, indeed intriguing evening when Lord Carrington, who was standing beside her, said something to the effect that BL was now going much better – 'Keep up the good work Michael', he said, with his usual charm. She immediately pounced on his words and said, 'So he should, he's paid more than I am.'

Now it so happened that only a week before we had had some actuarial assessments made of the cost of pensions for people in short-term posts, and although the present Prime Minister does not see her position as short term, the actuaries had understandably examined her job in this light. What it amounted to was that the salary approved by Parliament – about £36,000 – provides the basis for the pension, whether or not the salary is fully drawn, and a full and ample pension is paid from the date of leaving office, even if that happens to be only days after the appointment. This is of course very expensive to fund. When I began to point this out, she countered, 'I don't even take the approved £36,000 – I only draw £28,000 per annum.'

'But Prime Minister, you are not including the cost to the State of funding your pension – if you add that back, your job is worth £28,000 plus £70,000 a year, or approximately £100,000 in all.'

I thought Lord Carrington would burst. My conversation with the Prime Minister was helpfully interrupted by other guests saying farewell, and I left speedily.

People often forget the impact of pensions contributions. In fact MPs and even ministers are very badly treated – their pensions are pro-rata to the length of time they are actually in their hazardous roles and the cost to the State is minimal. But the Prime Minister draws a very reasonable pension (even if only in office for one day) and the additional cost of it is about double the face value of the salary. And why not? The job is onerous, and the risks are enormous. Certainly this Prime Minister earns every penny.

But this is a light aside describing the tail end of a very interesting experience – watching one of the greatest Conservatives entertaining a very Socialist French President. And how well they got on together; quite unlike the chilly atmosphere when I attended a dinner for President Giscard d'Estaing the year before. Of course, the Prime Minister and President Mitterand differ very greatly in political thinking – but they did agree to differ, which was a helpful start; an example of the statesmanship of a lady so often wrongly portrayed by her critics as a narrow-minded dogmatist.

The May 1980 dinner had set the alarm bells ringing, signalling the need for hundreds of millions of pounds. At the end of that year the Plan went in, and frankly when I looked at the size of the figures, I was not sanguine about our chances of securing government approval. The sum of £990 million over two years (with a requirement of £150 million thereafter) looked horrific to me. Admittedly we had the highly successful launch of Metro under our belts, and we had implemented all the physical actions laid down in our 1980 Plan, including the recovery programme announced in September 1979 and the working practices reform package, which was already bringing about tangible improvements in productivity. We had also set in hand a reorganisation which would sub-divide BL into four distinct operating groups – Cars, Unipart, Leyland and Land Rover. This was the logical next step in our plans for decentralisation, but it was also attractive to the Government in facilitating later privatisation and insulating the effects of a major strike in the volume cars business, from other parts of BL. We also set up Jaguar as a separate entity within the Cars operations, alongside what was to become Austin Rover.

My reason for being pessimistic about the funds was that the right-wing opponents of BL seemed to hold a formidable hand. The need for as much as £990 million sprang from a massive deterioration in BL's trading position (arguably attributable mainly to the Government's economic policies) which was likely to lead to total losses, after tax and extraordinary items, of over £500 million in 1980. The Board had therefore been unable to make a positive recommendation for the funds – it had simply said that a real prospect of recovery remained if the funds were provided, but that it could not oppose a government decision to close the business. This was the only honest course open to us. We had 'gone for broke' by insisting on a two-year period of committed funding to give us stability to plan ahead and encourage our hard-pressed dealer network – this was vital commercially, but the combined funding request added to the risk of the political decision going against us. The public expenditure constraints on the Government were still severe, given their overall economic policy, and there was some distrust of the BL Board on the part of some ministers. They felt, under the terms of the published letter I wrote to Sir Keith Joseph at the time of the funding decision a year previously, that we should have shut down when our financial performance deteriorated during 1980 – even though we had stayed within the Government funding limit for the year, and were achieving many of our physical targets. Finally, there was the thorny subject of privatisation, which by now had replaced employee relations as the Government's number one concern, in the arena of public sector industry.

It was in some respects surprising that privatisation should have become an issue between the BL Board and a Conservative Government. Shortly after my appointment to BL, I found myself saying to James Callaghan, 'I must be frank, I don't believe in state ownership of industry, but I will do my very best to bring about BL's recovery, regardless of who owns it', or words to that effect. The rest of the Board have always favoured free enterprise, and our ultimate aim has always been to return BL to the private sector. Unfortunately, the political and the commercial time-frames for achieving this did not match. The Conservative Government's time-frame was set by the four- to five-year duration of a Parliament; in addition, they looked to disposals as a short-term means of alleviating the burden of funding BL. The commercial reality, however, was that BL as a whole could not recover in time to attract significant private capital before the General Election in 1983/84. In these circumstances, the BL Board was still willing to take action in the shorter term where this was feasible – through the disposal of surplus assets and non-mainstream businesses such as Alvis, Coventry Climax and Prestcold, which raised no less than £53 million in 1981 alone. But it was not sensible to pursue privatisation in ways which put our recovery programme at risk – for example, by selling a business which was not separable from the rest without serious damage, or by selling prematurely when the price would be so low as to reduce BL's cash flow or seriously weaken its balance sheet. We also had over 80,000 private shareholders to consider.

The only justification for privatisation at the expense of recovery would have been if BL had no real chance of surviving and becoming profitable, and in the dark days of 1980, I'm sure there were several ministers who took precisely this view. Even then, to break up BL and try to sell off the bits, offered no easy way out for the Government. It was inconceivable that a buyer would have come forward for the whole of BL – even if the Government had paid them a substantial dowry to take it (which some ministers might well have been willing to do)! Nor could many of the individual units have been sold, and certainly not at worthwhile prices – the uncompetitiveness of the British economy combined with the worldwide recession in the motor industry saw to that.

Occasionally, prospective buyers came forward for particular pieces of our business without having adequately informed themselves of the true state or size or value of those businesses. The interest of Aston Martin Lagonda in MG, and of David Brown in Leyland Vehicles, were two well-publicised examples. Rumours of buyers for Land Rover and Jaguar arose from time to time in Whitehall or in the press. On each occasion, we faced a political flurry – but on closer inspection of the realities, the interest, or rumour of interest, invariably evaporated. The entrepreneurs had under-estimated the funds required.

So privatisation offered no real escape from the bulk of the cost of closing BL, if the Government had chosen not to support the Plan. But the Government's gradual realisation of this did not remove the difference of emphasis on our fundamental objectives – the Government's priorities tended to be privatisation (with recovery important but secondary) while the Board believed that further recovery had to be achieved *before* privatisation could become feasible. (Given adequate recovery, the Board were at one with the Government, that private ownership was preferable to state control.)

The processing of a BL Corporate Plan through the Government machine starts with a detailed examination of the Plan by an inter-departmental committee of civil servants, who then make recommendations to the appropriate ministerial Cabinet Committee. While the examination our 1981 Plan and £990 million funding request was still in progress, I was surprised to be asked informally by Sir Keith Joseph if I would be prepared to stay on as Chairman beyond my original secondment, which was due to end on the 31st March, 1981. (The secondment had already been extended for a few months beyond the initial three-year period.) The question surprised me because I had expected the Government to reach a view on our Plan before deciding whether or not I was the right person to carry it forward. But Sir Keith Joseph seemed to feel that, if the Board attached importance to an assurance of funding over a two-year period (to achieve stability) then I should be prepared to see this period through, until around the end of 1982. I was also surprised for another reason. The question seemed to give us a bargaining counter – if I and the Board wanted to use it. The Board saw it that way, and so did I.

I pondered long and hard, for I had been determined not to be involved in the public sector for longer than three years. On the other hand, I felt that I owed it to my BL colleagues to stay on, for three specific reasons. First, it was clear that our chances of securing the £990 million we then sought from the Government, would be much greater if there was no early discontinuity at the top. Second, although we had made progress, it was clear that what I had hoped to see done in three years, would in the event take all of five years. Third, we were being put under great pressure immediately to dispose of parts of our mainstream business – this I saw as a dangerous step from a timing point of view. Better to get the business back on its feet, than risk the disruption and loss of confidence were we prematurely to sell the jewels in the crown. If I was really wanted – which surprised me in some ways – perhaps there was a trade-off? I would not have raised the subject – it was distasteful to make myself the subject of a 'horse-deal' – but given that I was being invited to stay on, it seemed reasonable to explain the circumstances in which I would do so. I put the matter to the BL Board, and they pressed me to accept the offer, and to make it conditional. In fact they felt so strongly about the need to avoid hasty sell-offs that they asked to be associated with my letter, in which I said that I would consider staying on if we received an assurance of government funding for a reasonable period ahead, and were not forced to commit ourselves to any premature outright sale of our mainstream businesses.

I sent my letter to the Secretary of State on the 4th December. I don't think its message was very welcome in some quarters – phrases like 'a gun to the head' were afterwards quoted to me. This was never the intention. But it certainly stirred things up, and there were distinct signs of progress when I was invited to see a group of senior ministers a few days before Christmas. This was in Sir Keith Joseph's office, where the BL team of David Andrews, Frank Fitzpatrick and I faced a barrage of questions from John Biffen, John Nott, James Prior and Sir Keith Joseph. They were to report back later that day to the Prime Minister and the Chancellor of the Exchequer, and I left the meeting believing they knew all they needed to know about the Plan, and the Board's thinking, in order to reach their decision.

However, to our surprise, no decision was forthcoming before ministers departed for their Christmas and New Year break, although it later emerged from leaks to the press that only John Nott had stood out against approval of our funds. There was of course little enthusiasm for supporting BL, but the political and commercial realities were beginning to be recognised by his colleagues. Yet apparently the temptation to defer the decision had been too great. I was deeply disappointed that we could not now hope for a decision until after Parliament had returned in January – three months after we had submitted our Plan to the Government. I went to South Africa to spend Christmas at home – the holiday was not a relaxed one, with the Sword of Damocles poised above, and I was conscious of the damage being done in the market place – uncertainty kills businesses.

The lack of a decision was much publicised, and the uncertainty played on the minds of our managers, workforce, dealers and indeed everyone whose support was needed to keep BL going. I was heartened by the news in early January that John Nott was being reshuffled from Trade to Defence. Perhaps we could now get on with running the business! But I had not taken into account the effects of a lengthy break. Ministerial doubts had been nurtured by further reflection, and Sir Keith Joseph, in particular, had had a change of heart. Ministers met again under the Prime Minister's chairmanship. I know that Sir Keith Joseph had advocated to colleagues that the Government should support the BL Corporate Plan for 1982 onwards – indeed I was told later by a Cabinet member that a paper to this effect had been circulated to ministers before the meeting, and was therefore in front of ministers around the Cabinet table. The paper said, 'give them the money,' and Sir Keith Joseph – in what would otherwise have been a preamble to support the argument – said, 'I don't support the case!' By this time, after weeks of discussion, including debate between groups of Cabinet members and the Board, almost everyone around that table was a supporter or had been converted. Some saw the funding as the lesser of two evils. But there was no heavyweight view opposing the funds – only, but unbelievably the Secretary of State for Industry himself!

Why did he do it? He did it because at the end of the day he was too honest to do otherwise. Keith Joseph the man, does not believe in public support for loss-making industry, whatever its likelihood of ultimate recovery; he is not in favour of Government being involved in anything or any business that 'need not' concern the State – in short, funding BL was anathema to him, as indeed it was to some of his colleagues. The difference is that others were prepared to subordinate their fundamental philosophy to political reality, and Sir Keith Joseph was not. Admittedly, he had been prepared to follow the 'political' route at first – but he had since persuaded himself that he was not being true to his ideals, his basic doctrine – and who would deny that? He repented, and he did what his conscience demanded.

Sir Keith Joseph's volte-face seemed to turn the ministerial mood against us and we were not at first told that the decision, *in principle*, had gone our way – indeed, the outcome of the ministerial meeting was not revealed to me until some time later. Instead we were greeted with a stony silence by the civil servants, and with a summons to meet the Chancellor of the Exchequer and the Secretary of State for Industry at 7.30 pm on the 20th January, 1981. Although the Prime Minister's office had asked me to stand by to see her, she changed her mind and 'delegated' the task. She had reserved all the final decision-making powers to herself, but had helpfully 'delegated' to the right minister, for Sir Geoffrey Howe's common-sense proved to be a major factor in overcoming what had the makings of a crisis. At that point, all I knew was what the two ministers told me at Number 11 Downing Street that evening. They said that the scale of the funding requested by BL was considered 'horrific', and asked whether the Board would give a public commitment to seek to sell BL or merge with another manufacturer as soon as possible, in order to relieve the Government of this enormous burden. I explained once more that there was no easy way out for the Government, and that the Board could not hope to manage the business sucessfully while at the same time advertising it for sale. If the Government decided to close the business, then the Board would accept the right of our 99% shareholder to take such a decision, and would cooperate as required. This has been the Board's position throughout – we would not have resigned and walked away from a firm decision to close the business. In appropriate circumstances, we were prepared to see the closure through. On the other hand, if our employees, dealers, bankers and potential collaborative partners could be given confidence by a commitment to two years of funding, there were positive opportunities for further collaboration and for bringing in private sector equity capital as BL's recovery progressed. The discussion progressed, and I could feel the attitude of the two ministers moderating, as the commercial realities were brought out once again. Having anticipated some of their concerns, I was able to give them two notes describing what we would be prepared to say publicly about collaboration and two-year funding to ease their presentation problems. While it was all rather hypothetical, because they had to report back to their colleagues, the meeting ended with my being asked to provide a draft public statement, (to be endorsed by the BL Board) which would help the Government to handle the approval of the funds in the House of Commons, if that was to be the outcome. The meeting was something of an anti climax.

Although no decision was taken then, that meeting proved to be the turning point, in firming up on the Cabinet's tentative decision to back us. But even the next six days were by no means plain sailing! Having agreed the principles with senior ministers, I was amazed to hear by telephone on Friday evening, 23rd January, that the Prime Minister had got her teeth into the various draft statements which were due to be issued publicly on the 26th January and that she had made extensive changes which once again raised major issues of principle, for she wanted privatisation to have precedence over recovery of the business. At the time I was at the Dowty Group prize-giving ceremony in Cheltenham (at the invitation of their Chairman – one of our Board members, Sir Robert Hunt) and this occasion was disrupted by a number of telephone calls for me, as we tried unsuccessfully to resolve the problem that evening. We finally arranged a negotiating session with Sir Peter Carey at my home for the next day, Saturday.

The situation would have been difficult for any constitutionalist to comprehend. It seemed that having decided in the appropriate ministerial Committee to support our funding, the Prime Minister must have separately summoned officials to Number 10, apparently without any collective ministerial presence, to tell them of the significant changes in the business objectives she wanted them to negotiate with me – changes which in our view would have eroded the authority of the BL Board to carry through the recovery programme. In our view the act of privatising could severely inhibit recovery of the business. At my Saturday afternoon meeting with Sir

Peter Carey, his great ingenuity at drafting, as well as hours of argument, had to be employed to meet the Prime Minister's wishes as far as possible without undermining the Board's authority. Then we had 24 hours of waiting while the outcome of our discussions was sent out to Chequers for approval.

And so we had yet another unique experience at BL; a Secretary of State winning vast sums of money for the company's Recovery Plan, against his own wishes. Sir Keith Joseph did not enjoy the announcement he had to make to his own backbenchers on further funding for BL. His discomfiture showed, and I sympathised with him. But I too was about to face his backbenchers, for immediately after Sir Keith Joseph's announcement I happened to have a long-standing commitment to address the Conservative Industry Committee. In view of the sum involved – £990 million, actually approved, and a Corporate Plan which envisaged a further £150 million – the timing was opportune, for it seemed only right to give the backbench Committee an early opportunity to question us on the company's plans and actions. It was not for us to justify the Government's decision to provide the funds, but we owed it to groups of MPs – particularly hostile ones – to explain why we had sought these massive sums of money, and how we proposed to use them.

Accompanied by senior colleagues, I went to the meeting knowing that the far right wing were resentful about the Government's decision, and were somewhat puzzled at Sir Keith Joseph's apparent acquiescence in the process. In presenting the decision to the House of Commons, he had been absolutely loyal to the principle of collective Cabinet responsibility, and gave no hint of his personal contribution to the debate; but the agony of the conflict with his own personal principles, combined with the extreme reluctance of the Government as a whole to provide financial and even moral support for the company, had come screaming through. There was, therefore, a case for mollifying the backbenchers – cooling their tempers, and winning them over. The fact that we did not attempt this, that we took an entirely different tack, was due to a number of incidents that had occurred in the recent past. For example, in spite of all the pious exhortations that the public sector should behave commercially, 70 Conservative backbenchers had signed a motion *opposing* the closure of MG, completely ignoring the fact that it was losing money at the rate of £26 million a year. Furthermore, while we were trying to build bridges with the unions, having had a fairly torrid time over the past two years, right-wing MPs had (unwittingly I like to think) made extremely provocative statements on a variety of subjects, which had the effect of worsening relationships between management and workforce. We felt that we had been forthright, and certainly not soft, in our dealings with shop stewards and others; this was our job – no one else's! Gratuitous criticism of our employees by the right wing, or anyone else, was superfluous and downright unhelpful. Furthermore, much of the criticism was destructive and was hurting us in the market place – at home and abroad. This was the real problem and the one I planned to focus on that evening. At that time, January 1981, I found the extreme right wing just as unhelpful to our cause as the extreme left – hence the calculated aggression which went into the Industry Committee speech. My opening remarks reflected the frustration we felt at the time:

> Our job at BL is to run a business. Running that business is an uphill slog at the best of times. When, however, we are beset by extremist influences, whether they are Derek Robinsons or extremists on either side of the political spectrum, it makes the task that lot harder. Divisiveness in Britain makes world headlines; above all we lack and need greater unity of purpose. I for one am sick and tired of destructive criticism that makes it easier for our world competitors to sell against us. Because we are not militants or politicians we turn the other cheek in public – and despite the damaging effect on our market share and public confidence – we get on with running the business.

> The militants and the media we expect. It is surprising, however, to get uninformed, unconstructive criticism from people in this room, even when your own colleagues in the Government decide to keep us going. The Government owns the business – we have the unenviable task of running it. If the roles were reversed I wonder what you would do differently to what we have done.

I then proceeded to list the progress and achievements we had made in the previous three years, like drastic job reductions, low wage awards, large-scale closures and confronting militant elements in

the face of a sceptical public – including a number of MPs. To head
off the 'privatisation at any cost' political faction, I continued:

Can you expect the Board or the Government to reward a
moderate pay settlement, the most far-reaching reform of
working practices arguably ever introduced in the western world, the launching on time of the successful Mini
Metro, and the remarkable strike-free performance in
1980 . . . to reward all this by kicking all that into touch
and by kicking not the militants but the sensible average
employee in the teeth? No wonder the Cabinet decided
against closing the business at this time and in these
circumstances, despite the £990 million bill.

Given that, is there not some merit in pulling together
and *backing* the efforts of our managers to succeed? Let's
be clear, the BL Board has the objective of injecting
private equity and involving the private sector in our
business, but it must be on the basis of sound commercial
judgment. It is the Board's overriding objective to reduce
and eventually be free of State funding. But piece-meal,
ill-timed sell-offs are not the way. There is simply no
queue of buyers waiting for the 'sale of the century'.
Peripheral parts of the business have been up for sale for
more than two years with no dramatic cash intake as yet.
(Look at what has happened to the erstwhile MG bidder,
Aston Martin.)

It is pie in the sky to believe that any major unprofitable
part of BL is ready yet to return to the private sector, on
its own. As to the profitable parts – we need the attractive
parts of the business to attract the strategic collaboration
we are actively seeking as a major plank of the recovery
programme, and to fund our cash flow.

But confidence is the key – confidence of customer,
supplier, bankers, dealers, potential partners in collaboration; and there can be no confidence in BL's future
if there is constant sniping and pressure for disposals. As
we told ministers you cannot run a loss maker and try to
secure recovery while large potential chunks are being
advertised for sale. Try it. I promise you it is not on.

We can take constructive criticism – we cannot take

being a whipping boy for political dogma of any colour. BL's New Year resolution was to try harder. I hope some of you will endeavour not to – otherwise you may well neutralise our efforts. Please, can we now channel our efforts into making it work, rather than joining the lemmings in their rush to go over the top . . . For God's sake can we not have unity instead of continual divisiveness?

I have to admit my speech was not received with enthusiasm. I must also concede that those present gave me a fair hearing, and in the debate that followed they gave as good as they received!

The next day Spike Milligan wrote to me – he frequently writes encouraging letters – and pointed out that £990 million was a great deal of money. Could I spare some? I wrote back explaining that BL needed the whole £990 million, but I had a few quid to spare, and he was welcome to half of it. 'Herewith a fiver.' Since that date he periodically writes to invite me to dinner, and invariably encloses a pound note. That fiver will end up as one of my better investments.

That same week the Prime Minister unwittingly supported what I had said to her backbenchers, in an interview on ITV's 'Weekend World':

> Does it really seem to be the time to say to them, no I'm going to chop you off at the stocking tops when you've got a new car, [Metro] you're getting enormously increased improvements in productivity, you are in fact not having more people than is necessary to do the job, you're getting rid of your wreckers, you've got a new spirit of cooperation, and I know that many, many good firms in the motor car component industry, which is a very good industry, supply British Leyland . . . It was a difficult decision, I don't conceal that . . . I never want to take on another British Leyland. We shouldn't be in it at all, but now we're in it we have to choose the time and we have to back Michael Edwardes's judgment. He's the manager. I'm not the manager.

Then, and more particularly later when Patrick Jenkin succeeded Sir Keith Joseph as Secretary of State for Industry, I wished that the recognition of who was responsible for managing the business was always as clear as it appeared in her statement. But she had expressed the Government's dilemma precisely. I had hoped for less grudging support. But we had achieved what the press saw as something of a miracle in extracting such a major funding commitment from an understandably reluctant Government.

We had won the battle but not the war; we had won it by suppressing the difference of emphasis between the Board and the Government on objectives. We had not met, and could not meet, the Government's early aspirations on privatisation; but, in giving way to the commercial realities and to the 'threat' (as they regrettably saw it) in my letter of the 4th December, 1980, concerning my personal position, ministers had by no means been converted to the Board's point of view. Yet in agreeing to stay on until the end of 1982 (as part of the funding package) I had given myself a further task – to clear the air with the Government, so that my successor would inherit an atmosphere of mutual confidence and shared objectives.

There followed several months of relative calm in our relations with the Government. From January 1981, Sir Keith Joseph was supported at the Department of Industry by a very able Minister of State in Norman Tebbit. They made a good team. Sir Keith Joseph set the pattern of non-intervention, while on issues in which the Government really needed to be involved, Norman Tebbit provided a high level of understanding and realism, mixed with an appropriate toughness. He was also very probing.

This grasp of the situation helped us in particular over an awkward hiatus in the affairs of the Leyland Group, which looked after our worldwide truck and bus activities. The Board had been unable to approve the Leyland section of our 1981 Corporate Plan, and we had moved David Andrews and Ron Hancock to the Chairman and Managing Director roles at the beginning of 1981, and had asked them to take a new look at the whole strategy and management of that business – since the extent of its fundamental problems had not been fully appreciated by its own operating management. We had promised the Government a revised Plan by mid-1981, but by that time David Andrews and Ron Hancock were still only just getting to grips with the problem, and were some way short of a satisfactory solution. Eventually, they came up with their radical restructuring package in November. We owed much to the understanding of ministers and civil servants at the Department of

Industry that they continued to fund the Leyland Plan, despite the heavy losses of Leyland Trucks throughout 1981, and in the absence of a convincing recovery strategy. They realised we needed time, and they had the courage to face criticism while we thought it through. That we did is to the credit of David Andrews and his team.

In June of 1981, I proposed to Sir Keith Joseph that we should split BL into two free-standing companies, with two Boards; the Chief Executive of each would be supported by a non-executive Chairman drawn from the existing BL Board. This would make the two groupings – Cars and Land Rover-Leyland – self-sufficient and would thus be a logical extension of the delegation of authority which was progressively being made to my executive colleagues. It also provided greater insulation against major industrial disruption in one or other entity. This could well save half the company in the event of forced closure of one of the businesses. The proposal also had the great merit of spreading the top job across four broad shoulders – a technique which was in my view helpful if not vital to ensure ultimate recovery. It could not be right to continue to place an excessive burden on one man, now that the major painful actions had been driven through. At the same time, the proposal provided for the maximum possible continuity at the top of BL, which would be valued by our dealers, bankers and collaborative partners on whose confidence we depended. Sir Keith Joseph talked to colleagues, but there was no feedback.

In September 1981 both Sir Keith Joseph and Norman Tebbit were 'reshuffled', and I was sad to see them go. Nevertheless, my first impressions of Sir Keith's successor, Patrick Jenkin, were favourable. An introductory chat turned into a lengthy review of all the main BL issues, and I found it refreshing to be dealing with a pragmatist after the philosophical agonies which had afflicted his predecessor. Unfortunately, I was soon to discover that this pragmatic and politically sensitive approach had its disadvantages. The new Secretary of State turned out to have very little concept of, or even interest in, the strategic framework of the Government's relationship with a high-calibre Board of a state-owned company. He therefore lacked any instinctive check on the political temptation to intervene in our affairs.

Intervention therefore grew substantially, on a variety of issues which I felt were the responsibility of management. I often wondered whether the Prime Minister would have approved of the change of style at the Department of Industry, had she been aware of it – which I suspect she was not. The Secretary of State (although otherwise good about leaving employee relations to us) sought to influence the company at the crisis point of our November 1981 pay dispute; he intervened in our commercial negotiations with British Steel; he twice rejected our proposal to appoint an additional non-executive director to the BL Board; and he queried the company's right to take proposed legal tax avoidance action! The latter episode (which was to cost the Treasury some millions of pounds) provoked me to write a letter inviting him to ponder on the fundamental principles of the Government/BL relationship. Propriety does not permit me to quote from the letter, but I pointed out that whenever the Government intervened in commercial matters, it made it far more difficult to attract and hold first-rate managers. It caused entrepreneurial managers to eschew the public sector, and showed if the Government really did intend to leave commercial matters to the BL Board, then it should refrain from intervening not only when the Board does things the Government applauds – but also when it does things ministers happen to dislike.

Regrettably, Whitehall is always subject to the temptation to want to run the industries which it owns, and the capacity of Chairmen to deter or fend off such interventions declines as the end of their term of office draws near. I am sure that Patrick Jenkin's learning curve, combined with the appointment of my successor, has brought the Government/BL relationship on these secondary commercial issues back onto an even keel.

Some weeks after Patrick Jenkin had taken up his appointment, I told him that the question of my succession was now an urgent matter. With little more than twelve months to go before I stepped down as Chairman, it was important to provide stability and avoid speculation. He seemed to be unaware that this issue was on the table; which was fair enough for there were many issues requiring an incoming Secretary of State's attention. But the tensions caused by the change of approach in the latter half of 1981 made it very difficult to settle the broad strategy for the future of BL after my departure; a process of pressing the Government for organisation and succession decisions, which absorbed an excessive amount of my time for well over a year. Had the Government left these matters to the Board, they would have been settled in weeks.

But out of these discussions it emerged that we now had two

separate concepts – the Government were further heightening the priority they attached to privatisation, which was at odds with the objectives of the BL Board – objectives agreed only ten months earlier with the Chancellor of the Exchequer and Sir Keith Joseph which saw commercial recovery as a pre-requisite of privatisation, and which had been contained in the 1981 Plan approved by Parliament. Indeed, as this debate started the 1982 Plan was already on Patrick Jenkin's desk, and with hindsight it seems odd that the 1982 Plan was allowed to go through the Cabinet as smoothly as it did, with the Board's objectives still intact. Our strategy clearly stated that we would bring in minority shareholdings *in due course*, but we would not sell off major parts of the business, while we persevered with recovery as the main objective.

The 1982 Plan was consistent with the 1981 Plan in terms of funding needs as well as objectives, and the Government no doubt felt that in view of their two-year funding commitment (in January 1981) they had little choice but to let it go ahead. But when in January 1982 I pressed for an answer to my proposals for succession and organisation, the debate about objectives restarted in earnest. Although Patrick Jenkin and his Minister of State Norman Lamont argued strongly for the split on the grounds that the original Leyland merger was ill-conceived, they were turned down by ministerial colleagues. Consultants were to look at the organisation against the Government's privatisation objective. The BL Board and the Department were to be second-guessed.

Their subsequent report recommended *against* the split into two companies; they concluded it would *inhibit* privatisation.

The consultants' report recommended against the proposed split into two companies, because it was felt that this would inhibit privatisation – an incredible conclusion which I have never understood. We felt that the opposite was the case! Even more incredibly the report recommended that I should stay on as Chairman – incredible not only because it was my firm decision to go which had sparked off this whole debate, but also because they were questioning my judgment (and the Board's) on fundamental issues, and yet still believed that I should continue as Chairman! The consultants argued that, if I did not stay on, BL needed a full-time executive Chairman. I disagreed strongly, on the grounds that we now had the opportunity to move away from the excessive focus on BL and its Chairman, which was to the detriment of our individual 'decentralised' operating companies, and therefore to the recovery of the company. The business was under tighter control than it had been for many years, and day-to-day running of the business had been properly delegated – there was no longer the need for a high-profile executive Chairman.

When ministers met to consider the consultants' report, they came no nearer to endorsing its organisational recommendations than they had come to approving my own proposals. Their attention concentrated instead on privatisation. The consultants' report had a nasty sting in its tail; *en passant*, it said that the only part of BL which was readily saleable was Land Rover. This was outside the consultants' remit, and indeed constituted a . major commercial judgment based on limited experience and only four weeks of study. I responded to it by agreeing with the Secretary of State to commission an internal BL study working with our merchant bank advisers, to determine the full implications of selling Land Rover. However, ministers seized upon the consultants' throw-away line gratefully, without waiting for BL's in-depth study and the idea was debated at the highest level by the Government. Couldn't BL sell Land Rover quickly and thereby raise funds to obviate the need for the remaining £150 million of government funding envisaged for 1983 and 1984 in the Corporate Plan? Several birds would thus be killed with one stone – and all before the next General Election.

It took three months of hard argument in a very tense atmosphere to show that this was not in any sense a realistic plan. In addition to our own study which showed the impact on the rest of the business of the sale of Land Rover, we eventually had to commission the services of *two* merchant banks to demonstrate that in the short term the proceeds of such a sale would not be sufficient to relieve the Government of any of our forecast funding requirement. This arose because of the cash flow BL would lose from the separation of Land Rover. Indeed, the Government would probably have faced additional funding requests because of the loss of synergy between Land Rover and other parts of the business, plus the adverse impact of such a sale on confidence in BL.

The Board also had the interests of our 80,000 minority shareholders to consider, as well as the understanding we had with our bankers that the business would be run on commercial lines – and that we would not dispose of assets which provided security for their loans to us! In any case, we couldn't simply sell the business below 'book' value, which is what was implied. We could not depend solely on the negative side of the argument. We had to show that the continuing recovery of the business would make possible the ultimate return of all of BL to the private sector in a commercially sensible way. We also sketched out how we could make early progress towards this end by attracting private capital into our more profitable businesses.

As letters flashed backwards and forwards and meeting succeeded meeting on this issue, I feared for a long time that political dogma would overcome commercial sense and that ministers would use the obvious means of imposing their will, by looking for a new Chairman from outside the Board who shared their ideals and would 'do as he was told.' However, it was clear that such a Chairman would be difficult to find and would be most unlikely to be of the calibre to command the loyalty of the Board and senior management of BL. Rumours of a Government short list reached me which made my hair stand on end!

Thankfully the weight of our argument ultimately prevailed. At a meeting between Patrick Jenkin and the BL Board on the 6th July (for which the ground had been well prepared in advance by various informal contacts, particularly involving Jeffrey Sterling, a realistic and down-to-earth businessman recently appointed as Patrick Jenkin's special industrial adviser), a mutual understanding was reached. Ministers agreed that the Board's approach to privatisation was acceptable. We had not resorted to threats of resignation but had genuinely persuaded ministers that ours was the more sensible course. It is to the credit of Patrick Jenkin and his colleagues that they were open minded enough to be persuaded against their preferred course of action. The air had been cleared by the 'peace treaty'.

My relief at this conclusion was heightened by the outcome of the parallel discussions on succession and organisation. In order to concentrate on the fight against premature privatisation, we had decided not to press a reluctant Government on the case for a complete split into two companies. The Prime Minister (and some of her close colleagues) seemed to prefer a strategic overlay at the BL level – one board rather than two – to distance government from operational involvement, and in addition, they were concerned that the financial and legal work which would be involved in a complete split would be considerable. I accepted their point of view, with the proviso that the new Chairman was non-executive, so that the chief executives of each division would be free to develop the separate identities of their businesses within the umbrella of BL. Patrick Jenkin readily agreed to this concept, and as we approached agreement on the privatisation issue the Government specifically requested that one of the present Board should be prepared to take over the Chairmanship, so that there would be continuity in implementing the agreed objectives.

This brought the wheel full circle, since one of my main aims at the outset of the debate had been to maximise continuity. At Patrick Jenkin's request, I was delighted to take on, and eventually succeed in, the task of persuading Sir Austin Bide to accept the job, and Sir Robert Hunt agreed to act as Deputy Chairman. The pieces of the jigsaw had fallen into place. Although the long debate with the Government had delayed the announcement of the succession and organisational changes until the 1st September, 1982, this was still quite well in advance of the normal last-minute appointments of public sector Chairmen. Even more important was the absence of any leaks to the press throughout the long period of argument with the Government, which was to the credit of ministers and officials. Uncertainty amongst management about the succession issue was inevitable, and public exposure of debate about privatisation in its critical phase would have done great damage inside and outside the company. BL had been through one of its most serious crises without more than a handful of its employees fully realising it. As it was, there was some nervousness at my impending departure – not I think for any reason except the obvious one that uncertainty is not good for morale.

Is it possible to draw any general conclusions from this experience in dealing with government? It is perhaps unwise to generalise from the unique situation of BL, but the experience has left me with a number of clear impressions.

First, my conviction has been heavily reinforced that government should not own industry, except where absolutely necessary. Politics and business don't mix. Business cannot cope with changes of objectives in midstream, or with the shortness of political time horizons. Politics, with its focus on the day-to-day events which catch the headlines, cannot cope with the ups and downs of a company like BL, generating pressures to intervene to which ministers cannot and should not bow. Both politicians and businessmen find involvement with each other time-consuming and distracting from their more central tasks. *They are generally not on the same wavelength.* (In Patrick Jenkin's case it might have just been that he had little knowledge of the motor industry; when I met him during the 1982 Conservative Party Conference at Brighton I was within a month of leaving BL and we spoke of my forthcoming involvement in telecommunications as Chairman of Mercury Communications, I was surprised at his grasp of that subject and his perception of how the industry might develop. This despite the fact that his Minister of State, Kenneth Baker, quite rightly makes so much of the running in this field and in the application of new technology.)

Second, I had great sympathy with the Government in that its freedom of action in BL's case was almost zero. In the case of the traditional nationalised industry – the monopolistic utility – the Government can, to some extent, if it so wishes, regulate the affairs of the industry, for example through cash or pricing constraints, in line with its wider policy objectives. But for a company in trouble within a highly competitive worldwide industry, there tends to be only one possible route to recovery which rests on a number of tricky commercial judgments, and which generates an inescapable level of external funding requirements. This is tantamount to stepping through a minefield, with but one benign pathway. The Government can never assemble the necessary expertise, experience and information to 'second-guess' a Board's plans, and even its funding decisions are to all intents and purposes made for it. The only alternatives are to change the Board or to close the business. These were real alternatives in BL's case, but of course the one would have been drastic and the other extremely expensive. To be constantly presented with 'all or nothing' decisions is extremely frustrating for any government, and this combined with the day-to-day political pressures is bound to make the government/company relationship an uneasy one.

Nevertheless, my third outstanding impression is of the high intellect, conscientiousness and flexibility of all the civil servants with whom I dealt during the five years. During the difficult year which followed Patrick Jenkin's appointment as Secretary of State, the BL/Government relationship still worked in practice because the key people in Whitehall made up in intellectual skill what they lacked in managerial experience – and were prepared to make greater use of informal channels of communication to help us through our difficulties, rather than resting solely on the formal procedures for monitoring and approval set out in our *Memorandum of Understanding*. Because the borderline between the Government's and the management's preserve in the state-owned industries can never be absolutely clear, there was inevitably the occasional disagreement over what BL saw as unwarranted intervention, but the pressures on civil servants answerable for large sums of public money were understandable. Also important was their willingness during our battles with both governments to interpret their constitutional duty to ministers in its widest sense – not blind loyalty, but a constructive desire to find a way through to a result which was commercially as well as politically sensible.

In slight contrast, my fourth conclusion deals with a subject that I touched on at the beginning of this book. There is a tendency for managers and workforce in the public sector to relax the normal commercial disciplines: the mere fact of a government standing behind a company has this effect. My BL experience, however, leads me to the view that it is a simple admission of management failure to allow discipline to go by the board, merely because a company is state-owned.

Competition proved a considerable spur once an entrepreneurial ethos was established at BL, but even in more monopolistic organisations people always want to be seen to perform well and are thus capable of being stimulated into action if they see tangible fruits coming from their labours. No Board or manager should be let off the hook simply because a business is in the public sector. Similarly, the dramatic improvements in productivity in BL's car business over the last two years show what a public sector workforce can do when led by properly motivated and confident management. At no time did we allow government funding to be seen as a safety net against failure. In fact, it acted as a spur to success. The more serious problem in dealing with government in our experience was the danger that top management would become distracted from its internal tasks by the burden of meeting government's political and bureaucratic requirements. By concentrating our dealings with government on a small group of people in BL headquarters, we tried to minimise this, but I was on many occasions concerned at the amount of valuable Board time which was absorbed by government issues. This left insufficient time to be outward looking. While companies are controlled by the state, there is no ready solution to this – one can only be vigilant to the danger, and hope that politicians will become increasingly aware of their impact.

Finally, I believe that all these factors point to the need for government to subordinate other concerns about public sector industries to the absolute priority of recruiting and keeping high-calibre chairmen, and Boards, to run these industries – since this will be the chief determinant of success or failure. This means paying the going rate in the business world and allowing these Boards very great freedom of action. Neither of these precepts is easy to follow politically; and this course of action does not guarantee success, since sometimes the crucial choice of chairman or senior executives will turn out to have been wrong. But it is surely better to take the risk (and when necessary change the man!) than to perpetuate the mess which has been made of the British Government's ownership of industry over the last 20 years.

Here I must pay tribute to Margaret Thatcher. At no stage did she show the slightest inclination to interfere in our employee relations issues; even when we were in a crisis I had complete confidence that she would stand back and quite properly let us wrestle with the problem. Some of her lieutenants might have wanted to 'second-guess' us on these occasions – but never the Prime Minister. She knew our credibility would quickly erode if the government engaged in the commercial jungle that was ours to oversee. To be fair, apart from the one instance described earlier, neither Sir Keith Joseph nor Patrick Jenkin fell into the trap of becoming involved in employee relations crises. Like Eric Varley before them, they understood that intervention of this nature would only undermine the authority of the company. Next to the funds which the Prime Minister made available, the key factor in giving BL a fighting chance was that government should give us the space, the headroom, to resolve our employee and other commercial problems. This meant appointing the right Board and letting it get on with the job, even if it meant having to listen to the appointees voicing their concern about government policy – not an easy thing for ministers to live with, even in a democratic society! This Margaret Thatcher did, with no reluctance whatever. At times this must have required willpower and courage on her part.

12

Leadership, Change, and the Public Dimension

That we have a general leadership problem in British industry seems to me to be incontrovertible. Statistics tell the tale: in ten years wages have risen by 315% and productivity by 26%. We simply cannot blame successive governments – it is our job to manage, not theirs. Some pretty drastic changes are clearly needed if our loss of competitiveness is not to come home to roost, in the form of even higher unemployment and a substantial drop in our standard of living. But there are problems – not everyone wants change!

Conservatism – aversion to rapid change – is not the preserve of Conservatives with a capital 'C'. In fact, the present Government is criticised more for its radical actions than its conservatism! – radical actions which are calculated to change the way people think and act. For example, keeping sterling at an unduly high level was a radical action which forced fundamental changes, some of which were very necessary. Conservatism with a small 'c' – the reactionary kind – is not the preserve of a narrow sector of society. It is practised by boards, managers and unions, all with equal gusto. We all do it.

At an Oxford University lecture in 1981 I tried to address the problem of how best to do battle with those reactionary attitudes, wherever they may be – in management or among employees – and I touched on the problem of judging the amount and nature of the change needed. In effect, how does the changer know he is right? The momentum to effect change can snowball out of quite modest beginnings. Not so with BL. The company is at the other end of the spectrum, for we knew that if the Board couldn't bring about change, and quickly, the company would simply evaporate. While some people advocate the 'short, sharp, shock' attitude to change, I cannot regard this as a sensible approach to the management of change for two main reasons.

First, shock treatment may be justified but only if an evolutionary approach has encountered insurmountable resistance. If major changes are already in the process of being accepted – as they are by the vast majority of BL's workforce and indeed by management and trade unions in many other industries – then the application of shock treatment may well set back the very acceptance of change.

Second, the changes we need most in manufacturing industry are bread-and-butter changes of the sort we achieved in BL – acceptance of machinery which requires eight men to do the work previously done by 80, inter-disciplinary maintenance, and other workplace reforms. It does not help in the battle to achieve these changes if they are overlain with a political conflict at the macro-economic level which brings dogma into an essentially commercial and commonsense issue.

To those who have seen BL in the past five years as the practitioner of brinkmanship, all this may sound uncharacteristically cautious. In essence my message is simply: 'change needs to be manageable in order to be managed.' The BL Board was prepared to take unpalatable decisions affecting the whole of the company if circumstances required it. But this was a logical last resort – it could not be the preferred option while there was a reasonable chance of getting BL right.

Nevertheless, there are occasions when change is critically necessary – and when resistance to it really does need to be overcome. Reactionary attitudes, habits and prejudices can be diluted. Human nature being what it is, it is easier to lead a defence of the status quo than to lead people into something new, with all the attendant uncertainties, and the innate fears of the unknown, which change implies. Too frequently, change is seen by both senior, middle management and unionised employees as a personal attack; an attack on people who may have fought long and hard in the past for a particular principle, regardless of its long-term consequences – or even its current relevance.

To overcome inertia one must identify the actions needed and then lead people into facing up to personal responsibility; they must be made directly accountable for specific actions. People need to feel part of an overall strategy and feel they have some responsibility and involvement in decisions which affect them. No amount of table-thumping in the boardroom will achieve optimum performance from senior executives, middle managers or the shop floor if they do not understand the reasoning and accept some responsibility for their own actions. Equally, in public administration no amount of central direction from a Cabinet Minister will achieve the required objective, if the civil service machinery does not identify itself with the objectives and so share accountability for the results. The same goes for every other walk of life.

There is another catalyst for change – space. Not celestial space, but the very down-to-earth space people need within an organisation to carry out their particular contribution. People need to be able to breathe. This is a territorial imperative.

Space can happen (and be filled by anyone), or it can be created by a leader, and filled by the most appropriate person he can find. In that case action for change can be properly delegated. If a leader deliberately creates space and fills it, he will ensure that the person appointed in turn has the self-discipline to provide space for colleagues and subordinates. Simply allowing space, is to cooperate. Leadership requires innovation: that space be created. Equally, if one neither creates space for others nor allows others to use space, one is at best negative and at worst autocratic. A competent manager doesn't operate in that way. He is a team man, usually supported by top flight staff experts. The line manager is the key to change. He has to be positively motivated to play his part in changing attitudes on the shop floor, because he has the toughest job of all – of pushing through new ideas, new working methods, new technology in the face of a sceptical or outright hostile reaction. Therefore, he has to be convinced that he is right. He exists at all levels – from chief executive to foreman.

One of the very encouraging aspects of change within BL has been the way line managers have accepted – not without some initial trepidation – a much broader view of their role. Their jobs used to be narrow and operational – get on with the job in hand, avoid trouble if possible, and if there is a dispute call in the employee relations people. Things are now very different. We established a proper communications channel which involves managers, supervisors and foremen communicating with the workforce and the unions, about issues within the company; this, instead of abdicating responsibility for information dissemination to shop stewards, who often worked in isolation.

The strategy of going direct to employees on matters of importance, began within a few months of the new BL Board and management being appointed. Issues such as job losses, restructuring, changes to working methods were too important to the recovery programme to be passed on through shop stewards at factory floor meetings; or at mass meetings where the objective was not careful deliberation, but a show of hands.

When the 720 employee representatives met the new management team at Kenilworth on the 1st February, 1978, to hear our plans for rescuing the Cars operations, every employee in each of the 36 factories and offices was handed a summary of the proposals before they left work on that day. We also wrote to employees at home and where there was an issue of wider public significance – like the Recovery Plan ballot in September/October 1979 – we used newspaper advertisements to get our message across. This was, of course, in addition to the face-to-face debate between managers and the workforce on the shop floor itself, and in briefing groups.

Inevitably, direct communication from management to individual employees was regarded with deep dismay and anger by some employee representatives, and even by some district, regional, and national officials. It was 'going over the heads' of the elected representatives. But it was in our view, the only way in the early days of getting a fair hearing for management's plans and proposals. The existing process of establishing communication with employees in BL was not straightforward. The participation system of three tiers of consultative councils and committees had a momentum of its own and an ability to generate a paperchase up, down and across the organisation; it really was a wonder to behold. Furthermore, it did not achieve results: the direct message and urgency of action was lost in an administrative treacle.

The first step was to bring to bear on internal communications, the skills which the company possessed through its external communications and public affairs people. The responsibilities for communicating both inside and outside the company were brought together. This had the immediate effect of shortening the internal communication chain, and to elevate its status and importance in the company structure. This was a major shift, for it became clear to people that communication in its widest sense was a matter of direct concern to the Chief Executive; management priorities started to reflect this. The signal had to be given from the top, and the regular weekly meetings I held with groups of managers, either in London or when I visited our various factories, helped to infuse the new direct style of communication into management behaviour. It was not always successful: at the time of the dispute at Longbridge over parity in early 1980 we were slow to react to the campaign of distortion by shop stewards. They quickly convinced the men that they had earned the right to productivity money, when the facts showed otherwise. It took immense efforts by local managers to recoup the situation, but once they got the truth across, the strike was short lived.

Since that time more and more attention has been given to making sure employees receive a balanced view of any particular issue – and not just a union interpretation. They have seen managers move out from behind their desks and go out into the production areas and defend the company's actions on issues like new working methods, the need to increase productivity, the risks inherent in taking unthought-out strike action – and so forth. It has placed extra strain and pressure on those managers, but my assessment is that they were relieved to be able to reassert their managerial role, and regain control of a situation that was in danger of going by default.

I would argue that the manager British industry needs is one whose contribution to his company is two-fold. First, he must be a talented practitioner of his own profession – be he design or production engineer, accountant, chemist or metallurgist. He must have a thorough grasp and control of his direct functions and responsibilities (including his role as communicator) coupled with an appreciation of broad company strategy and direction. Second, if he is in a company which needs fundamental change to survive, he must be prepared to put his job on the line at regular intervals by pushing through contentious issues which could bring the business crashing down around his ears. And this last requirement leads to an attribute without which leadership cannot exist. Courage. If we are to bring British industry back to where it belongs, courage will be needed. This is not a job for compromisers, or for those who lean towards popularity – great courage will be needed, for this is a key attribute of leadership, for the problem solver of today and tomorrow.

Bringing about change in Britain is not easy; but handling the public aspect of change in a large state-controlled company is yet another dimension – it is rather like walking a tightrope. Top executives need to be articulate, and they need to be ready to speak out when the occasion demands. This can mean speaking on matters not immediately concerned with the business, like currency movements and local rates, but which impact on the business indirectly. When BL executives engaged in these debates there were always critics ready to pounce: 'He ought to be spending his time sorting out BL's problems instead of poking his nose into other people's business' – or worst still 'He's simply trying to distract attention from BL's own shortcomings.' As the solid progress being made in BL's recovery strategy became clearer, the second of these charges was made less frequently.

Although a company in trouble is usually more vulnerable to external factors than one that is profitable, I do not believe that any major company can afford to take a myopic view of its environment. Even profitable companies litter their Annual Reports with references to influences which are labelled 'external'. To mention just a small proportion, we read of the world recession, the fluctuations of currencies, the whims of Arab oil producers, the campaigns of the consumer lobby, the intransigence of the trade unions, and so on. BL's public statements have likewise not been entirely free of such references in the past. But how many of these factors are truly external, in the sense that management can do absolutely nothing to influence their impact? In BL, we were forced to rethink our attitude to this question.

The car manufacturer is uniquely placed in the public eye. On the one hand, he is a large employer and contributor to the national economy. Despite its troubles, BL has remained one of Britain's largest net export earners within manufacturing industry, with exports worth around £1,000 million in 1982. Furthermore, the car manufacturer makes a consumer product which is normally the individual's largest single purchase apart from his house – what is more, it is a complex product which (with the best will in the world) sometimes goes wrong. Add to these factors BL's particular circumstances: the entry of BL into public ownership in 1975 and its tradition as an employee relations flashpoint – and it isn't surprising that BL has suffered from considerable political and press exposure. BL cannot hope to hide from the spotlight, whether or not it would like to do so.

Having been engaged in a battle for survival, we were not strong enough just to shrug our shoulders if, for example, an adverse currency movement threatened to cost us tens of millions of pounds.

We had to fight to influence and shape our environment in the same way as we had battled to overcome trades union militancy, and raise productivity in our factories. In Britain, where the British pastime of self-denigration and mutual recrimination continues, regrettably, to prosper, a reference to 'external factors' in an explanation of indifferent results is automatically condemned as a mere excuse for poor internal performance. Perhaps there is some justification for this cynical attitude, since managers are rarely heard to mention external factors when these are working in their favour and producing good results. Not surprisingly, we hear more of external factors during a year of intense recession.

It is no longer sufficient for companies to concentrate on internal efficiency and merely to shelter as far as possible from any adverse influences in their external environment. Is it not essential to be outward-looking, to get in amongst these so-called external influences and try to bring about beneficial change, instead of acting defensively and accepting the political economic and commercial environment as immutable? It was for this reason that I kept up my Board membership of the International Management and Development Institute in Washington, which is plugged into the Washington policy-making scene. As the only European on its Board, I have been able to watch events there at close quarters. And the United States accounts for a useful $500 million of Jaguar sales, every year. For the same general reason I accepted Ray Pennock's invitation to join the President's Committee of the Confederation of British Industry. It was essential to contribute to commercial and trade and economic politics, and furthermore I learned a great deal in the process of contributing. The CBI's influence on events should not be under-estimated, whatever politicians may pretend.

For BL, the British political arena was of overriding importance because the Government controlled the shares in the business. I have described in the two preceding chapters BL's relationship with the Government and Opposition Front Benches. But what about the backbench MPs? One of the early questions we had to ask ourselves was – did they matter? Would it be cost effective to devote scarce expertise at BL to educate MPs in what we were trying to achieve? We had cut the number of people in our Public Relations Department at headquarters from 36 to 5 – we just didn't have the resources, to support a wide-ranging communications programme. Furthermore, it looked like a thankless task. A mass of prejudices confronted us, and in those few cases where there was no prejudice, there was general apathy. This was perhaps understandable in view of the many calls on an MP's time. We had to expect that lengthy written briefings from BL would be quickly and almost universally consigned to House of Commons wastepaper baskets. But it was disconcerting to have attracted only a handful of MPs to visit the pride of British advanced manufacturing technology at the new Metro facility at Longbridge (built with £200 million of taxpayers' money), only to find that the offer of a visit to Renault in France had attracted several times this number of MPs, filling the free places on the Air France planes.

We encountered many other difficulties in the task of briefing MPs. We could not always give them commercially confidential information, particularly after I found that remarks I had made to a supposedly 'private' meeting of MPs were very accurately summarised in the press the next day. In addition, MPs tend to focus, even more intensely than other audiences, on the top man in any organisation and a considerable amount of the Chairman's time is inevitably involved.

But such was the importance of political influence in dealing with BL, that we simply could not afford to keep our distance from Westminster. Quite apart from their impact on the Government and Opposition policies, MPs failed to realise what damage their public statements could do – like the three Conservative MPs who wrote to *The Times* inviting prospective buyers for any parts of BL to apply to them, for onward transmission of their applications to the (Conservative) Secretary of State for Industry. This naive approach frustrated our efforts to bolster the confidence of our hard-pressed dealers and potential collaborative partners. This and other similar incidents required individual briefings of MPs – MPs from the whole political spectrum – over cups of coffee in my office when I tried to convey that at heart I was neither an opponent of private ownership nor, as popularly supposed on the left, an enthusiastic union-basher.

Equally, I was pressed to make fairly regular appearances to address larger gatherings of MPs at the House of Commons. These personally delivered reports on BL's progress, by no means all 'soft soap', were more likely to gain widespread attention than the Corporate Plan which the Secretary of State placed in the House of Commons library on our behalf. BL's political exposure made us vulnerable. Not only were we obliged to debate issues we generated ourselves, but we also became unwittingly involved in wider parliamentary controversies. Two such instances arose in the latter part of 1981, when we found ourselves having to fight, at the same time, two Parliamentary Committees, the Industry and Trade Committee and the Public Accounts Committee.

The Select Committee on Industry and Trade – the All Party Committee with special responsibility for reviewing the activities of the Departments of Industry and Trade – had taken a considerable interest in BL over the years. In March 1981 I had given evidence to them at length about the factors which led BL to request the £990 million of further equity funding, which had been approved by the Government two months previously. The session in which I gave my evidence had been stimulating, and judging from the Chairman's generous summing up, had elicited a very positive response from the Committee.

We were, therefore, surprised and concerned to receive a rather peremptory letter from the Clerk to the Committee early in November of the same year. It noted that BL had just submitted its 1982 Corporate Plan to the Government, and requested that we immediately forward a copy of the *full* Plan to the Committee, with a view to my giving oral evidence shortly thereafter. The Plan comprised six volumes packed full of commercially sensitive information, including, for example, details of discussions with other manufacturers with whom (by mutual agreement) we had not publicly admitted to any contact. The normal practice was for us to provide a summary of the Corporate Plan for the House of Commons, omitting this type of commercially confidential information, after the Plan had been approved by the Government. The Select Committee now seemed to want to take over the role of government and to review and pronounce upon the merits of the Plan before the Government had taken a decision. Even more worrying was the belief amongst experts in parliamentary matters that this request was part of a wider crusade on the part of the Select Committee to assert its right to all kinds of sensitive documents which it thought would increase the effectiveness of its scrutiny over Whitehall. It had won a major victory over the British Steel Corporation on this issue a year or so previously, when they obtained such documents.

Having taken all the commercial, legal and governmental advice available to us, we quickly reached two conclusions. First, we could not afford to release our full Plan to the Committee. We had agreements not to disclose certain information to third parties (excluding, of course, the Government itself, in its capacity as our major banker and 99% shareholder), and we risked a major weakening of confidence on the part of those dealing with BL, if it became known that such information had been placed at the disposal of a Parliamentary Committee. The Committee did not help us with this problem when they reserved the right both to show the Corporate Plan to their extra-parliamentary expert advisers, and to publish whatever they thought fit 'after taking account of our views.' Our worries about Parliamentary Committees on this score were borne out a few months later when the Public Accounts Committee inadvertently published a figure which both BL and the Government had asked them to keep confidential.

Our second conclusion was that we had no grounds whatsoever to stop the Committee requisitioning the document, provided, at the end of the day, they obtained a resolution from the full House of Commons. If, after that, we continued to resist, I could find myself imprisoned for contempt of Parliament – my Board were intrigued at the possibilities! Surprisingly, the Committee had no power to requisition the Plan from the Government direct, but its powers in relation to companies and individuals were absolute; always provided it had Parliament's backing.

After some days of dialogue, when it appeared that we were heading for confrontation with the Clerk to the Committee, I managed to break the log-jam by telephoning the Chairman, the Conservative MP, Sir Donald Kaberry. Once the problem had been explained to him personally, he immediately saw the reasonableness of our compromise proposal, which was that the Committee should receive a truncated version of the Plan ahead of the House of Commons as a whole, with some additional confidential information covering the particular interests of the Committee. His attitude was a great relief. In January 1982 I again gave oral evidence to the Committee in public session, and once again the hearing was courteous and constructive, but probing. And thus a potential crisis ended satisfactorily, but not without consuming a great deal of time, not only of senior management but also of the BL Board. It is a sad fact that people and institutions – many well meaning I'm sure so often absorbed substantial amounts of our energy and effort without seeming to realise it.

While we were privately resolving the problem of documentation with the Select Committee, a more public confrontation developed with the prestigious Public Accounts Committee, which is Parliament's watchdog over the expenditure of all government departments. Again, the main issue was a more general one – the question of whether the Exchequer and Audit Department (headed by the Comptroller and Auditor General and in effect the staff support of the PAC) should have direct access to the files of state-owned companies and industries, as well as to the files of their sponsoring government departments. In its quest for this power, the PAC probably had the support of the majority of backbenchers on both sides of the House of Commons, and also, of course, the support of the press who saw the issue as one of secretive versus open government.

BL inadvertently became the focus of this argument after we had announced the sale of our Bathgate tractor business to Marshall & Sons. The sale was bad news for employees at Bathgate and their trades union representatives, since it meant the transfer of tractor manufacture to Marshall's facilities at Gainsborough, involving 800 redundancies at Bathgate. The only alternative was the complete closure of the tractor business, since our capacity vastly outstripped the sales potential, and we could not spare the cash to invest in new models for such a peripheral sector of our business, when we were under pressure to allocate funds to our mainstream products. Disposal was not only financially advantageous compared with closure, but it preserved more jobs – Marshalls had guaranteed to continue buying engines from Bathgate for their tractors for at least three years, and it would also create employment in Gainsborough. It was the best achievable deal all round.

The emotion generated by the severity of the cutbacks which we had to impose on Leyland and Bathgate gave rise to the use by the local Labour MP, Tam Dalyell, of the legally privileged environment of the House of Commons to make some very serious allegations of corruption relating to 'unnamed personnel' who had been involved in the negotiations between Leyland and Marshalls. These allegations were backed up by no specific evidence and if they had been made outside the confines of Parliament, would almost certainly have been the subject of legal action. We tried to persuade him to do so, as they were widely reported and, although firmly and properly refuted by our Leyland subsidiary, were highly damaging both to employee relations and to the general image of our commercial vehicles business; this at a time when its future was in the balance. We launched an internal investigation into the allegations, found no evidence of any impropriety and tried to persuade Tam Dalyell to produce any evidence in his possession – with no success whatever.

Tam Dalyell demanded an investigation by the Comptroller and Auditor General and thus involved the Public Accounts Committee in the matter. The Comptroller had full access to the files of the Department of Industry, but in line with the PAC's general policy, the Comptroller requested direct access to BL's files and, when we refused, he made our refusal public. We were in our view unfairly condemned in a *Times* leader. It was not often that *The Times* was other than scrupulously fair, but on this occasion we had a bad press generally, for the press misunderstood our freedom to act. Our refusal to make our files available was in line with the Government's general policy of resisting direct access to the internal documents of state-owned companies. The Government 'advised' us in the matter so the decision was technically ours – but we had good reason to heed the Government's advice. We had disclosed the results of our investigation and the details of the tractor sale to the Department of Industry, whose files were completely open to the Comptroller and Auditor General. We had made public our willingness to cooperate with any investigation by our own auditors, or even by the police, if there were any suspicion of criminal activity. To spare scarce resources to cope with yet another investigatory body seemed inconsistent with our remit from the Government to act commercially, especially when the Comptroller did not appear to have any special qualification to understand the commercial judgment involved in such issues as asset disposals. It was ironic – here we were being pressed by the Government to return as much of our business as possible to the private sector, and yet each individual disposal was arousing major controversy, requiring extremely detailed scrutiny. As I subsequently told Conservative backbenchers, it was hardly likely that we would get to first base in any disposals, if we had to pass a lengthy examination by the Department of Industry and the Comptroller and Auditor General before finalising each transaction.

The general controversy about the Comptroller's access to files continues, but on the specific sale of the tractor business the PAC found no evidence of impropriety and indeed criticised Tam Dalyell for making unsubstantiated allegations. They did, however, comment that the Department of Industry should scrutinise the sale of publicly owned assets much more thoroughly than had been done in this case. In the circumstances, I thought this unrealistic for to be more thorough than the Department of Industry would take some doing.

Again and again we had to fight unnecessary battles, and vast energy was consumed in the process.

The decision to stop MG sports car production created more public fuss and misunderstanding than anything in the whole five years – even greater than whole-scale factory closures and massive job losses. But trying to explain commercial logic to the public at large, and in particular to the vociferous and loyal MG owners and their allies in the House of Commons, proved a nigh on impossible task. This was perhaps the only occasion on which the Board's commercial judgment was seriously challenged, and it also brought home the difficulties and vulnerabilities of being determined to operate in a commercial manner – yet having highly influential and vocal MPs who saw their roles as being two-fold: first, to question BL's commercial decision-making in the role of surrogate shareholder – out to 'second-guess' the MG decision; second, to speak for their righteously indignant public. How dare the company get rid of a car that everyone loved, and that evoked nostalgia!

The public response and outcry was immediate. All our efforts to explain the commercial reality were nullified by this spontaneous outburst from outraged MG owners throughout Britain, and indeed throughout the world. Several hundreds of them demonstrated outside the showrooms in Piccadilly and presented a petition to us. Questions were asked in the House of Commons and I suspect the whole tone of aggrieved outrage and anger which the demise of MG generated prompted some of the opportunist approaches to take over the MG business. One of them was from Alan Curtis, who at that time was running the Aston Martin Motor Company. I have no reason to suspect that his approach was other than a genuine and concerned attempt to save the MG name, but it certainly turned out to be a long-running and indeed highly damaging episode which we suspected from the start would come to nought and which in the event did come to nought.

In retrospect the situation was made worse by BL's scrupulousness in refraining from making public some of the doubts that it felt about the validity of the bid; indeed for allowing the negotiations to drag on well past what was commercially reasonable. But having made the mistake in the first place of appearing to take the demise of MG for granted, we did try to give every opportunity to Alan Curtis to come up with a reasonable and viable proposition. This episode also involved Lord George-Brown, whose role was to be an intermediary; he tried his best, but in the event the cash just wasn't there and when eventually this also became clear to the other party (BL having come to that conclusion somewhat earlier) we brought the matter to a speedy conclusion. Within a few months of the MG bid dying Aston Martin itself was in some difficulty and Alan Curtis moved on.

The MG name is now proudly back on a BL product, and happily the MG Metro has been accepted by fiercely loyal enthusiasts as being in the MG tradition. The moral of the episode is clear: you mess around with famous marque names that are loved and cherished by motor enthusiasts at your peril!

Many of the external factors affecting the performance of BL and other companies can inevitably be traced back to government – not the reluctant owner of lame ducks, but government as in 'govern'. For example the impact it has on any large company through its general policies on a variety of issues – economic, fiscal, trade, regulatory and so on. As an industrialist, my natural inclination, is to keep as clear of the government bureaucracy as possible. There is a view that the successful companies are those which keep at a safe distance from the dead hand of government. An additional factor in BL's case was that, as a company still drawing substantial amounts of new equity capital from the Government, we were expected to keep our mouths shut about government policies which were damaging to the company because it was owned by government. Whatever one may think about the capacity of government to run a business or to assist industrial progress, it is undeniable that governments have a considerable capacity to do damage – often unwittingly. I therefore believe that industry needs to be active in seeking to influence government and shadow cabinet policy – not only through private representations, but on public platforms when necessary – and regardless of any deeper relationship between government and company, for the Government wears an entirely different hat as shareholder.

The need to fight to make the external as well as the internal influences work in BL's favour meant taking the battle to ministers – not in their capacity as shareholder, or proxy owner of the business, but in their functional roles, as people who made policy decisions that could do great harm, or, great good; or for that matter who could fail to make decisions at all and so fail to do things which might be helpful.

Unfair trading is a case in point. Throughout the reigns of Edmund Dell, John Nott and John Biffen, we argued and we battled. We cajoled ministers in private and in public; and no matter what we said and no matter what we did, we failed to persuade these various Secretaries of State for Trade to act against unfair trading practices. Cars poured in from Spain and the Comecon countries and none could flow the other way. The same situation exists today, with Lord Cockfield – the fourth, no less, Secretary of State for Trade during my five years at BL. The fact that ministers stay in these posts just long enough to learn the job is a great weakness in our system. It leaves great power in the hands of the civil service – not always a bad thing, but when it comes to international trade they tend to be more innocent than their opposite numbers in France, Japan and elsewhere.

'This payment in kind might be easing BL's overstocking problems, but a bit of cash would be useful!'

By courtesy of the *Birmingham Evening Mail*

Why did BL make so much of the issue of unfair trading? Not because we wanted protection; our whole argument was based on the need for reciprocal access to countries whose motor manufacturers were free to supply to Britain. We had to make our living by competing in international markets, and we could not understand why our Government's trade policies should require us to fight with one hand tied behind our backs. Labour and Conservatives were equally guilty.

Spain is the classic example. Due to protected investment by foreign multinationals, such as Ford and General Motors, the Spanish car manufacturing industry is now bigger than Britain's. Yet a long-standing agreement with Spain provides for cars imported into Britain from Spain to pay a duty of only 4.4% compared with a Spanish duty of over 36% on cars exported from Britain. Not unnaturally, this is likely to result in over 100,000 small cars being exported from Spain to be sold in Britain in 1983, while only a handful of Metros can be sold in the opposite direction, because the duty is eight times higher.

In addition, Britain receives some 30,000 cars a year from Eastern Europe without any reciprocal access for BL to their markets. Now imports are similarly building up from other highly restricted markets such as South Korea, Australia and South Africa. This, together with the long-standing problem of the Japanese, means that about 250,000 cars a year are being sold in Britain with British manufacturers being unable to reciprocate. When BL argued that the restrictions on exports to these other markets should be lifted, we were met with countless weighty diplomatic and bureaucratic arguments as to why nothing could be done. Yet when others, like the trades unions, argued that restrictions should be applied in Britain until such time as these countries changed their minds, the cry of 'free trade' was raised. It seemed to me that free trade operated only in one direction: BL therefore advocated 'free and fair trade'.

Late in 1980 I had an invitation from the Cambridge Union to debate the subject of fair trade versus free trade with the man who then mattered – John Nott, Secretary of State for Trade. We both accepted the invitation with alacrity, for we were poles apart in our views on the practical implementation of free trade and this would be a good opportunity to test the arguments in public. Independent television recorded the full debate, but without John Nott, who had been moved to Defence shortly before the debate took place; Cecil Parkinson, then Minister of State, stepped in to put the case for the Department of Trade.

There is no doubt that when the debate started the Union supported Cecil Parkinson's case. The theory of free trade is a compelling one to an academic audience with little business experience. But our opponents made two mistakes. The first and understandable error was to imagine that I was against free trade. I was not – I was against the naive policies being followed by the Government, indeed by successive governments, in the sphere of international trade. As I said at the start of my speech, I favoured *savoir-faire* rather than *laissez-faire*. As the last speaker for the proposal – 'Britain's free trade policy is not fair' – I focused on fairness. They, in their earlier arguments, had assumed I would object to the free trade aspect; that I would speak in favour of blanket import protection. On the contrary, with close to £1,000 million a year's worth of exports, the last thing that BL wanted was rigid restriction. Our case was that we would prefer total freedom of trade, but this doesn't exist in practice, and the facts should be recognised. My case was that the Government was not acting firmly and toughly against countries like Spain. I was able to give countless examples of unfair trading and my plea was that British industry must be able to compete on an equal basis and on fair terms with our competitors – 'If they beat us nevertheless, fine.'

I was getting into the swing of my argument when a quite extraordinary thing happened. Four people in outrageous paramilitary costumes burst into the Union and came up to the dais. There was an extremely tense atmosphere for a few seconds and even when they produced rag placards this did little to reassure anyone, for the IRA had entered a university hall in Dublin only months earlier, and had shot my colleague, Geoff Armstrong, in both legs. I stood my ground – what else could I do? – and with some relief watched cream buns being deposited on the Secretary of the Union and other officials. The fact that I stayed put seemed to deter the perpetrators from sharing their confectionery with me. The President, who prudently took refuge behind the 'throne', afterwards emerged to show his great displeasure, and to fine the perpetrators 'in absentia' for their very stupid act.

When I was able to continue I said, 'Mr President, that was certainly free, but it wasn't fair.' This brought the house down, and from then on it was plain sailing. As I argued the case, the Union swung to our point of view. This was facilitated by the other big error my opponents made. Ray Whitney, Conservative MP, attacked me personally – referring to BL's 'sleepworkers' and suggested that my time would have been better spent keeping our workforce awake at night – how in effect could I waste time in a debate when I should be working? Cecil Parkinson did the same. He went for me and the Union didn't like it. They knew that the new BL had sloughed off these practices of the past, and it was invidious to drag it all out again in 1981. Everything really had changed by then.

When the vote came to be taken we found we had won by 181 votes to 81 and I must say our team was satisfied with the evening's work. To be fair our opponents took their defeat in a very good-natured way, and no bones were broken. But more important I felt that Cecil Parkinson, now Chairman of the Conservative Party, was at least a little persuaded by our advocacy.

Of course, the Cambridge Union debate was as much a fun thing as it was a subtle opportunity to influence people. The fact that I participated when time was of the essence, merely serves to make the point that my colleagues and I were reluctant to miss any opportunity of taking the battle outside. We were mortified that a British Government could allow these imbalances to go unchecked. When personal representations to ministers failed, we made our position clear in public.

Two years later our efforts to change attitudes were rewarded. Patrick Jenkin told the motor industry at the 1982 Motor Show in Birmingham:

> There has been – quite rightly in my view – a lot of publicity given to unfair exports of cars to the UK. Many people urge retaliation against countries which export to us from highly protected home markets, of one kind or another, exploiting our good nature and our commitment to free trade. We do not like such inequities. If they threaten the stability and equilibrium of open trading relationships, we will take action.

I have omitted Japan from the catalogue of unfair trading because it is a very different case from Spain. The Japanese have certainly developed subtle methods of making life difficult for importers in their markets – from the inspection of every imported car with a fine toothcomb, to the tying up of distribution outlets by the local manufacturers. But the main fear of the European motor industry is that a society extremely well organised for efficient manufacturing and without many of Europe's social costs and constraints can wipe out its competitors around the world at will. Whether our governments are prepared to tolerate this is essentially a political matter. But the British motor industry looks with some envy at its French and Italian counterparts, whose governments are rigorous in keeping the Japanese share of their car markets down to 3% and virtually nothing, respectively.

My own involvement with the issue of Japanese trade came at the European level. (The talks between British and Japanese trade associations – which were intended to provide a basis for voluntary restraint on Japanese car and commercial vehicle exports to Britain – were covered for BL by Ray Horrocks or one of his senior staff.) The European motor industry has found it worthwhile to organise itself so that the chairmen of all indigenous European vehicle manufacturers meet periodically with the EEC Commission, at the highest level, to try to ensure that the Community uses its powers beneficially. Again, the use of a chairman's time in this way may seem an irritant, but it represents an increasingly necessary contribution for a chairman to make to his company's future prospects. In 1979, I took the Presidency of this organisation, known as the Committee of Common Market Automobile Constructors, for 12 months, when BL's fortunes were at their lowest, and my other commitments were heavy.

Such was the concern about Japan on the part of all the European manufacturers that in 1980 the CCMC resolved to seek a meeting in Tokyo with the leaders of the Japanese motor industry. Only by putting the problems to them face to face could we judge whether there was some hope that Japanese manufacturers would voluntarily moderate their export drive, or whether we needed to press for immediate EEC action, which the Germans, as ardent free traders, were reluctant to do unless absolutely necessary. The two meetings between the CCMC and its Japanese counterpart – the Japanese Automobile Manufacturers' Association – first in Tokyo in November 1980, then a 'return match' in Paris in May 1981, were fascinating in terms of the interplay between personalities, who together controlled directly or indirectly some ten million jobs across the world. But did they justify the time invested in them? The

Japanese in the end gave little ground, and the second meeting ended in open disagreement. On the other hand, their export drive gradually eased during 1981. I suspect that this was influenced by the often sharp exchanges with the CCMC and by the way in which the disparate personalities of the leaders of the European motor industry complemented each other, showing a united front and lobbying their national governments. We drew particular attention to the trade restrictions which had been forced on the Japanese in North America, trying to bring home to our Japanese counterparts, by personal contact, that they were part of a world trading system and had responsibilities as well as rights. In the longer term, this issue may prove to be more important for BL and other European manufacturers than many of the internal issues which preoccupied us from day to day during my five-year term.

I have already described my efforts to get 'free' trade policies converted to 'free but fair' trade policies. I was surprised but pleased to see the motor industry in the United States emerging from its traditional neutrality, to urge its government to act to help them through the recession. Whereas unrestrained free trade and the progressive tightening of safety and emission regulations were once accepted there as unshakeable norms – as 'external' influences which industry had to accept – these policies are now open to modification if the opposing case can be put clearly. With their four domestic manufacturers incurring losses of no less than $5.5 billion in 1980 and 1981, the United States has now implemented restraint on Japanese car imports, and eased the pressure which unrealistic safety and emission requirements had imposed on manufacturers' resources. And despite vast government aid, Chrysler in America, for example, has not been at all reticent in public comment on matters to do with the policy followed by the US Administration.

Typical of BL's approach (although incorrectly stated by the media at the time) was the 'oil in the ground' speech I made at the CBI Conference at Brighton in November 1980. I was widely quoted as saying we would do better to stop pumping North Sea oil – we should 'keep the bloody stuff in the ground.' Many influential people – even in oil companies – were upset at what I was reported to have said. What I had actually said was that the pound was over-valued, interest rates were penurious and the whole issue was being aggravated by North Sea oil – 'If the Cabinet do not have the wit and imagination to reconcile our industrial needs with the fact of North Sea oil, they would do better to leave the bloody stuff in the ground.'

I have great respect for the present Prime Minister's courage, and for the persistence and resilience of the Chancellor of the Exchequer. But I still believe that what I said at Brighton was right – we can and should have our cake and eat it. Of course pump the oil – but get the interest rate and exchange rate policy right, and don't undermine our competitiveness by causing or allowing the pound to be over-valued. In 1980 and 1981 the pound was heavily over-valued in relation to all currencies except the dollar, and the latter only because the Americans have been even less wise than we have been. Instead of cutting public expenditure, and so reducing the fixed cost of government, they funded their extravagances through the Treasury, put up interest rates, caused the dollar to be over-valued, cut exports and created high unemployment.

Industrialists cannot allow exports and employment to dissipate without fighting, and if politicians have good reason for putting us at risk, let them explain why.

Another external factor BL had to tackle was local taxation. In Britain this takes the form of rates on property levied by local authorities. With a total annual rates bill across the country of £24 million, BL could not afford to accept swingeing increases of 30%–40% without a fight. In 1981, we took legal action against local authorities which sought unrealistic increases. This helped to sharpen business opposition to irresponsible authorities who, in preference to cutting their own staff, imposed burdens on industry which inevitably forced companies to cut the wealth-creating employment in their areas. We saw our action as both a public and a company duty.

But the battle outside involves not only the 'authorities' in their various guises, but public opinion as a whole, for ultimately, it is the public who determine whether or not a company such as BL succeeds. BL operates in one of the most competitive and consumer-oriented markets in the world, and it is the consumer who has the ultimate right to decide whether or not it buys a particular company's product. Public acceptability is crucial.

In Britain there is a strange, national reluctance to support its own industries. This maverick attitude among some people manifests itself in the bizarre idea that to buy foreign goods is preferable to purchasing the home-produced or home-manufactured product.

This is not the case in other countries. In France, Germany, Italy and Japan, for instance, no public official drives a foreign car. Yet in Britain, leaders of industry, MPs, even union leaders parade their imported cars while bemoaning the fact of rising unemployment. In Britain the direct connection between a healthy home-based manufacturing industry and employment does not appear to register in many people's minds. Whether this attitude is a strength or a weakness depends on how one feels about the future of Britain as a manufacturing nation. Without a bed-rock of industries making and selling products at home and overseas, Britain's role as a major trading country must decline and with it the ability to influence events in the world community. The fact is that a 20% swing away from foreign to British-built cars would mean about 300,000 more cars being manufactured in this country and some 30,000 more jobs would be created in the British motor industry.

It was during the 18-hour flight to Tokyo with John McKay to sign the Honda collaboration agreement over Christmas 1979 that the seeds of a 'Think British' campaign took root. Perhaps it was the irony of joining with a Japanese firm to save British jobs that sparked it off, but something had to be done to create a more sympathetic climate of opinion, not just for BL but for other sectors of the beleaguered British industry. The result was a deliberately tentative and low key campaign which grew during the following months into a major debate, hotly contested by both the 'Buy British' and 'Freedom to Choose' factions in the correspondence columns of the daily newspapers. BL tried to convey its 'Buy British' message in an advertising campaign during 1980. Advertisements showed half of Britain sinking under water and an average British kitchen was used to illustrate just how much domestic equipment is imported. It is very difficult to quantify the result of this kind of appeal; the fact that it was initiated by BL may have been counter-productive as we were still fighting for survival. When Marks & Spencer say they are buying 90% British there is a greater impact. But there was market research evidence to show that by the time Metro was launched towards the end of 1980, the British public were better disposed both to BL and to the idea of buying British goods.

In the wider context of opinion-forming, so many people rely on newspapers, television and radio for news and for opinion that a very public – and newsworthy – company like BL has carefully to guard its reputation against unfair and inaccurate reporting. At BL we have found that it does not pay to stick our heads in the sand or even to be merely philosophical about errors of fact in the press. We have found that it pays to be vigilant, to act immediately to deal with an incorrect, biased, or malicious report, whether by phoning an editor or by moving quickly to field a spokesman on the BBC Radio 'Today' programme when they periodically unearth a militant shop steward who then undermines the credibility of the company.

One of the unhelpful by-products of becoming personally involved in public debate is that, inevitably, the media tends to concentrate on the individual making the noise. Once this happens there is this tendency 'to play the man, not the ball.' I've lost count of the number of times I've picked up a paper or watched a news bulletin to learn of a decision or an action I'm supposed to have taken; a decision that I haven't even been involved in. Of course personalisation cuts two ways: it was perhaps not a bad thing during the period when unpleasant and painful decisions about job losses and factory closures had to be taken, that there was a single target for the flak – I've no personal complaints on that score. But a preoccupation with an individual can mask the wider considerations, as I explained at an Independent Broadcasting Association lecture in early 1982:

> What day-to-day coverage of industry there is, is often concerned with the negative; the disputes, the strikes and stoppages and even less directly the threats of strikes which may or may not materialise, and which are often portrayed as actually happening. I make the point not simply to try to convince you that BL is now a reformed character but because of the 'knock-on' effect BL has had on the image of British industry as a whole, particularly abroad.
>
> The plea I would make to you is that just as you wouldn't judge the whole of ITV by one specific period of poor programmes, please don't let your perceptions of British industry be coloured by BL's antecedents or judge BL today by British Leyland of yesterday.

To be fair, when the facts were pointed out, many of the commentators were quite ready to acknowledge that the change in our situation was not being adequately portrayed. We now get a more accurate press.

A key part of a successful manager's role is to communicate – first and foremost to his workforce, to explain and to motivate – but he should also be prepared to take his arguments and judgments to a wider audience, if the circumstances warrant. It is not always easy to persuade industrialists to fight publicly – indeed we had to work quite hard to persuade our own managers to speak up, on a local and regional basis, and we arranged for some 50 executives to have television and radio training, but it still took time to break down their reticence.

I do not expect a middle manager to expound on strategic policy issues, but there is a case for him being interviewed where he is the one with the knowledge and the responsibility. Conversely, you can't expect the top man to agree to be interviewed on a matter which is the proper preserve of an appropriately placed *less senior* executive. There is a disinclination among broadcasters and journalists to take anyone but the top man for interview. Many times the BL communications people have suggested that this or that executive would be more appropriate, but often the response has been a feeling of affront from journalists that their particular programme does not merit the man at the top. In doing this they often reject the very man who would have most to contribute. Industry has to work very hard at improving the communications skills of its managers. The more enlightened companies recognise this and are taking steps through courses and training to correct it as part of the overall need for better management of businesses.

BL was greatly helped in its communications by John McKay, a very competent man in his role as Communications Director. He looked at his subject as being far wider than public relations, and reported direct to the Chairman and Chief Executive; therefore he knew exactly what was going on at the higher levels. He was fully in the picture, and to do the job properly, this was the only way to play it.

Furthermore, he chaired a most important sounding-board in BL – the External Policy Committee. This served a critical purpose: to find out how a highly intelligent and representative group of executives responded to various situations which we were facing or which might face the company. This meant that he was plugged in at all levels, and this set the alarm bells ringing more than once, so avoiding some nasty problems.

Communications are becoming more complex and more efficient, for its technology is becoming unlimited in its scope. In ten years' time perhaps most major companies will be taking the battle outside.

13

Why Go Now?

Looking back at the situation the new Board found at British Leyland in November 1977, one has to ask the question: how ever did the business get into such a mess? After all, the British motor industry was in a powerful position immediately before and after the Second World War. Technology licences were being sought and given, and paths to this end were beaten to Birmingham, and on the truck side to Leyland – from all over the world. The component industry was on the up and up, and many companies had built up useful cash reserves during the war. The rot set in, I would say, fairly soon after the war. Some British companies had remained market-orientated but many had not for they had been out of the competitive rat-race for five years; their total energies were taken up with war production. The transition back to the market place in the late 1940s and early 1950s was difficult.

In my part of the world, Southern Africa, the once popular Austin and Morris products soon gave way to Peugeots, Fords and vehicles from General Motors. The British product was not robust enough for local conditions, and the 'British end' always seemed unresponsive – full of inertia, always rationalising why things could not be done. There were always reasons why suspension systems and other obvious modifications could not be made to suit African conditions. That was my firm impression as far back as 1957, 20 years before I joined BL. Admittedly during the early post-war period, for perhaps 10 or 12 years, Leyland (truck and bus), Land Rover and Jaguar were customer-orientated, and had done well, but with the mergers and acquisitions there seemed to be neither the money nor the men to update the products. First the car products languished, and later so did the trucks; and even the much sought after four-wheel-drive vehicles were not updated. And neither were the manufacturing facilities. Much of this happened before the Japanese motor industry took off, in the early 1970s.

The Japanese began their remarkable rise as a vehicle manufacturing nation and exporter at the expense of British products in traditional British overseas markets. Some of them did it with British know-how. British products that were edged out of traditional export markets were nevertheless wished upon the British buyer at home who had come to expect the low standard he was given; standards across the British motor industry dropped lower and lower. And it was during the ten years before 1978 that some disastrous product decisions were taken which weakened the company's position and standing at home and overseas. The executives responsible for those model decisions carry a major share of the blame for subsequent events. And those models that were well conceived, like the Rover SD1 Saloon and the Austin Princess, were put into production imperfect from a product engineering and manufacturing engineering standpoint. Neither, as a result, fully exploited its potential, and indeed both were only brought to a high standard years after they went into production – in fact after the present Austin Rover team took charge.

Virtually all standards across the British motor industry dropped lower and lower. Why? I am not sure whether the successful attempt by extreme political groups to get toe holds – and then a measure of control of the car factories – was the cause or the effect of an erosion of management confidence. What I do know is that discipline in most British car factories reached the stage where – exchanging notes with Ford in 1978 – I found that we and they had been subjected to no less than 350 disputes over the previous six months. A motor business cannot be run on that basis.

The erosion of management confidence in the years until the end of the 1970s, meant a great loss of management control. The more management lost control, the more the vacuum was filled by the militants and the national union officers were pushed into a back seat by the stewards. The industry was in decline, with no end in sight. Even the profitable Ford of Britain had deep problems in its British factories, including restrictive practices, lack of discipline and low productivity; but the public perception of Ford has been enhanced by the contribution made to local Ford profits by a high percentage of imports from Continental Europe where sensible work practices and higher productivity made the product cost more competitive than in Britain. The extent to which Ford has become more dependent on its European factories to supply the British market is clear from the fact that in 1981 only 45% of Ford's British car sales were 'Made in Britain.' As a result Ford UK had a balance of payments deficit in that year of £164 million: exports totalled £919 million while imports reached £1,083 million. What could Ford management have done over the years to protect their position? Exactly what they did: step up manufacture in those Continental plants where sensible work practices and higher productivity made the product cost more competitive than in the UK. They had no other option.

By contrast, BL – with its less impressive profit performance – contributed nearly all its £884 million worth of direct exports to the British economy, as 97% of all sales were British-built vehicles.

BL of course had little option, for unlike Ford it had no efficient large-scale manufacturing operations in Continental Europe. The company was dependent upon its British manufacturing base, and if the pre-1977 management decided not to grasp the nettle – and that is my assessment of what happened – then it *might* have been because they simply did not have the cash flow to support a firm stand. Or that they did not have the unity at the top, or the confidence, or the determination to fight the battle. The fact is that few significant stands were made, whereas concessions were made left, right and centre, either by fair but tough negotiation on the part of the shop stewards or as a result of ruthless action which was usually unofficial and invariably unconstitutional. When management down the line have had their position undermined often enough through indecisive leadership, they give up the unequal struggle, and that is exactly what happened at British Leyland. My belief is that management simply lost control of the situation. Models were not, or could not be, updated. Quality and productivity fell to unacceptable levels, and disputes reached four to five times the sort of level that a 'continuous production' industry can stand. Weak management implies concessions, and concessions in practice do not make for industrial harmony. I could offer many other explanations, but as relevant as they are, none is as fundamental as the fact that management over a number of years lost their will to manage. Britain and the world blamed the unions, and turned their backs on British Leyland products. But the real blame lay with management, for they failed in their duty to manage. 'Management' is not an automatic right, it has to be earned. It is a duty, and if it isn't fulfilled it lets everyone down: employee, fellow manager, customer, supplier, and shareholder.

Other weaknesses and causes could be listed: the 'not invented here' factor, which is a myopic disease that causes engineers and others to assume that anything that owes its parentage *to others* is inferior – is 'foreign' or suspect in some way. Another fatal practice was the tendency for 'personnel' to be left to the employee relations function, to the relative exclusion of line managers. Managerial and organisational treacle made it difficult to establish and monitor the cost of the products, and the real value of inventories. Centralisation meant that decisions came to be made by the people furthest from the point at which the facts and the know-how were most readily available.

Many of these problems, and more, were addressed, and solved by the new BL Board and top team, but it took several years to achieve and many of these issues had to be resolved *ad hoc* and before a disciplined structure was established; progressively the decision-making and executive responsibility was devolved. This was vital – for one was never off duty at BL. Until I started the final process of handing over, about eight months before I left the company, I was totally absorbed in the business for every waking hour, whether I was in Britain or elsewhere; whether working or on holiday, the same applied. It so happened that each December while we were at our holiday cottage at Kromme River, there would be one or more crises building up in or around BL. Sometimes, the problems were to do with employee relations, and at other times to do with government approval of funds. Those hot sunny Christmases in South Africa always coincided with a bubbling cauldron of trouble in England. Even in December 1981, when there was no public crisis, there was an undercurrent of tension, for we were trying to settle the succession and organisation proposals with Patrick Jenkin and his senior colleagues. At that stage, after four years of obvious stress, the pressures had become more subtle, and in some ways more insidious. It isn't in the actual heat of the battle that one feels the physical strain. I began to feel enervated for the first time while the 'corridor' battle went on, knowing that the wrong decision by politicians could quickly destroy what we had built up over four long and arduous years. And it wasn't only our efforts that were in the balance, it was more than a billion pounds of taxpayers' money, and hundreds of thousands of jobs which are still directly and indirectly supported by BL as it moves towards profit.

The previous holiday had been rather more frenetic. The whole of the £990 million of funding for 1981 and 1982 was in the balance when I left for South Africa in December 1980 – and to add to the tension, there were employee relations problems at Longbridge which were simmering away when I left England. These related to the Longbridge 'riot' in which cars were damaged following problems and tensions in the seat-trim areas, and when management disciplined the culprits, strike action was called. Throughout Christmas and New Year, management worked to resolve the problem and the telephone lines between Britain and St Francis Bay were kept busy. That year the South African press picked up the fact that a large volume of phone calls was being channelled in and out of the St Francis Bay exchange, and there was a rather naive article talking of the vast cost of the exercise. The cost of the phone bill – R1,300 (or £700) – was nothing as compared with what was at stake – the cost of closing BL, at £1,400 million. I could only smile wryly, wonder at the innocence of some newspapers and ponder upon the degree of personalisation involved in the job.

I had arrived at the company in 1977 at a time of grave crisis, and not surprisingly the media focused heavily on me. It was a very public company in a very public mess. Then the battles started: the battles to change attitudes of managers and workforce, and to change working practices at every level in the company – to change an undisciplined organisation into a professionally managed business. Through all this the focus tended to be on me. Even when others took initiatives, good or bad, the media attributed them to me.

I know that the average worker feels I have done a reasonable job, for he tells me this quite spontaneously when I go around BL factories. The unions (at higher levels) say privately that they acknowledge that most of what I did needed to be done. But it is the public image that matters when it comes to selling the company's products, and my image was magnified out of all proportion by the media as 'the man who took on the unions'. The stage was being reached when the currency was diluting – when headlines like 'Edwardes offers 3% pay increase' might just have a counterproductive or emotive effect; when the militants might exploit the high profile of my public image to bring the whole company crashing down, as indeed they tried to do in the deliberate campaign on my apocryphal salary increase. And so the power of the media, which was often helpful in getting fundamental truths across, might well start to work against BL. As much as we tried to soften the impact by playing me down, the media would unwittingly build up the image again. Not always in an unfriendly way, for they were often generous, but in such a spotlighted way that it was difficult to separate the facts we were trying to get across from the personalised image.

The salary issue didn't help. Although my salary, for the size of the job, was among the lowest in the world motor industry, there is an unfortunate envy syndrome in Britain so that anyone who earns more than the average is branded 'highly paid'. When one earns a lot more than the average the freneticism builds up. (It always intrigues me that income from hard-earned life savings is described by the Inland Revenue as 'unearned' income! Regrettably the worst offenders are the press, and in particular the labour correspondents. When it was realised that my salary was £100,000 a year, hundreds of column inches of inaccurate information flooded the news-papers; much of it seemed timed to soften up management in advance of the 1981 wage negotiations. Some of it was so inaccurate that we had to take legal steps before editors – very reluctantly – retracted. What upset me was the lengths we had to go to persuade the media to retract statements which they knew to be untrue. The quantum of salary was accurate, but the rate of increase quoted bore no resemblance to the true facts. Reports in *Hansard* – both the Secretary of State and the Prime Minister had given the facts in Parliament – were apparently not enough. The fact is that the average increase in my remuneration over the five years would have been only 5.1% a year even if I had not taken a 35% re-duction in the last quarter of 1982, when my workload dropped sharply.

For one attempt to get the facts correctly conveyed, we were lampooned in the *Sun*, and amusingly so. At a year-end press conference, Arthur Large, the Company Secretary, read out the facts as substantiated by the auditors. Now to get auditors to give their names to a document does require a certain meticulousness in language that doesn't quite line up with the more colloquial lan-guage of a press conference! Although the statement was accurate to a fault, it was almost incomprehensible, and to the bulk of our media audience – it was gobbledygook. The *Sun* took us to the cleaners, by offering a prize for anyone who understood what it meant. I am not surprised that no one won the prize!

There were other media difficulties. From quite early on, whenever there were real or perceived differences between BL and the Government, quite respectable newspapers would aver that I was about to resign if I didn't get my way; on occasions, that the whole Board was about to resign. During the first four years, every one of these speculative pieces was a figment of the imagination. There were isolated occasions when the Board was prepared to dig its heels in and take what was coming – for example, over the pre-election issue of the closure of the Prestcold Scottish factory. We would have risked being dismissed on that occasion rather than do what was commercially unsound; in the final event we were not put to the test. The irony is that these genuine mini-crises did not become known to the press. Indeed once BL itself became disciplined, there was seldom any leak about our subsequent delicate differences with government. It was invariably when we had by no means reached the end of our tether that the press assumed that we had!

The only occasion when the question of resignation was a live issue was in October 1980, as my three-year secondment drew to a close, and Sir Keith Joseph asked me if I would stay on for a further two years. I agreed to do so subject to two conditions – the two-year funding and no *premature* sell off of parts of the business – and I was able to say that the full Board supported these stipulations. I know that some people construed this as a gun at the head of the Government. I am absolutely convinced that had these two points not been conceded by the Government, BL would not be alive and kicking to the extent it is today, for the two years of funding then agreed upon was crucial in building dealer and banker confidence, and the agreement that we should not be asked to sell off parts of the mainstream business (in parallel with securing the recovery) was the only way we could have completed a seemingly impossible task.

And so the press, in 'threatening' resignation on the Board's or my behalf, weakened the currency, for there comes a time when resignation can be a necessary instrument. If one has been perceived to cry wolf, the action when it happens loses its edge.

One of the new-found strengths at BL is the dramatic improvement in technological facilities and technical management. In 1982 the House of Lords sub-committee on Research and Development asked to see the new Metro facilities at Longbridge, and the new BL Technology establishment at Gaydon. The concept of BL Technology Limited came to me early on, for we had used a similar technique at Chloride – establishing a central technical facility, but one largely directed by the operating companies towards meaningful market-related work. This was accomplished by funding its work via the operating companies, in addition to a corporate contribution for more 'way out' projects. The members of the House of Lords Committee who made the visits were so interested in what had been done that they prevailed upon their remaining members to make a special visit. Following this second visit, Lord Nelson, at the time Chairman of GEC wrote inter alia:

> The quality and the dedication of the staff you have collected, the facilities which have been built and the work that is now being done were impressive, both on product design and planning and on product development. The excellent production facilities which have been created at Longbridge also demonstrate that Britain has the capability to produce competitively given the right circumstances.

> I believe we all felt BL should be given adequate time to prove it can be a successful motor vehicle producer in the world market.

There was more in a similar vein. These were generous comments from someone who doesn't believe in state ownership of industry. He felt that the progress being made to upgrade BL's technology merited further patient, but not open-ended, support: I am sure that like me, he expects further government support to be dependent on performance.

So why go now? Because I can leave BL with an easy mind. We have a much stronger management team than ever before – and with more resources at their disposal. I have referred in earlier chapters to the recruitment of top people from outside, to counter the in-breeding within the company, and touched on the far-reaching redeployment of managers. These things all start at the very top, helped by the Board which operates more like a 'Supreme Court' in that it is detached, objective and very strong. Anyone who temporarily forgets himself and engages in subjective special pleading would soon pull himself up, for in that company it would be seen for what it is. The directors have too much respect for one another, and indeed too much self-respect, to engage in subjective or partial debate. In short, it is an impressive group, all four non-executives being chairmen of substantial public companies, and having both David Andrews and Ray Horrocks on the main board was fundamental to the process of devolving executive authority, which had been my objective since I stepped into the company.

At one stage, as Chairman and Chief Executive, I had carried the whole executive load at the Board, and in an industry about which I knew very little. I was then joined by David Andrews, who at that time was primarily concerned with finance and planning, and top level central functions. Only when Ray Horrocks joined the Board and the executive operations of the myriad of profit centres in Britain and around the world all then reported to either Ray Horrocks or David Andrews, was I able to concentrate on my main function at the BL Board – that of Chairman. It took three years to get to that stage, but these appointments at executive director level had to be right: we simply could not afford to make a mistake. I have worked with the two of them very closely indeed, often for days at a time, and over weekends; on trips; and above all in crises – under very great pressure. None of us are perfect, but what these two men do not lack is courage – they hold their teams together without conceding on matters of principle when lesser men would give way to the temptation to win support down the line, by compromise. Their leadership of their teams developed the layers below into formidable management groups. BL managers now respond well to pressure.

What else does BL have? It has models that are acknowledged to be greatly improved – new models like the Metro and the Acclaim, the Roadtrain truck, the Titan double-decker bus, the new four-door Range Rover and the Land Rover V8 are already household names in the business; other models like the updated Jaguars and Rovers, have recouped their reputations after suffering from earlier quality and reliability problems.

The product range is however by no means complete – the 1980 to 1982 gap in the mid-car sector was the stuff from which nightmares are made, and it will be with vast relief that those in BL – and at least one ex-BL man – will herald the launch of Maestro early in 1983. This will be the first of the LC10 car family, the range on which the recovery of BL's car business will depend. With the subsequent launch of the LM11, one size up from Maestro, BL will have a range of cars, from Mini to Jaguar, that any company can be proud of. And when the XJ40 Jaguar and the new BL-Honda XX car hit the market in the mid-1980s the Car operations should be profitable and secure. The rejuvenation of the truck range will be almost complete by the end of 1983 – ready to exploit the upturn in that market which cannot now be long delayed.

In the employee relations field there are good points and there are bad points. In recent times, and in the past on specific occasions, the unions have cooperated far more than is publicly perceived. They have had some bitter pills to swallow, for on occasions the alternative to cooperation was apocalyptic – and they knew it. The less satisfactory aspect in this area is the sheer number of unions involved in BL affairs – some 16 in all. This is something that my successors and the General Secretaries will need to address in a strategic way: for the moment the negotiating machinery has been much improved at the tactical level.

Another area that is not healthy – and a weakness in most of British industry – is the 'we and they' situation in many factories. I do not believe that the differentiation drawn between 'white collar' and 'blue collar' worker in terms and conditions is tenable. There are, of course, costs associated with a change, and this alone is good reason for tackling the problem by deliberate evolution. But a start must be made, for the situation in which the 18-year-old daughter has staff status privileges for working in an office, which are not accorded to the 55-year-old father with 35 or more years' service on the shop floor, is an anachronism. In my view it is a form of social discrimination which is no more acceptable than other more recognised forms of discrimination.

There are, however, two areas in the minefield of employee relations where much progress has been made in BL. Both are the result of great teamwork between the staff experts in the employee relations field and the line managers, with encouragement from the unions. The first is in employee involvement which requires line managers to lead, to appear among the men on the shop floor, to communicate with them, to keep them in the picture, and to treat them with the respect they feel and deserve. Only then will there be mutual respect. This has required a change of attitude on the part of managers, and I believe that Ray Horrocks, David Andrews and their senior colleagues will drive through the further changes that can and must be made to optimise employee involvement.

The other major advance at BL is the increase in productivity which flowed partly from this new spirit, and which was made possible by new investment. Both political parties, while in power, had the wisdom and courage – and faith – to provide the necessary funds.

As a nation we export 33% of our gross national product. (This compares with the United States of America which exports less than 10% of its GNP.) To do this means competing with every nation on earth. If we do not match the productivity of our major competitors we will end up by taking it out of our wage packets, by low cost employment or by forfeiting jobs; which is the way things have been going over recent years. The only way to secure employment in Britain in the continuing world recession is to gain a larger share of world markets. I do not accept that unemployment is an inevitable price to pay for increased competitiveness. A healthy economy and cost-competitive companies are compatible with a positive strategy to reduce long-term unemployment. I am convinced the country can win back much of the ground it has lost at home and overseas. In 20 years Britain's share of world markets has virtually halved to 8.5% and each 1% lost is equivalent to 250,000 jobs lost in Britain. Every 1% of our home market we lose to imports costs us a further 80,000 jobs. I am sure that in a short space of time we can win back 2% of the overseas markets and 2% of our home market – that is 660,000 jobs. We can do this with a combination of effort from industry, unions, government and the British public.

Managers must, with the full involvement of employees, drive through changes – including new technology and the elimination of restrictive practices – and go for that 2% gain in world trade. The unions must work with management, as they do at BL, to make products more competitive. Even de-manning can be in a union's interest if the case is a good one; that is if it keeps the rest of the people in business until increased sales can restore the level of employment. And finally, government needs to give industry hope – to break through the 'no confidence' barrier by nudging the pound down (from the high level of the first half of 1982) and by cutting interest rates. In return industry can deliver an export-led recovery.

The British public also have a part to play; there is now a growing and healthy appreciation that buying foreign products when there are competitive home-produced ones, has a profound effect on our manufacturing industry. It keeps a worker in another country employed, while it puts another British employee on the dole. In the past there has been some justification for buying 'foreign' when British-made products have been unable to match them for quality and price. The lesson has been painfully learned and British industry needs the confidence of a recovering home market and support from British buyers to win back overseas business.

Gemini, the *Birmingham Post*

It can be done. Jaguar's 100% increase in sales in the United States of America in 1982 illustrates the point. Exports to Europe of Metro and Acclaim are rising as the reputation for higher levels of quality grows. Productivity – output per man – is the name of the game, and most parts of BL are winning on this front. Where there is the right management, productivity in Britain will escalate. It is up to managers to argue the case for rolling back restrictive practices, so that unions will see the need to forego concessions they have gained over the years. Those who don't – whether managers or employee representatives – will put themselves and their companies in jeopardy.

As I approached the fifth year at BL, I began to think about succession. Great management strength had been built at the top, and in depth; BL, which I believe needed me at one point, no longer needed me. That is the conclusion I finally reached in November 1981. Once it was widely known that I planned to go people often asked: 'Why are you going at the end of the year?' Earlier on the question had been 'are you really going?' Apparently the general feeling was that I didn't mean to go, and that I might easily be talked into staying. Nothing in the world would have persuaded me to stay beyond the five years, for I had come to the firm conclusion that five years was enough, from every point of view.

I was asked: Do you feel stale after five years? Does BL keep you awake at night? Do you want a different type of challenge? Was the public response – the high level of exposure – getting you down? It was none of those things. The fact is that I knew I would miss BL very much indeed, but I felt that the company would benefit from a change of gear, and that the time had come to divide the business into two discrete parts, each with a chief executive who could focus attention on his specific responsibility. That would effectively make the chief executive part of my (combined) role redundant. Given this, BL needed a Chairman who would adopt a lower profile, be strategic rather than operational. The answer was clearly to appoint a non-executive Chairman with strong chief executives running the two new divisions of the company; that this might well carry the recovery forward more effectively. At the end of 1977 it would not have worked, for there was so much to be done that the authority to do it needed to be concentrated, at least for three to four years. My report to the NEB in December 1977 – six weeks after the new team came in – described the scale of the job to be done. An unattainable

Corporate Plan for 1978 and beyond; an inadequate product range; serious design defects even in new models, compounded by lack of quality and poor reliability. Heavy losses in Europe, with an uncompetitive British cost base; heavy losses in South Africa and Australia; disputes in the Cars factories running at appalling levels; over-manning of huge proportions; an inadequate management structure, with too many staff men in line jobs. Factories out of control and some virtually controlled by militant stewards; an engineering resource that was not performing; a new product programme one year behind schedule, with major doubt about the viability of the model planned for the new small-car programme. Severe excess production capacity in the light of inadequacy of the models being produced; no agreed product strategy; the NEB pulling in a different – and arguably a more sensible – direction in this and in one or two other matters. Capital expenditure shortfalls against budget due to management weakness – the list was endless.

Many of these weaknesses have now been corrected, or are well on the way to being eliminated. We might not have done precisely what Sir Leslie Murphy and David Basnett, Lord Scanlon or Harry Urwin – or other NEB members – had in mind. But we had attacked the problems that my NEB colleagues of 1977 all agreed were there to be dealt with.

The fact that the future for the British motor industry is now much brighter than a few years ago was acknowledged by Patrick Jenkin when he spoke in October at the 1982 Motor Show dinner:

> Decline is not inevitable. Look at other European countries. Both Germany and France each produce about 69% of their own motor cars. If they can do it, we can do it! Throughout the industry, you have been making great strides forward – in management, in productivity, in industrial relations, in new models, in innovation and in manufacturing technology.
>
> Here, may I pay a particular tribute tonight to Sir Michael Edwardes who leaves BL in two weeks' time?
>
> He has built a management team of real depth and solidity. He has helped bring out the best in people in all parts and at all levels of the company. He has fought valiantly and doggedly – not least with successive Secretaries of State!

He went on to be complimentary about BL's achievements, and he hinted at a greater degree of moral support from the Government for Britain's hard-pressed motor industry:

> To the UK industry as a whole, I can say this. Perhaps for the first time the Government now sees real hope for halting, and reversing, the decline in UK car production and the rise in import penetration. That must be the right direction in which to be going. We see it as a trend to be supported and encouraged.

> Break-even for BL is now in prospect. And the company expects to seek private sector equity over the next two years for its mainstream businesses.

It will be difficult to attract private sector equity into BL until the recovery is further along the road, but as he went on to say:

> BL is now led by Sir Austin Bide. After Glaxo's recent performance on the Stock Exchange – well, as the Vodka adverts say, 'Anything can happen!'

The across-the-board improvement in the outlook for BL influenced my decision to move on when the five years was up – to create space for others. I felt I had served my purpose: by mid-1982 the de-manning was almost completed – some 90,000 employees, staff and shop floor, had left the payroll. The new test facilities and the advanced technology centre at Gaydon were established and in operation. Modernisation at Longbridge, Cowley, Land Rover at Solihull, Leyland in Lancashire and Freight Rover in Birmingham had transformed old-fashioned factories into effective production units. Our fixed costs in all parts of the business had been severely pruned, partly by de-manning and partly by rationalisation of production; by closing factories we did not need to match production capacity so that it lined up with market demand for the products, with sufficient headroom for expansion when the market recovered. Production time lost through disputes had been reduced to one-seventh the 1977 figure, and productivity had soared ahead. Management had regained control of the business.

Collaborative arrangements with Honda had greatly improved the Cars potential, as did the Cummins engine joint-venture deal for Leyland. Virtually all our models had been renewed, with the Maestro on target to go into initial production at Cowley in the autumn of 1982 for an early spring launch in 1983. Dealer networks in Britain, Europe, the United States of America and elsewhere had been retained and strengthened. Disciplines had been reintroduced after years of laxity in most parts of the company, and there was a new realism among employees and suppliers. Financial losses announced at the 1982 half-year were 57% lower than the first half of 1981, despite adverse economic circumstances. The target for 1983 remained 'break-even at the profit before interest level.'

The loans to underwrite all these programmes had been provided by willing and supportive private sector bankers, and the equity by a reluctant Treasury – with the company persuading two administrations over five years that funding was gradually becoming less of an act of faith.

And so I leave a very hot seat with more to be done, but with a feeling that the foundations are now well and truly laid; and that the continuing persistence and patience of the Board and top management, together with the products that are in the pipeline, will complete the job.

In October 1977 I wrote to Chloride's employees, to explain my decision to join British Leyland:

> If British Leyland fails to succeed it will have the most dire effect on jobs and investment prospects, not to mention the reputation of Britain and British goods overseas.
>
> The question you will ask is 'Can you really hope to influence such a situation?' I don't know. The task is enormous; some people would even say impossible.
>
> But I am going to try because I believe that British Leyland does have a future. It is a company which has talent at all levels. Talent that can and must be fully utilised. Given the right support from all in the company, and government – and that could mean facing up to some tough decisions in the future – it is still possible to restore its growth and realise its full potential.

Five all-absorbing years have passed since that was written, and I haven't changed my mind.

Index